And We Ate the Leopard

And We Ate the Leopard

Serving in the Belgian Congo

Margaret Baker Wente

iUniverse, Inc.
New York   Lincoln   Shanghai

And We Ate the Leopard
Serving in the Belgian Congo

Copyright © 2007 by Margaret Baker Wente

All rights reserved. No part of this book may be used or reproduced by any means, graphic, electronic, or mechanical, including photocopying, recording, taping or by any information storage retrieval system without the written permission of the publisher except in the case of brief quotations embodied in critical articles and reviews.

iUniverse books may be ordered through booksellers or by contacting:

iUniverse
2021 Pine Lake Road, Suite 100
Lincoln, NE 68512
www.iuniverse.com
1-800-Authors (1-800-288-4677)

Because of the dynamic nature of the Internet, any Web addresses or links contained in this book may have changed since publication and may no longer be valid.

The views expressed in this work are solely those of the author and do not necessarily reflect the views of the publisher, and the publisher hereby disclaims any responsibility for them.

ISBN: 978-0-595-46631-3 (pbk)
ISBN: 978-0-595-90926-1 (ebk)

Printed in the United States of America

*To the memory of my caring and intrepid parents
Lelia and Donald Baker*

ACKNOWLEDGEMENTS

Lovina Parmenter was the first to urge me to write the story she had heard from my parents about my family's life in the Belgian Congo. Throughout the long process of writing and revisions, she has continued to encourage me. I appreciate her letters and telephone calls.

Several of my friends and family read the first version of the manuscript and made helpful suggestions. Their support has been heartening. My thanks go to JoAnne Ramponi, Helen Wright, Diane Goldfarb, Marilyn Morgan, Lyle Smith, Terry Quinn, Marilyn Hunter-Torburn, the Vances, Lauretta Baker and Mary Mulvany. Marilyn Morgan suggested that joining Southwest Writers would be helpful to me as an author. The group confirmed her prediction month after month. Also, I thank Josephine Porter for her assistance in formatting the manuscript with skill and enthusiasm.

Two people responsible for significant revisions of the book deserve special recognition. My sister Grace, who lived through the events set forth here, helped correct and add to my memories. Mary Callahan, who never saw the Congo, helped me explain the setting of the story to make sense for outsiders. Their assistance has been invaluable.

Every author needs an editor to prune the excesses of a manuscript and tighten the writing. Many thanks to Dina Wolff for helping me see opportunities for such revisions while noting positively the special parts that should be left undisturbed.

The photographs of the *Oregon* and Captain John come from the Disciples of Christ Historical Society in Nashville, Tennessee. The rest are reproduced from the Baker family archives. Since missionaries freely shared each others' pictures to illustrate their work in the field, I cannot be sure that every photograph in our family collection was taken by my father. If I have not credited a picture correctly from our collection, please accept my apology for the omission. A special thanks to McGarvey Ice, Michael Callahan and Will Wente for lending me their expertise in converting the photographs to the proper form for printing.

I wish to thank Dr. Gene Johnson for allowing me to quote from his book *Congo Centennial*; and the United Christian Missionary Society for giving me permission to quote from *I Saw Congo* by E.R. Moon, *Fifty Years in the Congo* by Herbert Smith, some Congo Newsletters and the brochure, *Congo Portfolio-Mondombe*—all published under its aegis. These publications were helpful far beyond the selections I have quoted.

My husband, in his loyal and loving way, gave me the time to get lost in my writing without interruption or attention to the clock. I have appreciated the freedom from guilt. My children Clara, Will and his wife Christie have been helpful in many ways. Without their computer assistance, I could never have finished the book in a manner compatible with printing. They have been supportive throughout the years I've labored to complete the book. Family and friends kept me focused and made the effort seem worthwhile.

CONTENTS

ACKNOWLEDGEMENTS vii
MAP OF THE BELGIAN CONGO xi
MAP OF MONDOMBE xii
PREFACE xiii
CHAPTER 1: CONGO BECKONS THE BAKERS 1
CHAPTER 2: PREPRATIONS FOR A TROPICAL MISSION 11
CHAPTER 3: SETTING OUT AND SETTLING IN 19
CHAPTER 4: A DIFFERENT WORLD IN 1933 32
CHAPTER 5: TRIPS, TRIBULATIONS AND VARIETIES OF VISIITORS ... 41
CHAPTER 6: BOXING THE LEOPARD 49
CHAPTER 7: FETISHES OR MEDICINE 62
CHAPTER 8: TIME FOR FURLOUGH 73
CHAPTER 9: MONDOMBE'S STAFF AT WORK 79
CHAPTER 10: BUILDING FOR THE FUTURE 90
CHAPTER 11: HYGIENE, LEPERS AND A LITTLE FROG 97
CHAPTER 12: *NATIONAL GEOGRAPHIC* WONDERS 108
CHAPTER 13: HOME ON THE STATION 120
CHAPTER 14: CRUISING ON THE *S.S. OREGON* 137
CHAPTER 15: SHADOWS OF WAR IN THE CONGO 146
CHAPTER 16: PROPITIOUS TIMES 160
CHAPTER 17: THE END OF MY CHILDHOOD IN CONGO 167

CHAPTER 18: GOOD THINGS COME SLOWLY 173

CHAPTER 19: GRAPPLING WITH GROWTH IN THE FIFTIES 180

CHAPTER 20: THE LULL BEFORE THE STORM 189

CHAPTER 21: THE END AND THE BEGINNING 199

EPILOGUE 209

BIBLIOGRAPHY 213

INDEX 215

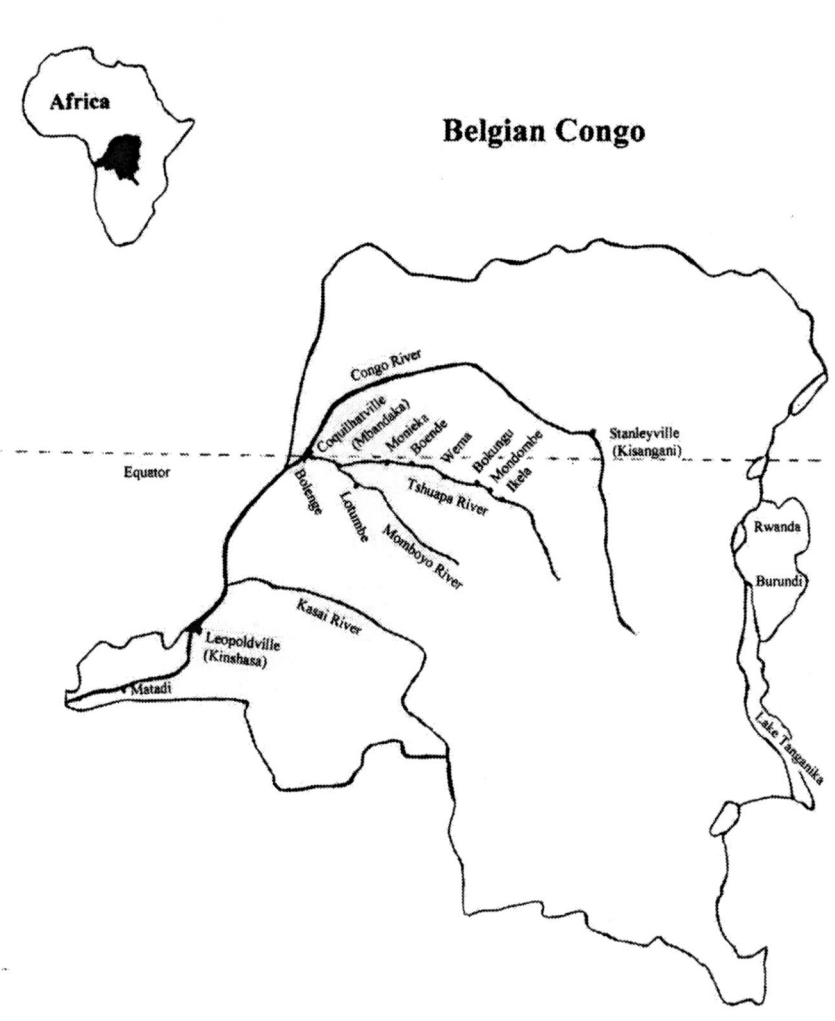

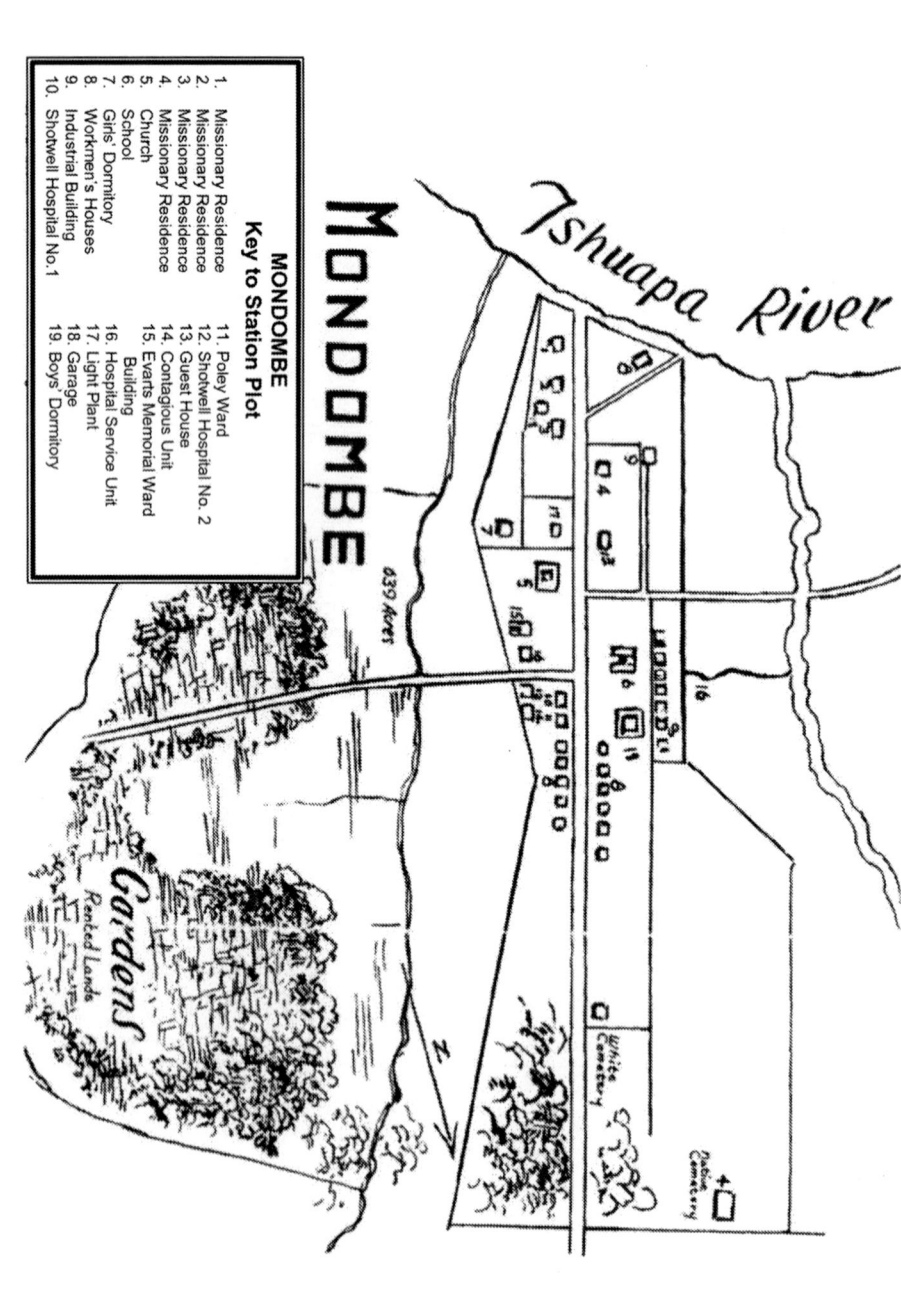

PREFACE

Passing through an arched trellis in Hawaii a few years ago, I found myself instinctively ducking and scanning the vines overhead. That's what growing up in tropical Africa instills in you. Since there were no snakes in Hawaii, I consciously made myself stop. But in the Congo, there were lots of snakes.

From the time of my birth in the Belgian Congo in 1933 until 1960 when the colony became independent, I stayed closely bound to a remote area of the immense African tropical rain forest. This little spot was a mission station named Mondombe. My attachment to it grew strong through fifteen years of first-hand experience as a child. Later, after I returned to the States, I stayed in touch by letters and conversations with my parents—a doctor and a teacher.

A short visit to Mondombe in 1959 renewed my ties to the people and their activities. Although birthplaces usually look diminished from an adult perspective, this one still shone beautifully green. The smiles of the dark-skinned inhabitants welcomed me even more warmly than in my recollections. The coming troubles hardly flickered on the horizon.

A year later I was the first to meet my parents after they fled the crumbling Congo in its first weeks of independence. For hours I listened to stories pouring from my mother as she tried to cope with her fears for the safety of the Africans she cared about. The whites had been evacuated, but the peaceful Congolese that she knew were left to handle the rampaging military as best they could. As the inexperienced new government flexed its power and encouraged the people's anti-colonial rage, would all things Western be destroyed? My parents' lifetime work seemed at risk along with the educated population.

Reading Barbara Kingsolver's *Poisonwood Bible*, as so many have, inspired me to return to the stories from my childhood and later. If so many readers flocked to a skilled, fictional portrayal of a "bad" missionary and his family in the Belgian Congo, surely there must be some interest in a historical picture of authentic missionaries.

What was it really like to experience a tropical night? Full of the cacophony of shrill insects and the "knock-knock" of the fruit bats, the darkness always induced the fear of marauding leopards and the even more likely bite of an infected mosquito. With my life brought to death's door by malaria, this was not idle anxiety. The capture of a snarling leopard on the station generated the title for this book.

Half the missionaries in the earliest days of missions died on the field or returned home with severe medical problems. Could one live there and raise children in health and happiness? Having a doctor in the family served better than an apple a day, but freedom from disease and adequate nutrition were a struggle faced daily in a land lacking sanitation, grocery stores and quick transportation. What did a missionary doctor and teacher actually do to raise a healthy family?

Over the years my parents worked to heal and educate the Bantu people in their region of Congo. In fact it was the missionaries who provided hospitals and schools for the native population for the first thirty-five years of the colony. Not till after the Second World War did the government open state schools and health centers in any significant numbers.

How could one understand the beliefs and customs of people still living in the Iron Age? Their way of life would surely fall before the overwhelming influence of Western intrusions. Letters from the early years contain descriptions of historical and cultural significance. I have drawn heavily from correspondence by my parents in the thirties and forties.

My parents kept in touch with one to two hundred friends, relatives and supporters by means of general letters written two or three times a year throughout their years in Congo. These letters, written on the field, were sent to the mission headquarters in Indianapolis for duplication and mailing. Letters sent directly to close friends and family members, with my dad's idiosyncratic spelling, added to my treasure of information. The historical context in which these letters were written must be considered when judging some of the now outmoded vocabulary.

Rereading twenty-eight years of stories from Congo has been a joyous exercise for me. I have chosen passages from these letters that best illustrate the people and the life my family led in this foreign land. The selections show my parents striving to bring the best of their culture to help the Congolese move into a future completely different from the one known by their ancestors.

This little-known period of history gave birth to the nation that called itself Zaire for a time after independence but has now renamed itself the Democratic Republic of the Congo.

Albuquerque, New Mexico
August 2007

Donald and Lelia Baker

CHAPTER 1

CONGO BECKONS THE BAKERS

My parents arrived in the Belgian Congo in 1932, only fifty-five years after Henry Morton Stanley fought his way past the cannibals for more than a thousand miles down the Congo River. His epic canoe trip proved that the Lualaba River became the Congo, not the Nile. The mission station where the Bakers first stopped lay three miles from the Equator—halfway up that thousand miles. In the early days of the mission station, an elderly member of the African community living there still remembered the day Stanley's crew beached their large dugout canoes on the nearest island in February 1877. The event remained etched in his memory.

Stanley's exhausted, starving men eyed the village of Bolenge across the mile-wide, silvery channel warily hoping they wouldn't have to fight off yet another savage attack of cannibals. They wanted to trade for food. As Stanley recorded in his journal, the tribe agreed to bring their bananas, goats and manioc to barter for beads and cloth. This amicable tribe may have saved the expedition from starvation.

When Stanley, the journalist of "Mr. Livingston I presume?" fame, published the narration of his trip, he became an international celebrity. Large audiences crowded auditoriums to hear him describe the hardships of travel through tangled jungles and down the dark, swiftly-flowing Congo with its seven-mile-wide expanse. The people living along its banks had to fend off the Arab slave traders at its upper reaches. The lower river tribe had been in contact with Portugal since 1482. In that year Diogo Cão, a Portuguese explorer, was the first European to reach the mouth of the Congo. He landed after sailing his small caravel down around the hump of Africa. The date of his arrival is known, because he planted a stone monument of Portugal's King John II on a bank of the river. Located much later, it identified the date and the discoverer.

1

The Portuguese set up forced diplomatic relations with the coastal tribe, taking hostages to ensure a positive reception. A lucrative trade in slaves and other merchandise was established between Portugal and the Kingdom of the Kongo, a highly organized tribe along the mouth of the Congo River. For 400 years an unequal trade gradually degraded the Bakongo (the people of the Kongo) and their neighbors. This early history of the Congo is well told by both Peter Forbath in *The River Congo* and Robert Edgerton in *The Troubled Heart of Africa*.

The people in the middle Congo basin where my parents worked showed some early trading connection with the downriver tribes. Stanley recounts being attacked with muskets, which fortunately were old and shot inaccurately. But, insulated from the coastal connection to the outside world, the inland tribes lived in their pole-and-mud houses thatched with sheets of palm leaflets, ate the manioc they grew in clearings in the trees, and hunted or fished for their protein. Their loyalty was to their clan within the larger tribe, and each clan spoke its own dialect, of which there were 150-200 in the Belgian Congo. Along the Congo River and its tributaries a trade language called Lingala assisted groups to communicate across tribal lines. These people, excluding the pygmies, were mostly Bantu—the true Negroes of Africa.

By the time my parents arrived in Africa, the continent had been divided into colonies with boundaries drawn by European governments. That process began in November 1884 when representatives of the European states with holdings in Africa met in Berlin. The conference settled claims and established ground rules for trade, navigation and missionary endeavors. King Leopold II of Belgium hired Stanley to represent his interests, which focused on central Africa. People everywhere were eager to hear Stanley tell of his exploits; he alone could describe the Congo Basin. His singular experience made him an inspired choice as agent to the King.

By the end of the conference three months later, Leopold had won personal ownership of the Congo, an area 76 times the size of his small country. He was given Matadi, the Atlantic port, and additional land to build a railroad around the cataracts at the mouth of the Congo River that blocked navigation to and from the sea. In exchange, Europeans had a hazy notion that Leopold would open the land to international trade, philanthropic development and the abolition of slavery.

Leopold named his new land the Congo Free State. He lost little time shedding his implied humanitarian goals, although his regime did win a war defeating the Arab slave traders. While still publicizing his aims as altruistic, he hired Stanley to establish administrative posts along the river connected by steamboat service. Once the infrastructure was in place he set about stripping his private domain of its wealth in ivory and rubber. When the indigenous people didn't collect enough wild rubber to satisfy the quota set by the State, they were severely whipped, mutilated or killed.

In 1892 Leopold's military began to fight the Arab slave trader forces of the famous Tippu Tib. Earlier Tippu Tib had helped Stanley in his explorations by making some of his great resources available for Stanley to hire. Thousands of African and Afro-Arab soldiers battled for control of the riches of eastern Congo. By January 1894 Leopold's Congolese *Force Publique*, or Peoples Army, with its European officers, had won the Arab War gaining the Congo Free State a fortune in ivory, military materiel and freedom from the murderous slave trade. This was perhaps Leopold's greatest gift to the Congo. The war freed Leopold of all competition in his ruthless control of wealth harvesting.

Reports of unbelievable cruelty and exploitation began surfacing as early as 1890. Missionaries with the Southern Presbyterian Mission and an American traveler on the scene sent their observations home. An astute British trade representative named Edmund Morel noticed discrepancies in invoices, which hid the imported wealth. Adam Hochschild in *King Leopold's Ghost* details Morel's realization that not trade but slave labor was being imposed on the Congo. Roger Casement, a British consular service officer, joined in the crusade against Leopold.

The atrocities became widespread news as Morel and Casement kept up the pressure. Newspaper articles exposed the brutality of Leopold's administration. Pictures of beaten and mutilated men, women and children with hands and ears cut off accompanied front-page articles. Worldwide horror grew.

The Belgian government finally bowed to international pressure. It assumed responsibility from its now discredited king for a colony it had never wanted. In doing so it paid the king for his land and accepted the debts he had incurred in developing it. Leopold so cleverly hid the fortune he had made that it took Belgium two decades to sort out his front companies and investments. Little was recovered. The country's reluctance to accept the administration of a colony is shown in the incorporation papers. They clearly state that no Belgian lives would be spent in its defense. That may have foreshadowed the haste with which Belgium divested itself of the Congo years later. Belgium renamed its colony the Belgian Congo and formally took charge in 1908.

Decades later when proper censuses had been taken, the death toll of the Leopold era could be gauged. Ravages of the slave trade in eastern Congo, slaughter by the administration, new diseases from which the people had no resistance, and the results of exposure and starvation from fleeing into the forest from slavers as well as government agents probably reduced the population by half. In the mid nineteen twenties there were ten million people in Congo. That put the estimated death toll at ten million.

There has been a lot of criticism of Belgian colonial policy and administration since the colony gained its independence. Whether Belgium's development of the Belgian Congo was totally self-serving, as some assert, or a reasonable balance of a developing economy supporting both the administration of the colony and furnishing a just return to its commercial companies is a judgment for students of colonial and economic policy. World attention to the Congo receded after Leopold reluctantly gave up the Congo Free State and didn't return until the turbulence of the newly independent country. Very few writers showed any interest in the colony until 1960.

In evaluating Belgium's role one should place it in its historical timeline starting with the condition of the Congo when Belgium inherited it and its civil administrators. The new administration had made verified progress in reversing Leopold's disastrous policies by the time Belgium was invaded by Germany six years later at the beginning of World War I. With the help of German reparations after the war, Belgium had just recovered when the Great Depression hit. Before the economy fully recovered Germany once again invaded Belgium with the start of World War II. Belgium's economy took a nose dive, the government fled to London, and Congo worked to aid the Allies with little direction from its colonial master.

The little mother country came out of World War II in a shambles. The Congo, however, had seen some advancement. Its resources had served the Allied war effort well. Especially coveted were rubber, copper and the uranium used in the atomic bombs.

My parents arrived on the mission field just as the effects of the depression began to hit the colony and the gifts to the foreign mission board decreased. In preparation for this life overseas as missionary teacher and doctor they studied French, Lonkundo (the local language used by the mission) and Bantu culture. They spent six months in Belgium, where my father passed the tropical medicine course in French to qualify for government subsidy of his medical practice in the Belgian Congo. About the time of my older sister's first birthday in February 1932, they saw the dark brown waters of the Congo River mixing with the blue Atlantic Ocean. They were still two days from shore.

The Congo River is unique among the great rivers of the world in dropping directly into the ocean without first slowing down, losing its silt and forming a delta. A great trench at the mouth of the river extends into the Atlantic, worn away over eons of scouring by the great volume of water. That dark water my parents saw mixing with the Atlantic stays sweet for one hundred miles before becoming salty.

After leaving the States in mid-July of 1931, stopping over in Belgium for the months of studying tropical medicine, and completing the trip down the coast of Africa, the three Bakers found new adventure traveling up the Congo River in a small Mississippi-style steamboat. The following description of their trip up the river comes from one of my parents' earliest general letters, which were usually written collaboratively:

> Because of the treacherous sandbanks our little river boat dared not travel during the night. Consequently, each night found us tied up to the river bank at a wooding post [a place to buy fuel for the steam engine]. The dense tropical jungle formed a wall that quite effectively cut off whatever breeze there might be. The natives dressed themselves in a manner which they considered worthy of our honorable presence and came down to view the activities. We in turn lined up on the deck to watch them across a narrow space literally peppered with millions of insects. Our boat was close enough to the shore to permit the crew to span the distance between with a length or two of planks. This gave easy access without getting one's feet wet, except, as happened a time or two for the wood carriers, when the planks slipped off the middle trestle. The wood was loaded on board until two or three o'clock in the morning. Night after night we went to sleep hearing armloads of wood bang as they were thrown down by the carriers, listening to the beating of the *lokole* (the native drum), the singing and bantering of the natives.
>
> When we had mail, the steamer tooted for a canoe. A dugout started out from the bank with two or as many as half dozen paddlers, standing erect, and paddling in unison, half on each side of the boat. Our steamboat slowed down so as to let us coast up alongside of them ... [and the mail was handed over].
>
> Often times as we passed a native village, the canoes came out with food. It was held up to see if our captain wished to buy it. If so, we tooted, and slowed down, and they came closer. If not, we sailed right on past. One day we bought a big specimen of the catfish family. It must have been at least five feet in length, and was not yet quite dead. It tasted very good at supper.
>
> Several times a daring crew bore down upon us while we were going ahead at full speed, and held on to the side of the boat, (the

lower deck was only a couple of feet from the level of the water), while they bargained with our crew over the dried fish which they had brought. The man in charge of the cabins and dining room (*maître d'hôtel*) told us that what they were doing was very dangerous, and it looked it. They were a well-muscled group and handled their frail unstable craft in a dexterous manner. However, later another canoe, in starting away from our boat, overturned, and crew, dried fish, and money, all tumbled into the river. Of course, these men all swim very well. (General Letter 3-20-32)

On Bolenge, the oldest mission station of the Disciples of Christ Congo Mission (DCCM), my parents met the first missionaries with whom they would be working. It took another two weeks of travel up a tributary of the Congo River to reach the post to which they were assigned. Almost a year had passed since leaving the States when they finally reached Mondombe in May 1932.

The station named Mondombe had been established twelve years earlier on a strip of land about a third of a mile, stretching back from the Tschuapa River between two swamps. Dominated by the enveloping forest, this clearing already contained permanent buildings and a small, dedicated group of Americans and literate Africans eager to achieve great changes in the surrounding population. At last they had arrived to share their skills, compassion, and beliefs with a people who seemed eager to learn the "white man's" knowledge. They came with a matter-of-fact approach to religion and a wish "that we can combine the evangelistic with the practical everyday demonstration of Christian living, with all that that involves," my father wrote.

What kind of early experiences would lead a person to set off resolutely to a place where, my mother said, in the beginning she felt dismayed at being unable to distinguish one dark face from another? Geographically this place was 7,000 miles from home but centuries away in cultural development. These friendly inhabitants had still to learn the operation of the wheel or the skill of joining wood. Household utensils and furniture were either carved out of a single piece of wood or tied together with jungle vines or twisted twine. By anthropological description, hunters and gatherers are still a step away from herding and farming. The local tribes had taken a small step in that direction with their manioc cultivation.

The people in this area knew the smelting of iron. They worked metal into utilitarian axes and knives and also hammered iron into ornate spears or cast brass into valuable anklets. They wove raffia cloth and fired simple clay pots.

How could an Ohio farm girl and a youth from rural Pennsylvania expect their lives to influence positively these people of central Africa?

Lelia Barber, my petite, introspective mother, grew up on a small farm near Lima in west central Ohio. As a child, she remembered seeing the log cabin once occupied by her homesteading great-grandparents. They had first claimed the land from the Indians. Her childhood was a time of one-room school houses, riding a horse to class and running swiftly to outdistance her younger brothers. During one weekly Saturday bath it was discovered the cause of her itching wasn't the harsh linsey-woolsey but a case of the chicken pox already abating. Only two inches over five feet tall with light brown hair and blue eyes, her lithe frame held a remarkably concentrated resolution and perseverance.

A ruptured appendix took the life of her mother when Lelia was nine years old. She clearly remembered being called in to say goodbye, as her mother left for the hospital, and thinking that harvest activities had caused irreversible neglect of her ill parent. As she promised to be a good girl and take care of Grant, her two-year-old brother, she knew it was a solemn pledge even if her mother didn't realize the finality. Honoring those words focused her for the rest of her life.

Her young parents' remarkably active examples of responsibility served as her role models. They taught the adult Sunday school class in the small community church, something her father continued to do all of his life. Lelia pictured their heads bent over the table one evening as they collaboratively wrote an article for the monthly farm magazine.

By the age of thirty, Bessie, Lelia's mother, was gone. Within the year Lelia's father had married the hired girl to help him raise his young family. It was a long and happy union, but to Lelia the new wife never took the place of her mother.

Perhaps living up to the promise of being a good girl and carrying an idealized picture of a mother, who had been active in leadership at a young age, motivated my mother to stretch beyond her horizons. Following grade school Lelia did not marry and settle down as her friends were doing. Instead she finished high school, which was in another town. Then she attended normal school for one year to attain her credentials for becoming a teacher. She taught in a one-room schoolhouse for two years, where some of the older children towered over her.

The family chuckled that she started teaching before reaching the age of adulthood. Fortunately, her eighteenth birthday occurred in mid-September allowing the school board to pay her legally. She saved her salary for an advanced education and graduated from Hiram College in Ohio with a liberal arts degree in psychology and education prepared to teach English.

During college she decided how to spend her life using the knowledge she had so diligently gained. She would become an educational foreign missionary. Undoubtedly her parents' active participation in the life of their church influenced her to choose a religious-based career.

In 1925 there was no way she could foresee that foreign missions would change the world. A seventy percent European Christian preponderance in 1902 slid to a vastly reduced twenty-eight percent a hundred years later. In that same century, Africa moved from eight and a half million Christians to over 350 million. My mother contributed to that transformation.

Study of the purpose of the church in those days "… put the needs of the world before American Christians, who responded by the millions to support missions," said Dana L. Roberts, professor at Boston University School of Theology, during the centennial celebration of the Mission Education Movement in 2002. My mother was one of those millions who responded to the appeal to serve on the foreign field.

After making her decision she joined the Student Volunteer Movement (SVM). This organization consisted of idealistic young men and women who wanted to go out in the world to help the needy and teach them the joys of the Christian religion. At a conference of the SVM my parents met and fell instantly in love, as recounted by many of their friends.

As Mother told the story, she arrived at Oberlin College in Ohio for the SVM conference. Almost the first person she met was her college roommate's brother Donald Baker, an alumnus of Hiram College. They had undoubtedly heard of each other. Stories still circulated about my father's student escapades during his days at Hiram, perhaps kept alive by one or the other of his two sisters, who were still attending the school.

After Lelia received her dorm room assignment, she turned to walk there. My father circled the nearby column and appeared beside her offering to carry her suitcase. She unpacked and returned to the dining hall for supper. As she hesitated at the door, her roving eye caught sight of a turned-up chair beside my father. Right away she knew that it was saved for her. The romance quickly became serious. They shared a deep conviction. They should carry their faith to a distant land where they could bring a happier, healthier life to the people.

Although my father, Donald Hall Baker, lived part of his childhood on a farm in Pennsylvania, his parents were not farmers. Both were college graduates and had been professionally employed—his mother Elizabeth had been an English teacher before marriage; his father Almon, an ordained seminary graduate, engaged in what we now would call inner city missionary work or storefront preaching.

Almon Baker supported his family as a postal worker, first in Germantown outside of Philadelphia and then as a mail sorter on the Pennsylvania Railroad while living on the farm as his children finished high school.

All his adult life my father cherished those years on the farm. When driving through the countryside, he always drew in great breaths and exclaimed, "Just smell that wonderful farm aroma." The scents of silage and manure were equally as acceptable as freshly mown hay to him. From his years on the farm came my father's life-long interest in agriculture. Foreign language study in high school–four years each of Latin and German–undoubtedly helped him later acquire fluency in other languages. And declamation exercises instilled the self-confidence later used with such success in public speaking. Although he stood only five feet six inches tall, his shoulders were broad. He claimed his work in the steel mill to support his brother through medical school developed this muscular build. His exceptional energy added the component that carried him far and long. Sporting glasses and a small, trimmed mustache with his prematurely graying dark hair he projected a forceful, outgoing personality.

In deciding how he could best spend his life, he knew he wanted to help others. He settled on becoming a medical missionary abroad. His college work and medical education focused on preparing himself for this career. The decision reflected both his father's practice of evangelistic preaching and the stimulus of the overseas missionary movement. Whether news of the work of Sir Wilfred Grenfell, the famous British medical missionary to Labrador, had already spread to Ohio by the 1920's to inspire this career choice, I don't know. Certainly the ground swell of interest in foreign missions in the early part of the twentieth century flowed through a denominational college such as Hiram. Missionaries from foreign fields would have been invited to speak at colleges and conventions. Perhaps my father heard an inspiring address at the national Centennial Convention of the Disciples of Christ that he attended as a boy of twelve in Pittsburgh.

My father was more than halfway through Western Reserve Medical School in Cleveland when he attended the momentous Student Volunteer Movement conference and was introduced to my mother. That meeting resulted in a June marriage two years later. By then she was teaching English in Parma, a suburb of Cleveland, while he was entering the last year of medical residency with a focus on surgery.

Three more years passed before they could pay off his medical school debts and be ready for training for the mission field.

CHAPTER 2

PREPRATIONS FOR A TROPICAL MISSION

Whizbang, Oklahoma, immortalized in the children's story *Boomtown Boy* by Lois Lenski, had been sedately renamed DeNoya by the time my parents moved there in the summer of 1928. My father bought a medical practice there from Dr. Brady, an older colleague from Western Reserve Medical School, expecting to pay off his medical school debts. With the oil field booming, Dr Brady had retired his loans in one year before heading off to the mission field in China. He and Mrs. Brady lived in DeNoya before spending the last half of the year in nearby Kaw City.

The drive west excited my parents, who had lived up till then only in Ohio and Pennsylvania. Aside from the challenge of the move and taking over a new practice, they would have a house of their own to make into a home. Mother wrote to the family:

> Approaching DeNoya we entered the oil region, the largest field in the U.S. The green hills were marked off in checkerboard fashion with an oil derrick at the corner of each square. When on the top of a hill, one could see dozens of them with little clusters of cabins that mark a town or center of the oil industry.
>
> DeNoya is such a town. Its business section is concentrated along one street, which is about eighty feet wide; but its residential districts are scattered over several acres. Streets (mud roads would be more descriptive) lead out to these various districts from the business section, not in block style such as is found in a well-planned city but in a very intricate, lacy design. What does it matter if one has to ford a stream once or twice before arriving at one's destination? (LB Letter to Family 7-18-28)

The oil companies built the houses for their workmen. The companies also provided utilities, safe water, and dugout shelters, which furnished security during severe windstorms. Cables, anchored on both sides of the houses, extended across roofs to add more protection from the wind.

Nearby towns offered banks and churches. One boasted a paved street. Another had a roofed boardwalk fit for a movie scene. These towns, like DeNoya, had boomed and passed their zeniths.

Mother's letter described their house:

> … Our home is located on the Sinclair lease down in the business section of town. Except for the black and white shingle on the front porch, it looks very much like the rest. Thanks to the oil our town is entirely free of mosquitoes and not very plentifully supplied with flies. The kitchen looks very nice with Dr. Brady's new gas range and linoleum and our deep cream walls and white painted woodwork. As soon as we can, we hope to paint the examining room and, perhaps, the living room. (LB Letter to Family 7-18-28)

A confinement case demanded my father's services the first day on the job. Because this baby exceeded the birth weight of their other four children, the parents named him Gene Tunney, after the boxer. "What a pretentious name for the poor, helpless thing," Mother felt. She assisted at birthings dressed professionally in a white uniform, trained by my father.

Dr. Brady's practice, although thriving at the beginning of his year, had fallen from $500 a month to half that amount at the end. My parents were grateful to be almost matching the lower rate within their first two weeks, although only half of the eighty dollars worth of care provided had been paid.

Living in DeNoya meant that patients knocked on the door any time from 7:30 A.M. until eight in the evening. Until they were financially more secure my parents realized they couldn't be too choosy about their office hours. They anticipated being paid the first or second week of the month when their patients received their pay checks.

While my dad gained professional experience that would sustain his medical practice overseas and income to rid him of debt, his daring was tested on the "frontier," as he called DeNoya. One night during the sheriff's gun battle with one of the lawless types a stray bullet came through the wall of my parent's house, passed through another wall and the top of a small table. That small folding table with the bullet hole remained in the family for decades. It, as much as life in Africa, seemed proof to us children of our parents' fearlessness.

The streams, formed after a heavy rainfall, drained quickly off the surrounding hills and across the dirt or gravel roads. They thrilled my father who wrote in his preferred phonetic spelling:

> But the fords themselves! To roll quickly over the bank of a stream, cross the gravely or rocky margin and move gently thru water at least to the running boards, perhaps with gentle spray if the plunge be made too suddenly, then to climb out on the opposite bank, as tho having taken a swim by proxy—oh! That is a pleasure you more civilized folk cannot enjoy. It makes one feel like a pioneer. (DHB Letter to Family 7-28-28)

The enjoyment of life's rousing moments differed between my mother and father. Years later when they were retired and living again in the States, my mother, who didn't drive, disliked a heavily traveled one-way street with many lanes full of cars charging up a hill. She characterized it as part of the American "rat race" to my father, who was driving.

"Is that how you think of it?" he responded. "I think of it as a chariot race."

The young couple happily found a busy place for themselves through the fall and winter joining the limited social activities of the community. They served the injured and the sick and took their turns in leading programs at church and PTA meetings. There was no ignoring that the boom had busted. Although they could pay their expenses, little remained each month to apply to their debts. They needed to devise some other strategy to repay what they owed.

For a time in the spring of 1929 they looked into the possibility of moving to a booming area in the southern part of Oklahoma in the new oil fields. Mother feared that "oil fever" might infect my father along with the many others rushing to the latest gusher. She remained less enthralled.

They drove to Asher. Four weeks before it had been a sleepy little town with a hotel, railroad station, a few stores, a bank and two churches. Then a wildcat well was shot that flowed 3100 barrels daily. Two weeks later they found throngs of people arriving in trucks or covered wagons. Short-term leasers had snatched up all land in the vicinity of the well. Drilling for new wells had commenced. Already 150 new families had arrived and half a dozen company houses were moved in.

Dad stopped to talk with a carpenter about prices and lots. "I wonder whether the next boom will be here," he said.

"Don't know where the next boom will be; the last one is here," the carpenter said.

Dad returned ten days later to evaluate the possibilities. The feverish pace had continued. Walls for a theater were going up. A new doctor and a new druggist had arrived. Seventeen oil rigs were in place.

Finding no guarantee that they would do better in Asher, my parents stayed in DeNoya for the time being. They put an ad for a medical position in the *American Medical Journal*. The ad must have been successful. By fall my parents moved back to Ohio. There Dad assisted a doctor in Bellevue with his large practice.

In evaluating their year in DeNoya, my parents discovered their accounts came out almost even, perhaps fifteen or twenty dollars and some furniture and instruments to the good. They also had paid back fifty dollars of Mother's debt. Unfortunately, the money owed them for their house and an appendectomy was uncollectible. The debtors moved without leaving forwarding addresses. Despite the losses my parents never regretted going to Oklahoma. The year had furnished valuable medical experience. The adventure proved to be good practice for establishing a home in an unfamiliar setting.

Few letters from the year in Bellevue survive. I remember my mother saying that it had been a difficult year professionally. The doctor was a hard man to work with, but the job did provide the income they needed to pay off their debts. The time had arrived to let the United Christian Missionary Society (UCMS) know they were ready to begin their missionary careers.

By spring the correspondence from the UCMS assured them they would be sent to Africa, either in 1930 or after preparation at the Kennedy School of Missions in Hartford, Connecticut. Doctors in the field were urging differing courses of action—go to school or come straight out. Meanwhile, my parents were tutoring in French expecting to complete their first year of language study before leaving Ohio.

Mother wrote in March 1930 of a visit they made to look at a Dr. Weir's collection of butterflies in Bellevue:

> The collection was beautiful. He has at least 125 boxes 8x12 and he said that he had a lot of insects that he has never had time to put away. The boxes are green. The cotton has been tinted and the butterflies placed against it. The cover is mostly a rim that holds down the thin glass-like material—I can't remember the name of it. Don and I have decided that that would be a good hobby for Africa if photography proves too expensive. (LB to Family 3-30-29)

During the many years my father was in Africa he caught butterflies of all varieties—little white ones and beautiful richly-colored blue and black ones. They were asphyxiated in a jar of cyanide, then gently dropped with tweezers into the protective corner of an envelope and kept dry in a tin can with silica gel. When a can filled, it was sent to Dr. Weir in the States. I've always wondered if those hundreds of specimens were ever placed on display anywhere.

By early September the year's contract in Bellevue ended. Dad and Mother moved their belongings to Hiram, Ohio, to his parents' home for sorting and repacking. The decision was made; they were to attend school before leaving for the mission field.

Planning to live in furnished quarters at the School of Missions in New Haven, Connecticut, allowed them to sell their furniture. That helped them pay off their loans and left a comfortable sum in the bank. With the rear of the car packed to bulging. They set off for school by way of the Finger Lakes in New York and Niagara Falls. Along the way a cabin cost a dollar a night, if one furnished one's own sheets, or a dollar per person for provided linens. For the first time Mother saw and admired stone fences. Dad enjoyed the white spires of fine old New England churches. The excursion thrilled them both.

Once settled into pleasant accommodations in Thompson Hall, Professor Hensey and his wife assisted them. The Henseys had been missionaries to the Belgian Congo starting in 1905 during the Congo Free State era and served until arriving in Hartford in 1930. They were talented linguists and knew the mission field well. Mr. Hensey negotiated the opening of a new station in 1920 that later became my parents' home. The Henseys became good friends. About thirty other members of the Disciples of Christ church were enrolled at the school. Although members of the same church group, they were not all destined for service in Africa.

The ten families in Thompson Hall represented such varied countries of work as Arabia, Portuguese West Africa, the Philippines, the Sudan, China and Japan. A white couple from Alabama slowly adjusted to living next door to an African-American family in the States on furlough from the Baptist mission in the Belgian Congo. A Dr. and Mrs. Horton were headed to the Disciples of Christ Congo Mission (DCCM), as were my parents.

My parents' classes consisted of French, Lonkundo (the African dialect they would use on the mission field), African Native Life, Introduction to Africa and some practical work in "Missionary Character and Efficiency." My father wrote:

With any language study there is always a lot of good hard labor, because there is always a lot of memory work which can be learned in no other way. Lonkundo is proving to be very interesting, and we are fortunate in having one of the men who wrote the language since it was only a spoken language until the missionaries transcribed it. Just think of the amazement of the natives upon learning that the words they spoke could be set down on paper and carried from one place to another. Prof. Hensey is perhaps the best authority on the language, and he is a most patient teacher. I would like to tell those of you who know nothing about the lingo that it is one of a very few languages (I am including the Bantu group of tongues) which have alliterative prefixes to its words. For instance, the noun comes first (subject) and sets the first sound for each modifying word and for the verb. The object of the verb may set another sound for its modifying words.

To give an example, *Banyango bakiyo basato baboma isweswe ikiyo issato*—Brothers their three kill ducks their three. The preceding is the literal translation, which would be in English—Their three brothers kill their three ducks. It is distinctive in that it does not classify nouns according to gender, but according to personal relationships, derivations from verbs, etc., into eleven classes. (DHB 10-6-30)

In addition to being president of Thompson Hall, or perhaps because of it, Dad was elected the representative from Thompson Hall on the Student Council, "probably one of those jobs which sound good but don't mean anything," they wrote home. It meant that they took an active role in the life around them.

By October Lelia was into her fifth month of pregnancy. Hints showed up about her condition in references to a protective step taken now and again, or a quick nap needed. Still life continued at full pace.

The Model T Ford they owned had belonged to my father's sister Betty and her husband Everton Smith. The Smiths, both Hiram graduates, had left for the Congo mission field the year before. The car was named Balboa, because it "had seen the Pacific" during a trip they had taken to California.

With Balboa my parents were able to offer rides to the Henseys, who did not have a car. It simplified and enriched all their lives. The young couple managed short and long pleasure jaunts as time permitted. These included picnics and visits to churches of the area and to Yale University campus with its Gothic architecture.

Although their religious convictions were well formed before the year at Kennedy School of Missions, the lectures and speakers they attended undoubtedly helped shape and reinforce them. Mother wrote approvingly that the dean of the school had agreed with a visiting speaker from Columbia University. He advocated a mission policy for the future, as she wrote in October, "giving them the Bible for their own and being willing that they discard any of our doctrines which they didn't find agreeable and advocated scrapping our formal type of conversion." Not everyone agreed with such liberal thoughts, I'm sure.

By the end of February reservations were made for a mid-summer departure. The UCMS informed them that berths were booked on the *S.S. Pennland* sailing from New York on July 17, 1931, direct to Antwerp, Belgium. My parents filled out sheaves of papers, which included their passport applications. They ordered groceries to eat for the first eighteen months of their term. They studied the Montgomery Ward catalog searching for specific articles and prices from diapers to garden hoes.

With help from Prof. Hensey they bought some steamer trunks of durable construction.

My father wrote about them in the February letter:

> The vulcanized fiber required for the tropics must be quite hard and the rest of the outfit must be capable of standing lots of banging around. The locks, which we had ordered as per the sample trunk, were not duplicated when the others came, and the trunk company had to make it good by sending out a locksmith, who changed them. (Letter to Family 2-23-31)

They were to stop in Belgium for the tropical medicine course and would study French intensively from July until classes started on October 1st. This schedule projected their arrival in Congo in February 1932. They wrote:

> School is out May 27th, and the ordination and appointment service at Indianapolis [headquarters for the mission board] is to be held sometime during the first week of June. That will leave us almost six weeks for packing, visiting and the trip to New York. Lelia says so many kind relatives are encouraging her to let them do some sewing that she is going to take advantage of their good natures one of these days and parcel out some sewing on the African supplies....
>
> The other evening Don saw one of the Thompson Hall fathers in the basement washing diapers and jokingly remarked, "I suppose it

has to be done." Thinking of the possibilities of his own future he called back from the stairs, "It won't be long now." (Letter to Family 2-23-31)

A daughter was born four days later. They named her Lauretta Ann.

CHAPTER 3

SETTING OUT AND SETTLING IN

Looking somewhat like steerage immigrants with their mountain of baggage, the Bakers boarded the *S.S. Pennland* for Belgium in July 1931. Packing for a four-year absence had proved to be as difficult as anyone could anticipate. Last minute strategies recounted later on shipboard included staying up all night, buying extra containers, leaving some possessions behind, even rolling some things in a blanket and tying them. They rejoiced at being on their way at last.

On shipboard Mother answered the many goodbye notes from her Cleveland friends. Over the years she wrote to these members of a Sunday school class she had attended during the two years she taught in Lakewood, Ohio, after graduating from college. These letters were saved by members of the Philathea Class, as it was named. The treasured packet of mail was given to me at the time of Mother's funeral in 1970. In Mother's response to the Philatheans, she thanked the group for flowers and a five-year diary:

> … A few friends were down to the pier [to see us off]. The familiar faces helped one to keep on smiling when the space between the ship and the pier began to widen. For there is an ache. If we were not leaving so much behind, we should not have so much to take with us. If the days behind were not so bright, we could not make the days to come happy for ourselves and those among whom we shall work. So we frankly admit that we are giving up much but we recognize also how much we are gaining.
>
> What shall I recount of our shipboard thrills? The vastness of the ocean, the long, sunny days, the ship viewed from forward deck silhouetted against a moonlit sky, the fun with deck games, the menu cards giving strange names to familiar foods, people from many

countries are all new and strange and thrilling. When the sun lights the whitecaps against their deep green background, I think the scene is superb. Then at night the moon paints a bright, ripply path across the inky blackness and I am sure *that* scene surpasses in beauty. (LB Letter to Philathea Class 7-27-31)

The ship docked at Antwerp, Belgium, after ten days at sea. The Bakers settled in, boarding with a kindly Belgian family in Brussels who spoke no English. French lessons started immediately. In addition to French tutoring Mother learned to ride a bicycle. She also was learning to use the typewriter. When everything strange overcame her, Lelia took refuge in her room with the baby for a while.

By October first the tropical medicine classes commenced. Adjusting to lectures in French "destroyed the superiority complex" of those who were novices to the language. However, for my father, the content was not particularly challenging..

In December Dad wrote:

> … The didactic work at the school is practically finished, and will be so by Christmas. We do not know when the exams will start, but there will be one or two weeks of interval to assimilate what has been given. We have studied parasites in specimens of blood from crocodiles, leeches, turtles, pigeons, dogs, cattle, horses, and human beings, so are prepared for everything. Lion blood must be pure, or too difficult to get, for we haven't seen any specimens of it, as yet. Perhaps they are not concerned about saving the lions. (DHB Letter to Family 2-?-31)

By this time Lauretta delighted her parents by saying "Mama" and "Dada." Her Belgian hosts admired that she cried little. And she had sprouted her first tooth "lower right incisor," said Dad with his usual clinical precision.

Lauretta was learning to drink from a cup. Word had come back from missionaries traveling by boat to Congo that sterilized milk was available on the ship, "so if we can teach Lauretta to drink from a cup it should not be so difficult to reach Matadi. From there on we shall probably have to use Klim [powdered whole milk] and carry boiled water with us …" Klim, milk spelled backwards, became the milk the Bakers drank all the years in Congo.

By early February they were on the ship headed south for Congo with stops at beautiful Tenerife in the Canary Islands and Lobito in Angola along the way. Aboard ship they wrote:

> ... We have been interested to learn that each of the boats going to Congo takes about one hundred and fifty passengers on the trip out, while there are around three hundred for the return trip. Of the three hundred, about fifty return to Belgium, knowing that they will have to hunt for work there on their return. All of which means that the white population in Congo is steadily decreasing at the present time, due to the Depression. That is good and yet it is bad. White civilization with its commercialization, and the attendant evils and temptations of town life have come too quickly for the Negro, but on the other hand, the decline of business carries with it decreased revenues for the government, and in turn decreased expenditures for governmental projects, including health measures. In recent years, the administration of the Belgian Congo has been quite liberal in its appropriation of funds for bettering the sanitation and living conditions of the Congo, as well as for taking active measures against the multitude of maladies which are found there. As I recall, the percentage of the expenditure for these purposes has been higher even than among the British Colonies, who have long held a justly deserved reputation for managing colonies.   (Letter to Family 2-20-32)

The two-and-a-half week trip was filled with relaxation, socializing, and steadily warming weather. Special festivities celebrated crossing the equator. These rites of passage usually included ducking the first-time crossers in a tub of water. Since the missionaries hadn't specifically agreed to being "baptized," they were left out of the usual practice. A few years before an American hunter had forcibly objected to being immersed, so the exercise had been discontinued for awhile. Its resumption was accompanied with some uncertainty, but mostly the men were ducked in a big pool made of canvas and the women were sprayed with perfume. The 5600-mile trip came to a close at Matadi at the mouth of the Congo River.

Helped by Swedish missionaries stationed at Matadi, the arriving missionaries collected all their baggage and traveled the next day by train to Leopoldville, the capital of the colony. The beauty and variety of the flowers surprised and delighted my parents. Roses bloomed all year long they were told. In a minimum of time they were on the state-run boat headed up the Congo River.

Accommodation to the dangers of life in the tropics began on the river boat with malaria prevention strategies described for family members:

> … This night was the second night under the mosquito nets, and we have been under them ever since. I used to wonder what a mosquito net was; now I know. They put you in mind of the old four-poster beds, with the drapes. Fine netting, which cuts off what little air there might otherwise be circulating, hangs from supports at the top and bottom of the bed, forming ceiling and walls. The bottom edges are tucked in under the mattress. Please don't think from what I have just written that we spend all of our time under them. However, from now on, they will be a necessary evil while we are in Congo. On the boat, the young man who looks after the cabins closes the nets at five o'clock. During the day they are hung up out of the way.
>
> We started taking quinine at Lobito, and expect to keep on taking it each evening with our supper. I left two pills out on the top of a tin can on our cabin shelves last evening, and this morning the sugar coating was pretty well gone. The ants infest this boat, as I guess everything else in Congo, and they had been feasting on the sugar. (Letter to Family 2-28-32)

After four-and-a-half days of traveling up the Congo by daylight, the Bakers and another missionary in the group arrived at Coquilhatville, the capital of the Equator Province and the point of disembarkation for the Disciple mission. An idea of the quantity of luggage they were managing is given as "four trunks with which we started from the States, plus three steel trunks which had been purchased just before leaving Brussels, together with two cases of powdered milk, a sewing machine for Dr. Horton, a crate of the bicycles, and ten small packages of groceries from Antwerp." There was also the hand luggage.

The next two months sped by as they met other missionaries at Bolenge, the nearby mission station. They attended the crowded local church and participated in the biennial mission conference. Dad spent one of the months working in the government hospital in Coquilhatville and another two weeks helping at the Bolenge hospital. He felt fortunate to be able to assist in the removal of an elephantiasis tumor big enough to fill a bucket.

"I had been hoping to see one before I went up river where they are larger and more numerous," he wrote. Caused by a tropical parasite the tumors resulted from a blocking of the lymphatic system.

To their joy they were housed with the Smiths, Dad's sister's family, for the conference. They were disappointed, however, not to be assigned to the same station. The conference decision remained firm to keep them posted up river to Mondombe.

And so it was to Mondombe that they steamed up the Tshuapa River on the mission paddlewheel, the *Oregon*. This station was the newest and farthest up river in 1932.

What a story was the founding of Mondombe! Eighteen years after the establishment of the mission at Bolenge, a Mr. Edwards and Mr. Hensey, later the professor, assembled the village elders on a "... delightful stretch of rising land, nestling in a bend of the river" high up the Tshuapa. The area had been pillaged in the nineteenth century by the Arab slavers. The people had so few resources that they were called the *botaka*, the "naked" or "ones lacking in much."

The missionaries asked the group of elders whether they wanted to have the missionaries come to live with them. After debating the issue the elders gave a disappointing response. They turned down the offer with a simple negative and no explanation. Sure that there were other sites available to them, the Americans returned to the steamer and fired up the boilers. Before they could leave there was a commotion on the beach and the elders appeared and asked to talk again. They had changed their minds. An early missionary described the scene:

> "Why the change so suddenly?" asked the missionaries.
>
> There was silence. Finally one of the elders stood and told what had happened: "After you left us, one of the adults in the village who does not have any rank among our elders spoke plainly about our lack of wisdom. He said we were a sorry lot to lack foresight when an opportunity came our way. We were angry and scolded him back, because an elder cannot allow anyone to talk that way to him. But he kept right on and this is what he said:
>
> "'Those white men would do us a lot of good if they came to live near us. They would not only teach our children wisdom but they would heal our children when they are sick. Our young men could work for them, and there would be some money in the village with which to pay our taxes and to buy cloth. Moreover, they are men of God and they would teach us the way of life. You have driven them off. God will now leave us stranded because of the ignorance of our elders.

"Now we don't like men talking to us like that. We may be unwise, but we do not like anyone to show us up before God. Now you come and teach us." (H. Smith, pp. 62-64)

Three years of preliminary work brought sixty-five Congolese teachers from down-river stations to the new site to work under the capable supervision of a down-river preacher. In 1920 the station named Mondombe was officially opened with the assignment of three American missionaries. A brochure of the Disciples of Christ Congo Mission describes the early years:

> The first ten-year period witnessed a prodigious amount of building. Bricks were pounded and burned. From the mill in Bolenge came large supplies of better quality lumber. New brick structures included a church, an industrial building, two units of a hospital, boys' and girls' dormitories, three residences for missionaries, and ten cottages for native leaders. Less obvious but just as well done was the work in evangelism, education, and medicine.
>
> By the end of the first decade most of the preacher/teachers from down river had been returned to their homes and replaced by local evangelists and teachers. The head preacher, Bokese Paul, stayed on until 1936 to lead and strengthen the church.
>
> From that early group of Christians has developed today's leadership for the church. One of them, Ntange Timothy, is the fine and conscientious pastor of the Mondombe church. His counsel and judgments are greatly respected. (*Congo Portfolio—Mondombe*, brochure of the Disciples of Christ Congo Mission, 1952)

Twelve years after Mondombe opened, the Bakers arrived to join an already thriving work. Mr. Lewis Hurt, an American preacher, headed the evangelistic work, while his tiny wife taught in the school. Miss Gertrude Shoemaker, who had been at Kennedy School of Missions with the Bakers, headed the education work. Miss Buena Stober, a nurse from Oklahoma, helped at the hospital. Everyone took his or her part in the building program, supervising the students and African staff, as well as helping in the outlying evangelism, education and medical efforts.

The medical work taken over by my father included treating well-known tropical diseases such as malaria, leprosy and yaws. Parasites were another ubiquitous form of illness causing such misery as elephantiasis. Tropical ulcers, which grew to unbelievable dimensions, took a long time to cure without antibiotics. And Western diseases from measles to syphilis claimed a large toll. Whenever a patient's resistance was lowered by disease, malaria struck, too.

Along with treatments for disease there were surgical and obstetrical demands, training of nurses, Belgian patients coming for examination, treatment clinics at nearby coffee plantations and supervision of first aid clinics in some villages staffed by mission nurses. Less frequent were the emergency calls for the doctor's help from the next station down river, but even that occurred within the first month of their arrival at Mondombe. Although proficiency in the African language still eluded them, the active life of the missionary started immediately.

The extreme deprivation of the tribes around Mondombe almost overwhelmed all other impressions for Mother at first. By December she could distinguish individual faces and was deeply into her share of the station work. In addition to teaching in the women's school in the afternoon, she had charge of the little girls in the girls' dormitory. These were the daughters of back country teachers, who wanted their girls to grow up on the mission in a Christian atmosphere away from the heathen customs of the villages. Mother expected the six children to be increased shortly by four or five more.

Mother assigned work and inspected rooms after devotions at six in the morning. She gave her charges sewing lessons at our house, and in the afternoon they attended school. Her plans for them included bringing in native women to teach them how to make baskets, pots, sieves and other useful handwork. She expected them to keep their rooms neat, their bodies clean and the jiggers removed from their feet. (The tropical chigger or jigger is the common name of the chigoe flea. The female chigoe digs into the flesh of the foot and lays eggs, which enlarge in a small sac causing a painful sore. The ailment was a natural consequence we all suffered from going barefoot.) For good work the girls received little rewards of beads, cloth, magazine pictures, safety pins and other trinkets.

"I'm quite firmly convinced that in Africa, as elsewhere, the home will be no finer than the woman who directs, guides and influences it," she often said.

She wrote again to the Philathea Class:

> Don is outside talking to a leper who has made a broom of native materials. Don helped him tear an old one apart to see how it was made and since then the fellow has turned out some crude but firmly made brooms. We thoroly clean them off with disinfectant before using them and think that removes danger. He is a nice, bright-eyed young chap of much more than average intelligence and industry.

We can't think of the time coming when the spots will develop into sores and he will start losing fingers and toes. We hope the time won't come, because folks think he is better than when he came in for treatment months ago. Whenever he goes along on the path, he is always working at something....

Gradually we are finding our place in the station work. One must take it slowly because of the language. Of course the doctor [Dad] has been doing his work at the hospital from the first. There is much to be done in this vast region and only one doctor to do it. It is four days down river to the nearest doctor and there isn't any in the other directions. He has had patients make a nine days journey to come in for treatment or operation. He has been averaging three major and a few minor operations each week and around 150 patients a day. His heaviest day was 228 patients. How horribly diseased these people can be. Yaws is terrible. I saw one man whose lower jaw was eaten off leaving his tongue hanging and his eyes drawn down. It was horrible. Fortunately a remedy has been discovered by which the sores can be cleared up with one injection. The patients are encouraged to stay for a few extra treatments just to be sure that the disease is completely cleared out of their system.

The natives know nothing at all about protecting their numerous ulcers from dirt and further infection. They fill them with native medicine made from powdered leaves and filthy, magic potions. That, naturally, means more infections and bigger ulcers. They can't comprehend the naturalness of it because their primitive minds believe that diseases are caused by curses, witch medicine and "old women" (apparently spirits of dead women who seek to do evil) ... (LB Letter to Philatheans 12-20-32)

Life was never humdrum. Despite being remotely located, visitors arrived with consistent regularity—a British couple, the Belgian administrator and his wife, the boat captain with his wife and child needing help with an abscessed tooth. Little trips provided other diversions. Dad wrote of some in September:

A couple of weeks ago we three made a trip up river to a coffee plantation. In fact there are two of them some twenty miles apart. They sent their motorboat (since ours was not available). The wife of one of the managers was in need of examination, and we have been cooperating with them along the medical line. We furnish them with a native hospital nurse, and they pay him and supply him with house, etc. So far it has worked out very well, and we have changed nurses every six months. It gives us a chance to get their cooperation, and extends the sphere of our influence.

The motorboat arrived in the late afternoon, and we left at eight the next morning, arriving in the early afternoon. We saw thirteen wild ducks, which let us approach almost to touching them, and one crocodile. Of course I had left my gun at home.

We stayed there three days. Don made the trip from one plantation to the other on his bicycle, and on the way saw elephant tracks in the road, some native dancing at one of the villages, and other interesting sights of native life.

We came home in a long steel canoe with twelve native paddlers to replace the engine. A thirteenth (the natives are not superstitious) beat the rhythm, on a small wooden drum. They not only sang songs, but they sang out their thoughts, sang to villages and passing natives, and told who they were and where they were going, and why. They sang, "The work which we are doing is the work of men." Don asked them not to beat the boat itself, but to beat the drum, since the latter was not so disturbing to Lauretta. They sang about that for awhile. (DHB Letter to Family 9-6-32)

Later in the month Dad wrote more about his work:

Some time ago I discovered a tiny hole in one of my teeth. Mr. Hurt had a big one in one of his. So we got together, and I filled his cavity with some gutta percha filling [a tough plastic substance from the latex of several Malaysian trees], and he in turn filled mine. Now I have found the cement filling which I brought out, and we are hoping to do a more permanent job soon. One of the Belgians on a nearby coffee plantation is hoping to get down for a filling also.

I have been very much interested in my diabetic patient in the hospital. In the first place, it is said to be very rare here. In the second place, I almost missed my cue as to his illness, due to the difficulty of finding out what his symptoms were, tho I realized that he was a very sick man.

Diabetes, as you know, is not so formidable at home, as it once was, due to the discovery and wide use of insulin. Now it happens that some three years ago, while we were in Oklahoma, I had a sample bottle of insulin given to me by a salesman of the Lilley Co. It was only a bottle of a little over a teaspoonful of liquid, but I have carried it around in my bag ever since to have for an emergency.

The man was desperately ill, and had almost reached the stage of coma. He is nothing but skin and bone, yet his life is hanging on the slender thread, or rather, the few drops of liquid in that sample bottle. I doubt if I can get more in this country, and when that little bit is used up his life must flicker out, if he cannot get straightened out before.

After the first injection he made a remarkable transformation, and has continued to improve, tho I am using the insulin very sparingly, and he has still too much sugar in his urine. He is on as restricted a diet as I feel he can be on and live, and I am greatly interested in the outcome. It is dramatic to think that he can live, or could live with just that little something more, which I have been able to give him now, but may soon be unable to supply. I am glad that diabetes is a rare disease here. (DHB Letter to Family 9-21-32)

Dad's surgical patients waited in turn for their chance to be operated on. With only one set of operating drapes, gowns, towels, etc., it was necessary to wash and dry one afternoon, sterilize them the next day and operate the following day. That only allowed about three operations a week, and left them unprepared for emergencies most of the time.

Nurses' schedules posed another problem. Since the nurses who helped with the surgery were the same who worked in the hospital, they had other work to do, also. They attended regular mission school in the afternoons and an hour of medical school each morning. Preparing for one operation and helping with it and clearing up afterward completely filled their time. A number of them were very young men not past twenty. Dad wrote about the nursing staff:

At present we have a dozen students and three of their wives who work in the hospital. Having their wives is a good idea. It gives them an understanding and appreciation of their husbands' work; it gives women patients a feeling of security; it popularizes the hospital among the women. Eventually, thru the women, nurses must help to dispel that trust in the witch doctor and fear of white man's medicine which lurks deep down in all their hearts, especially the conservatives, the women. It gives women's work a dignity and value, and an equality with that of the men. Each morning at six we have a song, a scripture reading and a prayer, and often times—usually—the reading is stretched out into a teaching, simple but good. I really think they help us greatly with the day's work.

After these simple exercises, which are for the nurses only, one of the nurses gives a little scripture reading and talk for all of the patients. One wonders how much they are affected by it as they sit all huddled up in the often times quite chilly, foggy morning air, knees hugged to their chests, with perhaps the scantiest bit of cloth for decency's sake. (DHB Letter to Family 9-21-32)

Congolese patients came to the hospital with their families to care for them. There were no hospital wards in those early days. They wouldn't have known how to stay in them in any case. The few huts that existed accommodated the relatives, too, and were a familiar setting. Obviously, these were not very clean conditions by which to reduce the chances of infection, but the practice of medicine in Africa was far from ideal in many ways. Dad used to say that postoperative infections were not a particular problem in spite of the housing.

Thatched houses for hospital patients and their families

Although mail arrived at Mondombe every other week on the State boat, correspondence to the U.S. took a long time. My parents were already sending home their wishes for a merry Christmas in their October 19th letter. Not until November first did they receive the news that Dad's father had died on August

27th. For two months they hadn't even known. They felt exceedingly remote in the grip of their loss, far away and unable to help. "Perhaps that is where missionary sacrifice comes in. We have had so few hardships," Dad wrote to his sister.

Mostly their daily lives passed rapidly with fun and hard work, as described here:

> A gentle rain is falling outdoors, which makes us thankful that we transplanted some collard and eggplant shoots before supper. We are hoping, too, that it will cool off the atmosphere a little at the end of this, another, exceedingly hot day. The thermometer only went to 93 degrees F. but it seemed as hot as yesterday at 97 degrees F.
>
> That didn't stop us from taking a ride on our bicycles yesterday to a nearby native village, for the afternoon "teaching" which was given there by one of the student evangelists. It was the first time that Lelia had taken such a long ride on her bicycle, perhaps two or three miles, or that Lauretta had done so either. She enjoys it so much.
>
> Now when we say village, you doubtless have a mental picture of something resembling a large camp. You would be surprised to find the villages here are generally one-street towns. Sometimes where the people are more numerous there are houses on both sides of the street, but often there will be two or three or more houses in a group along one side of the road, and no others in sight. Further along there will be another group. Thus a "village" may extend for several miles, and yet have no very large population.
>
> Today Lelia is paying the penalty of her excursion. She says she doesn't remember when she has been so tired. However, she made her work today as usual. Lauretta is a bit fretful, with some new teeth, and a slight cold, and maybe you don't think that doesn't keep us both busy....
>
> We laughed at Ntaate [the student houseboy] the other day. Lelia had told him to soak his dishcloths in cold water overnight and they would be easier to wash. He didn't have sufficient cold water in the kitchen one night, so she found him pouring boiling water over them. She exclaimed and he calmly replied, "It will soon get cold." (Letter to Family 11-21-32)

My parents laughed afterwards. A sense of humor helped carry them through the strains of a new language and different culture. So many times they met totally unexpected reactions or frustrations. Mastering a couple foreign languages necessary to accomplish their daily chores challenged them daily. Proficiency in both was vital to reaching the goals they had set for themselves. A sense of humor helped.

CHAPTER 4

A DIFFERENT WORLD IN 1933

The government, which my parents called the "State," asked the doctors, whose work it financially supported, to take medical census in selected villages. The books they used were huge with twelve columns for as many years and the subsequent annual examinations. Once the censuses were completed, the State would have a valuable collection of information about the health of the people. The doctors were examining for sleeping sickness, yaws, syphilis, tuberculosis and leprosy.

This first census trip revealed only a small percent of anyone with the above diseases. Some people didn't show up for the examination because they were sick. Dad would like to have seen them also, but from the description of their symptoms, he guessed they had pneumonia. During the first census Dad wrote:

> I am supposed to write down the names and family connections of the men, women and children of a nearby group to the total of about five thousand people. I figured that as a result of the four days work we got something over a thousand. In each large village at a central point the State has appointed an acting chief or *messager* who is subject to the chief of a much larger territory. As part of the duties of these *messagers*, they see to the construction of a large mud house for the use of white folks—largely state men—who may pass that way. The house in which I stayed was fairly new and was not at all bad....
>
> The *messager* in this village directs about two thousand people, so is not without authority. He was very friendly and had folks bring us chickens and eggs and other food. He took a great liking to my canvas leggings and repeatedly told me that he wished to have them....

We went to the village, part of the way in the launch and part way by bicycle ... We saw a number of interesting things....

We saw a big steel screw press, placed by the State so that the people of that region could squeeze out their palm oil from the nuts in a more economical and efficient manner. Incidentally that helps them and helps business. There is a huge oil company which buys the oil, for your Palmolive soap, if you please.

At another place we saw a very elaborate grave of a woman, roofed over and planted with decorative plants, including pineapples. I asked the nurses if anybody ever ate the fruit from them and they said that was a big taboo.... For the first time I saw a clay image of the deceased, marking the grave. It was reclining under the shelter.

We were interested in the number of men whose wives had left them, often for men of the same village. The fathers however would continue to care for the children of the first union. One man who presented himself with his children had lost his wife the day or so before. He was blackened all over with charcoal, and wore a cap of leaves from a ferny vine which grows all over in the forests here. He sneaked into the house from the rear and avoided being seen by the group of people standing in front. The nurses said that that is the way of those in mourning. One other time we passed a widow, evidently on her way home from a burial and she wore the same cap of vines, but turned her face to the ground so that we were not able to see it as we passed....

I must admit another interesting feature of the trip was the medicine men who wanted to talk with me. On the way home some women passed us, and we found that one of them was a medicine woman, who was hurrying home because word had arrived of our work in another village where she was treating some sick. Her work differs from that of the men, tho I didn't have time for many of the details. She is supposed to take care of those suffering with demons. But in treating them she does not use knives or bloodletting as do the men. Her treating apparently consists of rubbing, exhorting, and some medicine by mouth. She told the nurses who were with me that she wanted to talk with me. I too am eager to question them tho it is difficult thru an interpreter. A professor at the School of Missions was of the opinion that it was wise to conciliate them and even help them out with harmless remedies such as salts. I am not so sure that it is wise to help them and thus prolong the period of their existence.

They are interesting as relics of a bygone time, and have an immense hold on the people. You would be surprised at the number of people who bear the scars of the bloodletting of these medicine men. (Letter to Family 1-31-33)

Following Dad's census trip, a long hiatus in letter writing can be explained partially by the baby announcement written in Dad's poetic meter:

> God took our circle,
> Welded for three,
> Joined in another;
> But miraculously,
> Increase of circles
> Enlarges e'en more
> The surfaces bordered,
> Now, since we are four,
> The depth of our love
> And the breadth of our ties
> Have widened far more
> Than the circle's new size.

My birth and an extreme "busyness," as Mother called it, she included in a letter to her friends in the Philathea class in August:

> The nicest and most important event was the arrival of our second daughter, Margaret, on the morning of July 17th. In the four weeks since, she has added two pounds to the original seven and one-half, a second chin to the first and is beginning to show promise of a third. She looks like her daddy, especially around her nose and eyes and on the top of her head where the hair is scarce. Lauretta likes her little sister but thinks her old Kewpie [doll] is a better companion. The natives exclaim over the blueness of her eyes and her size. Their babies average about five pounds and gain slowly. [I've been told that, whereas Lauretta resembled a little curly-haired doll when born, I could have been filmed for Gerber product advertisements with my blue eyes and bald head. My father delivered me at home with help from Gertrude Shoemaker, the teacher, in the absence of Buena Stober, the American nurse, who was in the States on furlough.]

The same month it was time to prepare for our July *ekitelo*—teachers conference. We hold them twice a year. The [Congolese] teachers come in from the back country stations to present followers for baptism, to attend school and lectures, to get school supplies, medicine and renewed inspiration. We were somewhat concerned because the financial situation [due to the Great Depression] demanded a big cut in their six months salary of four dollars and twenty cents. They were very loyal, however. Only one man left us to work on the coffee plantation upriver where wages are higher. The rest of the sixty men went back to their towns knowing that six months later may find us in even more straightened circumstances.

The last Wednesday of the *ekitelo* was an exciting day. About two o'clock in the morning the big drums of Lingoma, the long village that stretches away to the north of us, beat out the news of a fight between the two antagonistic sections. Since some of our Christians are from that village they were deeply concerned although they were not anxious to get into the fray. At breakfast time, they said the State-appointed chief had been cut off from his friends, severely wounded in the side and no one knew what had become of him. A *capita* [supervisor] had been killed. The two ends of the village were still fighting. A number of the residents had been over on the river fishing, and all morning long they streamed back home to help with the fighting and the mourning. Women hurried by with gasping sobs. Men strode along with great shields which would offer protection for their full height, grasping their spears and knives, their bows and arrows. The doctor felt that he should go to the rescue of the chief. So Mr. Hurt, Dr. Baker, two nurses and the head preacher who is invaluable settling disputes among natives started out on their bicycles.

They rode for two hours seeing mostly women and children, sitting around daubed with dust and ashes, and weeping and wailing as only African heathen women know how. The few men whom they saw were hastening along with bows and arrows on their way to the fight. At last they came to the last group of houses in the first section of the village. Here, on this side of the valley which divides the village in two, was grouped one side of the fighters smeared with the black clay which the witch doctors had given them to assure success in battle and well armed with native war implements. They learned that two men had been killed. The head teacher talked with them about the foolishness of their fighting and appealed to them on their long established code of justice—a man had been killed on each side. The accounts were squared. Then they rode to the camp at the opposite side of the valley and talked with those men. They were resigned to ending the battle since one man had been killed on either side. Suddenly someone shouted that the enemy was advancing, the big drum boomed out a signal and everyone started forward with arrows in bows and shields on arms. The mission men ordered them to stop and rushed to the opposite side of the valley to halt the villagers. While the native preacher talked with them Dr. Baker and his head nurse, a Lingomo native, went back to the opposite side. The armed men were going down the hill and difficult to stop. The doctor succeeded by taking out pencil and paper and preparing to write the names of all who passed a certain spot. The heathen are dreadfully afraid of having their names written down. Thus ended the activities. The State agent sent out soldiers to corral the guilty parties. When he made his decision on the case, fifteen were ordered to go down river to the Coquilhatville judge. (Letter to Philatheans 8-20-33)

Call this "The Last Battle." It ended fighting in the upper Tschuapa River region during colonial times. Peace pervaded the interior for almost thirty years. The up-river tribes appreciated the freedom from war enforced by Belgium's rule. The interlude included not only the end of intertribal fighting but also freedom from domination by the larger, better-organized down-river tribes.

A week following the excitement of battle, the steady "put-put" of a motor launch sounded around the bend of the river in the pitch dark. Surely someone must be ill. No one traveled through the black nights except in emergencies. Indeed, the boat brought the governmental administrator of the territory and his wife. My father determined that the young man was suffering from acute appendicitis, which required an immediate operation.

Extreme anxiety ensued as the staff prepared for this procedure under the crude conditions that prevailed. Linens and instruments were carefully re-sterilized. The brightest gasoline and kerosene lamps were collected. One missionary held a flashlight to spotlight inside the incision as needed.

With too little light and too many insects drawn to the scene, Dad and his African and missionary assistants removed the ruptured appendix at one o'clock in the morning. Thanks to my father's competence and the assistance of all his helpers, the patient lived. No antibiotics existed yet.

While the missionaries busied themselves with the teaching *ekitelo* and medical concerns, the Africans took advantage of an unusually long dry season to replenish their food supply. The river flow dropped well below the level where drooping green branches usually trailed through the brown current. For days the women streamed out at dawn to the creeks of the nearby swamps. They dammed the water and then scooped up the little fish left floundering in the drained pools. Happiness came with a good catch that not only could feed their husbands but would also leave some for them and their children after the men finished eating. Such havoc with school attendance resulted that the women's school was closed for several weeks.

Meanwhile, the men did their fishing on the river, usually at night. Gleams of light from a lantern and faint songs for courage to frighten away evil spirits wafted over the dark water. They had little to keep the darkness and cool night air from chilling their almost naked bodies.

Tschuapa River catfish

Finally the day arrived toward the close of the season when the natives from all of the villages of the region fished out a lake situated up river from Mondombe. All of the native dugouts from the canoe beach and the big, steel mission canoe carried our station folk on their outing. Coming home at the end of a happy day the overloaded steel boat capsized within a few rods of shore. The water was deep. In spite of their valiant efforts to aid each other three drowned. The loss of one young man especially saddened the missionaries. Such an intelligent, capable and industrious young Christian! He and his wife had developed a fine companionship—a thing almost unheard of among Africans where men were masters and women were property.

A long letter from Mother to the Philathea class, written over a two-month period, thanked her friends for items they collected and mailed to her for use in her work on the station. She continued:

> Since the first of April, Mr. and Mrs. Hurt and their daughter Virginia, Miss Shoemaker, my husband and I have all had malaria. It seems as if every white person in this region has been ill. One woman at a company post a few hours away died of blackwater fever after four days of illness. Previously she had had trouble with malaria and fevers over a period of several months. What a dreadful disease blackwater is. Either one dies very quickly or one recovers slowly. And after recovery resistance in the tropics seems to be low. In three days Madame's red blood corpuscles were eliminated so rapidly that only 10% remained. There was nothing one could do except to make her comfortable and provide her with plenty of liquids to drink. The only known warning is an extended period of malaria and low fevers. Needless to say we are taking every precaution against malaria and its carrier—the mosquito.
>
> I want to thank you for the box of bandages. We certainly need such things for they have been giving around 200 treatments a day at the hospital, operating about three majors a week and a few minors. Dr. Pearson [the previous doctor] worked hard to build up confidence in the white man's medicine and laid a very good foundation in the work. Don has tried to continue the good work. Last week, a doctor, who was inspecting medical work in this territory, remarked about the large number of women among the patients and said, "That speaks well. It means that you have the confidence of your people."
>
> Some heathen just went past the house with the corpse of a woman who just died in childbirth. They didn't bring her to the hospital until the third day and that is too long to wait. Of all heathen scenes, a wailing is the worst. They yell and scream, throw themselves about, and roll on the ground. It is awful. The poor things have no consolation of any kind and they are beside themselves with fear. (LB Letter to Philatheans 8-20-33)

The primeval village life around Mondombe struck not only Mother but also her sister-in-law Betty Smith, when she visited in 1933 from her down-river station. Down river the people had moved away from the primordial life of the upper river. Here the village women she saw mostly wore only three-inch-wide loin cloths attached to a string and perhaps a greasy, short grass skirt. Heavily-oiled "Raggedy-Ann" coiffures, as Mother called them, served with heavy brass anklets and bracelets as adornment. Facial scars announced their tribal affiliation. Housing, gardening and cooking were all accomplished with the simplest of tools to cope with the harsh jungle conditions. Aunt Betty kept remarking about the primitive life around Mondombe from the chattering monkeys and parrots to the men in their monkey skin caps and animal pelts dangling from their belts.

Language formed a barrier to communication. With each tribe speaking its own dialect, the earliest Disciple missionaries learned the local one in Bolenge's Lonkundo-speaking area. This became the language used to translate the Bible and write texts for the schools. As the missionaries progressed up the rivers, they brought the Lonkundo dialect with them. Although the Mondombe area spoke Ladia, a different dialect, the people quickly learned Lonkundo without formal instruction. It challenged my parents, as Dad wrote, "to learn a language here where the people themselves do not converse in it among themselves." Practicality made it impossible to translate and print materials into several dialects.

The State used the local trade language. There were five of these simplified languages in the colony, Swahili in the East being the best known abroad. Dad learned phrases of Lingala to speak directly with patients, for it was generally used by people all over the central Congo. "It is a polyglot," Dad wrote, "lacks the niceties of declension and conjugation, and delicate expressions of meaning. In fact it is difficult to find in it, we are told, sufficient words to convey abstract and spiritual ideas."

The spiritual beliefs of the people directly impacted the medical work. More about these beliefs will appear in a later chapter, but in 1933 the fear of the spirits after death almost brought one woman to a premature end. Mother wrote about the patient:

> Ekila lay in her hut slowly starving to death with a gangrenous tumor sapping her strength and vitality. The terrified neighbors, realizing that she could not get well had already beaten the drum telling of her death, and had refused to give her anything to eat. They are more afraid of death than of poison, and no one would lift a hand to help her.
> Miss Stober [the nurse] found her, and, undismayed by the sight of the tumor or the smell of it, insisted that a pole be brought, a sling be constructed under it, and carriers be found to carry the woman to

the hospital. At the hospital we amputated the major portion of the tumor, supplied the woman with nutritious food, and she has made an uneventful recovery. (Having made the protest that recovery of any kind was uneventful, I was informed that this is the scientific way of saying all went well.)

When she recovers from her malnutrition and anemia we hope to remove the rest of the tumor, although it seems at present to be causing no difficulty. The woman herself is as cheery and grateful as she can be. (LB Letter to Friends 5-1-33)

In 1933 Miss Stober had left for furlough in the States with no assurance that there would be funds for her return at the end of her year of home leave. This left the medical work very short handed. However, the staff rejoiced in October when the mission board scraped up the funds to return Mondombe's second educationalist and expert linguist, Hattie Mitchell, to the field.

Because of the Depression the future looked grim for the mission. Missionaries home on furlough were forced to delay their return; those on the field ready to leave had their terms expanded to a fifth year of service. The Mondombe staff, both black and white, toiled doggedly to maintain their gains, but expanding the work was impossible.

CHAPTER 5

TRIPS, TRIBULATIONS AND VARIETIES OF VISIITORS

Mondombe's remote location insured that the missionaries traveled often for their work. They welcomed the companionship of visits from other whites in the area. One day the Belgian director of the coffee plantations and his wife came to say goodbye before leaving for Belgium. Another day the local State Agent and his wife stopped in and were invited to have noon dinner with us. By this time in 1934 professional governmental administrators had replaced the brutal adventurers of the Congo Free State. The State demanded that these young men—most that we knew were young—spend two-thirds of their time off their posts traveling in their regions. (Contrast that with British colonial policy of fifty percent of the time in the bush.) Dad wrote:

> [The Agent] had been having such a severe toothache for three or four days, that it was impossible to work and so he returned from the itineration that he was making and came to seek relief. The afternoon in which he arrived first, I was out on a thirty or thirty-five mile (each way) trip, running down some smallpox cases, and vaccinating those who lived nearby. Miss Shoemaker and Miss Mitchell hunted up the bottle of oil of cloves, and by packing that in the cavity of the State man's tooth, were able to give him relief. The next morning he returned and I was able to extract the molar, which was badly abscessed at its roots. He has had no pain since, and ate dinner with

the rest of us that noon. That afternoon it rained, and so they stayed for the night. They are somewhat above the average in education and are very pleasant neighbors. Living five miles away, and spending twenty days out of every month on the road, does not give them much time to visit, but we are happy when they can come. (Letter to Family 3-27-34)

Another day the Americans motored in the Mondombe launch to the State Post to have tea with the State Agent and his wife, the Dedoyards. From the beach the visitors walked up the hill to the thatched mud house with its turrets at the corners. Flowers grew alongside the house. Madame Dedoyard served grenadine on the porch as they sat looking out over the lawn at the river. Mother marveled at how easily the conversation flowed from a discussion of ill neighbors to new Victrola records.

Later, the party moved inside when Monsieur Dedoyard arrived from the office. The living room windows were draped, but with no screens, and provided with shutters to close tightly during the many months the Dedoyards spent in the bush. Coarse bricks formed the floors. Chairs covered with blue cretonne and scattered bric-a-brac created an attractive home. A snake skin six feet long stretched out on a plank to dry and canoe paddlers singing on the river emphasized the Congo atmosphere.

Of the formal tea, Mother wrote that it:

> ... consisted of strong coffee and thin pancakes spread with jam and rolled into compact form. The Belgians are just as much amused by our making a meal of pancakes as we are by their using them as a delicacy....
>
> When ready to leave, a little before five, two of the spark plugs in the launch's Ford engine refused to work. Monsieur helped the two natives and after about half an hour we were able to start. But then the pump wasn't working. So we pulled in to the bank and worked on it a long time. By six o'clock it was quite dark, and Miss Mitchell was holding a flashlight so that the men could see to work. Fortunately, we didn't have to return to the beach in the canoe which M. Dedoyard had send for us, altho we did have to call on the paddlers to help push us off a sandbar which lay between us and the deep current. We came home in the dark, in an hour instead of the usual forty-five minutes. How the natives know where to go on this winding river in the dark is

beyond me, but they seem to have a sixth sense on the matter. (Letter to Family 3-27-34)

Fifty-five miles south of the Equator, night fell quickly at six o'clock deviating only fifteen minutes before or after the hour throughout the year. During a full moon one could literally read a letter by the light of the moon. The rest of the month the pitch black gave Dad full opportunity to study the stars in the clear beauty peculiar to the tropics. He pointed out the constellations to us spinning out their attendant Greek myths. Being in the southern hemisphere the North Star lay on the horizon out of sight and the Big Dipper swung in a half circle only. The Southern Cross disappointed him, lying on its side looking more like a kite and "lop-sided at that." In spite of the Africans' uncanny navigation in the dark, their folklore and knowledge indicated little familiarity with the constellations or their movements. Perhaps they spent little time outdoors at night except when dancing in the moonlight. Then the light from the moon hid the stars.

Belgian Catholic missions covered the whole colony. At times the competition for converts and government finances was quite fierce in the colony between the missions of Belgium's predominant religion and the struggling Protestant missions. My father always laughed telling the story of a Catholic priest in pre-ecumenical days. After a visit to Mondombe, the priest generously concluded, "Well, we regard you Protestants as being one step ahead of the Africans. At least you recognize that there is only one God." Usually meetings with the Catholics were more cordial, as Dad relates here:

> Day before yesterday we had a visit from a young Catholic priest. He spoke English, tho we suspect that if our French sounds like his English, they must get many a good laugh behind our backs. He is new to Congo, enthusiastic, and very pleasant. He had come two hours bicycle ride thru the hot sun at noon, and wearing his long white robe, tightly buttoned at the neck. That is not my idea of amusement. The Catholics of this particular region are reputed to be much more liberal than those in other sections, and so far we have had nothing but the most pleasant relations with them. We have heard hints tho, that there were times, not so long since, when the local situation was not so pleasant.... (Letter to Family 3-27-34)

One year two white-wimpled nuns in their full-length habits bicycled several times from the Catholic mission to Mondombe to visit with the single female missionaries. The priests, who controlled the activities of the Sisters, soon stopped the trips. We heard that the priests thought the nuns were getting too chummy with the Protestants.

The time arrived in June for the next biennial conference and another sojourn to Bolenge. The mission steamer, the *S.S. Oregon*, blew its thrilling three-tone whistle unique to the river and swung expertly into its mooring against the bank at the boat beach. It came to transport, in one run, all the up-river delegates, which included all the Americans and a few Congolese from Mondombe, Wema and Moneika stations. A second shorter trip up the Momboyo River to Lotumbe would include the Smiths. In a general letter my parents recounted the preparations for the trip:

> Before we left Mondombe we gathered together all necessary clothes, wash tubs, buckets, beds, food in tins and from the garden, and everything else necessary for a month and a half trip away from home. Then we stored what we left in such a manner that it would be least likely to be reached by beating rains or by the destroying mud trails of the elusive white ants. No one knows what may happen when possessions are left over a long period, miles away from any other white man, but we are hoping not to suffer any great losses during our absence. It is rare that someone does not have possessions destroyed by white ants during Conference time. (General Letter 7-2-34)

The twenty-five-year-old *Oregon* appeared small when compared to the freighters plying the wide Congo River. Although speedy for its size, it took the better part of seven days to reach Bolenge traveling only during the day time. Twenty-one American adults and children squeezed into its three tiny cabins, dining room and narrow decks. Those sleeping on the deck during a rain storm risked being drenched under the rotting roof. "Like the Mission itself, it [the *Oregon*] has fallen on hard times, but pushes forward with courage and energy, looking to better days," my father wrote.

Living arrangements were crowded at Bolenge, too. Each household there took in an upriver family. The families took turns putting food on the table. It required considerable planning for the upriver cooks to bring all their supplies, but that equalized the expense. Few of the missionaries were able to live on their depressed incomes with the low value of the dollar abroad.

One interesting development announced at the conference was the adoption of a single name for all of the Protestant churches in Congo. The Congo Christians had been disturbed by the divisions of the Protestant churches and taunted about it by the Catholics. Now the Protestants would be known as the Church of Christ in Congo. Each evangelizing group would then add their name, *e.g.*, Church of Christ in Congo, DCCM. My parents took pride in the fact that the Congo Protestants unified sixteen years before the National Council of Churches of Christ in the United States of America was born. They strongly supported ecumenism.

Descriptions of the conference indicate that its business occurred in harmony despite the shortage of operating funds. The African delegates shared their work and challenges. The missionaries, meeting separately, exchanged details of their work and examined the financial and human resources available. To fill critical needs in staffing Miss Stober, newly back from furlough, and others were temporarily reassigned.

During the time of the conference the missionaries found an itinerant dentist at Coquilhatville. To go for five years without seeing a dentist was too long unless, as Dad wrote, "your teeth are on two good plates." Although the cost seemed expensive, being comparable to those in the States, the dentist did very good work, so my parents were only too happy to utilize his skills. Dentally restored, spiritually refreshed and socially renewed they boarded the *Oregon* for the two-week trip against the current up the river to their remote station.

Their work followed familiar patterns, but unexpected excitement kept it from ever being dull. In September the most feared predator of the region came calling:

> Had another leopard scare last Sunday night when three more goats were killed on the hospital grounds. Only one was carried off, so that the meat wasn't all lost. However, our table lad insists on getting home before dark or with company thereafter, and spears are in the hands of those who do travel after dark. The night sentry has moved the drum inside of his kitchen so that it can be beaten at 9:00 p.m. and at 5:45 a.m. without venturing into the dark. Made a box trap and are hoping to catch something in the next few months. (DHB to his Sister Ruth 9-9-34)

While the leopard watch started on the station, itinerations continued year round. These circuits from one teaching and preaching outpost to another gave the distant representatives of the mission both professional and concrete support in the way of advice and supplies. In October Mother wrote about an opportunity to become acquainted with the station outreach program:

Last Friday with Miss Mitchell, I started on a weekend trip which was to be my introduction to the back country work. "Do you have a little money with you? Are you taking your bicycle pump? What did you do about that weak tire?" she asked.

"I have done everything except give Don his final instructions on self-protection from the children during my absence," I assured her. (General Letter 10-16-34)

Lelia Baker setting off down Mondombe's main path

To travel in the back country for three days or three weeks meant hiring porters and collecting the necessary gear and food to be almost self sustaining. While fruits and vegetables might be obtainable, one couldn't count on it. Although Mother was leaving for only a weekend trip, the list of gear included cots and bedding, folding table and chairs, food and utensils, lantern, bucket, and materials for distribution. The carriers left at six in the morning. Those on bicycles had time for breakfast—but then it rained half the morning. One day earlier or later really didn't matter among these unhurried people. Mother and her companion left the next morning before the fog lifted. Mother's description continued:

> The sounds of children's voices calling *"Bisikleti"* (bicycles) preceded a merry tinkling of anklets and bracelets and announced our arrival at every village.

There is a monotonous barrenness about these forest villages. The path widens and is bordered on either side by palm trees. Beyond is a narrow, well-swept door yard, and then the low mud or bark huts with thatched roofs. An especially ambitious gardener will have some bananas growing nearby. Around one or two doorsteps a few pretty-leaved plants are to be found; but be assured that it is not for beauty's sake. They are the plants from which the hunter makes his charms, assuring success in the hunt, or the witch doctor concocts his magic potions. Bordering this tiny clearing, shutting out the beauty of sunrise and sunset, and holding in the heat of noonday, is the silent, thickly-woven green of the forest walls.

While resting in the shade of the unwalled "City Hall" [the palaver house in most villages furnished only a roof], we frankly exchanged curious stares [with the villagers] and listened to their still more frank remarks about our personal appearances. We returned confidences, chose the cleanest and the dirtiest of youngsters and praised and lectured their mothers much to the delight of the audience. Conversation never lags among the Bantu. It was all very amusing and entertaining but we dared not linger long for the sun was rapidly climbing. Brief goodbyes were called as we rolled out on the path.

It was a steaming path at that hour. The hot sun was rapidly evaporating the previous day's downpour and, unfortunately, there was no breeze to carry the moisture away. We didn't attempt to ride even a part of the way uphill but were content to walk, and rest a bit, while the bicycle lads pushed the bicycles to the top. That they too, were becoming tired was evidenced by the curt reply given by my lad in response to the common question of the morning. At the sight of a gray-haired and a brown-haired lady they were constantly asked "Mother and child?"

This time my helper, smarting under the implication of inferiority in his assisting the younger, snapped out "You, what do you mean calling her the child? She is the wife of the doctor and the mother of two children."

"You don't mean it!" Then with a doubtful gleam of the eye, "If she has two children, where are they?"

"At home with their father." A silent clapping of hands, a solemn rolling of eyes, and a discreet silence followed this announcement, for who ever heard of a good mother running off like that without her child on her hip. (General Letter 10-16-34)

The trip continued until mid afternoon when they arrived at the village of the first teacher. As with most back country locations, the teacher served also as preacher, and the simple chapel served during the week as the school room:

> We arrived at the first teacher's location in time to briefly inspect the school being conducted in the little chapel. Mud walls extended up about half the distance to the thatch roof, and along the walls at either side of the central aisle were neat seats made by driving stakes into the earth and then spreading bamboo mats over their cross braces. The various classes were reading from the beginners' charts which hung from the ceiling between seats, working problems which their teacher had written on the small blackboards, or reciting for the teacher as he passed from class to class. The school was quiet and well organized, and the children clean and responsive.
>
> Before breakfast was finished the following morning, the village *lokole* was drumming forth the message which called the people to worship. We went over to take our places of honor on the little platform at the front of the church. It was well that we arrived early for soon all of the seats were packed ... The central aisle was filled by those who carried their own chairs: a large leaf, an uncomfortably small stick, or a tiny native stool—no self respecting native can be accused of sitting on the ground. (General Letter 10-16-34)

The dignified service impressed Mother with the changes in the people during the short period of mission influence. The people listened intently, their weapons sheathed, few amulets in sight and bodies clean. Hattie Mitchell sang "My Task" in her rich contralto voice. Then the earnest young preacher spoke to them of his new faith. He had courageously accepted the call to teach and evangelize far from his own tribe and the support of the Mission. Mother found it a moving experience.

The second full year of the Bakers' work at Mondombe with its trips, triumphs and tribulations closed as the others had. The preacher/teachers traveled to Mondombe for their *ekitelo*, or ingathering. The medical census was ongoing. Optimism prevailed in spite of financial setbacks in the States.

CHAPTER 6

BOXING THE LEOPARD

A snuffling leopard, a splashing hippo and a reeking elephant trunk kept my parents focused on their jungle surroundings in the third year of their term. New modern air service from Brussels to Coquilhatville, seven miles from Bolenge, didn't adulterate the customs Dad found doing census in the local villages. Even the birth of a new daughter underlined the distance we lived from supportive family. Letters home continued to describe the wonders that made up our days.

In late January 1935 a back country teacher remarkably killed an elephant with an old muzzle-loader, the only kind of gun most natives could afford because of government taxes and restrictions. The teacher's wife arrived at Mondombe a couple days later with an elephant trunk for sale. Even in that short time the meat smelled too pungent for anyone to want it. Hungry as the students usually were, they announced to Gertrude Shoemaker, their guardian, that she needn't purchase it for them. "Our stomachs couldn't stand it."

The natives in the area of Mondombe did not know how to kill hippos. When they spotted the rippling wake of a hippo's head, they yelled and grunted until the next sighting. Mostly, only the hippo's eyes or bubbles appeared. The animals could be dangerous for a canoe and its passengers. Generally hippos left the river only at night to forage.

One night during the short dry season, when the river level had dropped, the sentry who lived by the boat beach thought he heard someone stealing his chickens. Imagine his surprise as he started out toward his chicken coop to find the hippo behind his house. Both hurried back to cover.

The most exciting animal sighting, however, occurred the next month:

Early one morning in February we heard a call: "Doctor, come quickly, there is a leopard in the trap." The excited voice of the hospital sentry thus announced the news at one in the morning and urged full speed to the big wooden box trap near the goat pen at the hospital. [The trap had been baited with a goat enclosed in one end]. When it was opened and the goat let out, we looked thru the slats of the middle partition, and sure enough, there was a beautiful young-adult leopard in the other end. The flickering oil lanterns showed an excited circle of almost-naked natives surrounding the trap, each man's spear poised for use should the leopard make his escape. The trap had been made six months earlier, and lumber exposed to the sun, rain, and white ants does not last long in Congo. Would the planks and nails hold? A huge hunting net was brought and wrapped many times around the box.

"How shall we kill him?" No rifle, powerful enough, remained on the Station. A shotgun would probably ruin his beautiful pelt. Chloroform was suggested. Why not? The box seemed reasonably tight. Four ounces of chloroform were poured on bits of cotton and pushed thru the trigger hole to the leopard. We waited. No sound from within save a muffled breathing. Again we looked. Mr. Leopard looked drowsy but was far from being asleep. Again we waited. Mr. Leopard growled a deep-throated roar of resentment.

"Why not use poisoned arrows?"

"But does anybody here have them?"

"Do they? There are lots of them!"

"All right then, let's have some." So again we waited until a student teacher, who is a hunter, returned with his bow and arrows. The first glanced off the leopard's skull. The second embedded itself in the thick skin of his neck. After a half hour of waiting, and since we did not know at that time that the leopard had not removed the second one, we decided to give him a third. A hole was bored in the side of the trap and the third arrow sent into the black and yellow skin. He died quietly, twenty minutes later....

The next morning was a regular holiday for us. Very little work was done, and the folks from the adjoining villages all came in to see the leopard. He was tied up to some poles so that his full length—six feet three inches—was easily seen. The visitors came with their shields and spears, and danced and cavorted around in a truly barbaric and entrancing manner. Miss Mitchell took a bunch of photos, and we are hoping to have some souvenirs of the occasion. I skinned the animal myself and am hoping to have a nice skin, after it has been tanned. Skins are unusually difficult to preserve here. (General Letter 4-25-35)

Most feared of all animals in our part of Congo, the natives universally hated the leopard. Ordinarily these huge cats kept their distance from man and his fires, contenting themselves with his goats, chickens and dogs. However, they carried off a child or attacked an unwary woman filling her bucket at sunset at the spring whenever opportunity offered. Occasionally, they became man-eaters. Our State man recorded such a leopard several years before in a tribe just a few miles away from Mondombe. Over one hundred persons were killed by the beast before he was finally speared in a hut.

To skin our mature trapped leopard with sufficient care to prevent nicks in the pelt required several days of skilled surgical effort in the time available. Keeping the carcass chilled presented a problem. The only refrigeration usable was our well-insulated chest called the IcyBall. Two chemically filled, connected spheres about the size of basketballs served as the refrigerating mechanism. Every twenty-four hours one ball was well heated over the laundry fire, then plunged into the water in a rain barrel. This heating and cooling of the refrigerant caused a reverse flow from one side to the other. Frost immediately formed on the ball that fit inside the box, chilling the contents of the IcyBall sufficiently to freeze ice cream.

I can imagine my mother's reluctance in emptying the IcyBall of food in order to clear room to chill the carcass. Such a large animal completely filled the space. When the animal was skinned, my father also denuded the skull for preservation. What days of wonder and excitement for four-year-old Lauretta.

The next year on furlough in the States, her retelling the leopard adventure assumed folklore dimensions. Lauretta's version metamorphosed. When asked about the trapping of the leopard, she explained solemnly, "Well, the goat ate the manioc. The leopard ate the goat. And we ate the leopard!"

The beautiful skin, preserved in Congo and professionally tanned in the States during furlough, maintained its fierce aura draped over the long-toothed skull on our piano. In the tightly shut house of wintry Ohio, its musky cat scent soon permeated the living room, driving us out. My parents reluctantly removed the magnificent pelt to storage in the attic.

That furlough was many months after the leopard was trapped and the box trap carefully stored for future use. No ordinary person could legally obtain a leopard skin today with the restrictions placed on endangered species, but there were no Park Rangers back then to save us from a dangerous animal.

Leopard caught in box trap

Dad returned to the back country in March for the next medical census of 9,000 people. Mother carried the load for the five weeks he was gone. She didn't deplore his absence, because she enjoyed reading his accounts of the people and folk customs he observed and recorded:

> On such a trip, where an effort is made to see every individual, one senses the depths of misery and suffering of these underprivileged people ... One such was little Botshikala who called to me as I rode past on my bicycle, "*Mbote ming*i!" (Many good wishes!)
>
> Botshikala has never walked in all of his eight or nine years. His little legs are almost completely paralyzed. Fortunately for him, the thigh tendons at the knee have not greatly shortened, as is so common here, and the lower legs can still be straightened at the knee. I stopped to examine him, for it was a new road to me and I had never seen him before. His little toes still wiggle. One leg can almost be bent at the knee by its own muscle power. Expensive braces could certainly

put him on his feet and prevent tendon shortening. Crutches would probably not be sufficient. What else can be done for this cheery son of Africa, sentenced from birth to a life denied even of ordinary locomotion, of wife, of family, and of average human happiness? I know not what. He is just one of the many human wrecks unfortunate enough to be born in Central Africa instead of the good old U.S.A., where, under other circumstances, he might become president. Oh for a miraculous power to straighten those withered limbs!

Occasionally however, the refrain was of another tempo and we were encouraged. As: "Doctor, are you there?" An eager voice put the question-greeting in a local tongue I do not well understand. I hastily searched my poor memory to place this smiling middle-aged woman among the thousands who have come and gone at the hospital at Mondombe in the last three years. Conversation being difficult, she waved her left arm at me. Then I remembered that poor forearm. Both bones had been broken for a month, when she greeted me at Mondombe on my return from Bolenge last August. How we had worked with her, with extension and cast and splints! Her useful, well-healed arm and happy smile repaid me more than ever she could pay me with this world's goods.

And then there was Ekila! Ekila whose life Miss Stober had saved [the patient described in Chapter 4].... Her gratitude, as in perfect health she came to greet me, was immeasurable. (General Letter cont. 4-25-35)

In a personal journal of this census Dad recorded several instances of native customs. This first one concerned their administration of tribal justice:

"Augh! Augh!"
The chatter of conversation hushed to listen to the rapid beating of a large drum at the end of the village.
"What does the drum say?"
"A woman has just died."
"What was the matter with her?"
"Two weeks ago her child was born. It was very difficult. After the first day or two she was asked the names of the men with whom she had been indiscreet during her pregnancy. Before her child could be born she had confessed the names of eight men. The child was born dead. It was the fault of these men. One of them has already been

seized by the chief, and the others will also be brought to trial. For the death of the child they will have to pay the father twenty native moneys and two brass anklets. Now that the mother has died they will have to pay her people 100 native moneys, a fine in francs, and spend some days as prisoner of the chief. It is a taboo among us. The men have caused her death. They shall have to pay."

The woman died in her father's house where she probably had gone, as the custom is, for her confinement. She was carried that afternoon to the husband's home where she was buried the next day. He will have to make a reasonable exchange of native moneys with her people as is customary at the death of the wife. (DHB Census Diary 3-1-35)

The elders of the local clans spent the next morning settling the price to be paid by the husband. They decided that he immediately should pay seventy knives and spears plus two brass anklets to his wife's relatives. The wife's family in turn would give him the wife's younger sister as wife. As was the custom, she would drop her name and assume that of her dead sister. The husband should also give his in-laws ten chickens and one goat. These metal and animal assets formed the wealth of the people.

One quiet Sunday morning Dad bicycled for an hour and a half to another village and the same time back, stopping for a short church service along the way. Another day he met the grandfather of our house servant. The grandfather's hands had been cut off at the wrists by the Arabs many years before. Dad recorded seeing other mutilations, which had been inflicted by brutal Arab slave traders in times past. Their defeat by King Leopold's soldiers stands as one of the few positive accomplishments of the Congo Free State.

In a bantering mood Dad philosophized about the survival of the fittest:

> It's a good thing that Lelia didn't cut my hair before starting on this itinerary. I don't have much at best, and I need all the padding possible when entering these houses or passing from one room to another because of the low doorways. Perhaps that is why helmets save so many travelers in the Congo from dying of stroke. Those that go bareheaded probably die of fractured skulls instead of sunstroke. How my poor head has ached from the bumps on the tops of the doorways during this trip! If you believe in the law of natural selection, it would help explain the shortness of stature of the people of these parts. Only the short ones have survived the constant blows

on the head, or have had the agility necessary for constant ducking. (DHB Census Diary 3-5-35)

Most missionaries in those days scrupulously wore pith helmets—as protection from the sun, not bumps. On the boat trip out to Congo my father and another doctor decided it was unnecessary to burden the head with such a heavy covering. A light straw hat would provide sufficient protection. After that first term my family put aside helmets and wore wide brimmed straw hats. I remember loving mine with its decorative circlet of suspended little blue yarn balls.

Still on census Dad wrote to Mother describing another common recreation of the Congolese on bright moonlit nights:

> Park your anklet and join the dance! That is what one woman did here tonight. Most of them would come off with difficulty, but hers was of the hollow variety and perhaps they are parkable.
>
> We have been entertained, in the bright light of a half moon plus the help of Orion, by nearly a dozen women and girls, in what seems to be the current Liondo [village] dance. All told, we totaled nearly fifty, as we stood or sat, and watched the women circle in a follow-the-leader fashion. One of the thin, melodious triangular drums furnished most of the music, tho two tiny drums such as our little one [of the talking drum kind made of a hollowed out log], were used for rhythm and to augment the noise ... Once the group paused in a semi-circle opposite the drummer, and each advanced in turn, solo, dancing, to salute the drummer. (DHB Letter to LB 3-16-35)

Dad some years later filmed a musical entertainer, such as he describes next, in a fifteen minute segment. Unfortunately, sixteen millimeter movies were silent in those days. One can only imagine the song as the elderly man, crouched on a low stool with his eighteen-inch-long instrument, strummed the strings with both hands, sang and rocked, as his monkey skin cap slowly edged down his forehead and was pushed back up between measures:

> Last evening we were entertained by a local musician with a *bonjimba* [a stringed instrument] and his songs. Being unable to understand him I don't know what they were. Iyemo [the nurse] tells me that he has no other way of earning money but manages to pay his tax each year with what he has given him. He selects men of position

or wealth, or both, and by singing for them, to them and of them he usually is rewarded with a cash gift....

The *bonjimba* is the Congo equivalent of a guitar. This one has six strings. He has several combinations of chords, but with any one particular song he uses only one set of chords, varying a little their intensity from time to time. It gets somewhat monotonous, especially when one does not know what he is saying. It makes a real Congo atmosphere, however. First he twists a long curling feather into the hair at the side of his head. Then he tunes his instrument, as any violinist might do at home. Then he plays and soon sings, accompanying his music by rhythmic motions of the parts of his body not occupied with the instrument. It is held lengthwise on his legs and played with two hands. He can still wag his head and contort his trunk. (DHB Letter to LB cont. 3-16-35)

Through the years we children loved the letters Dad sent to us, illustrated with skilled pencil sketches. This census he wrote to Lauretta about the butterflies he had netted, "three blue ones, and one which is red and blue."

Two months later on June the fifth Grace Elizabeth joined the Baker family. My parents must have been expecting a boy for Lauretta for weeks had been asking, "When is little brudder coming?" Another poetic announcement flowed from my father's pen:

> We've a pink-fleshed, blue-eyed stranger,
> Darling little cosmic ranger.
> Bounds this precious bundle small
> The Universe: laws, forces, all—
> Life, and love beyond dimensions,
> Sacrifice past comprehensions.
> Could one solve this riddle blind,
> God, beyond, he'd surely find.
> (Birth Announcement, June 1935)

Grace was colicky at first. Mother sat on the porch hour after hour rocking her, joining her in exhausted crying and wishing her aunts were near to relieve her. After a month Grace grew into a "bonnie wee lass" as an English friend put it, a contented and happy baby. By two months this little doll-like baby knew to duck her head when I attempted to give her an affectionate bear hug.

The Hurts left on furlough in June. Their activities were added to the work load of the remaining four missionaries—my parents and the two educators, Gertrude Shoemaker and Hattie Mitchell. In spite of three young children to care for, Mother did her share. She supervised the baby clinic and the girls' dormitory. She taught the Sunday school teachers, the inquirers class, and a class in the morning school while Dad was home for breakfast.

Dad directed the making and burning of 18,000 bricks. He taught a hygiene class and supervised the garden work for the patients. Then he had breakfast and started his regular hospital day. Taking over for Mr. Hurt, he assumed responsibility for all official correspondence for the station. Paperwork sometimes filled his afternoon.

Aunt Hattie and Aunt Gertrude, as we called our neighbors, supervised the three station schools, the student-evangelists, the boys in the compound, and most of the church activities. Their capable hands carried a tremendously heavy schedule.

As Mother acknowledged, they couldn't have kept the station going "if it weren't for the staunch support and intelligent help and cooperation of some of our fine native leaders. They are on the job each day and ready to mediate and give counsel when difficulties arise."

Mother wrote her sister-in-law Betty Smith:

> Don preached his first sermon two weeks ago. I didn't hear it but reports were good. They are starting to call on me for public prayers in Lonkundo so I can't enjoy any meeting. Public prayer in English is responsibility enough. (LB Letter to Betty Smith 8-10-35)

With her quiet personality, Mother found public speaking difficult. It was a skill she acquired only after much practice. Years later she remembered the morning during her first furlough when she returned to her college town to speak at the morning church service. Exceedingly nervous she looked out over the congregation filled with friends and august professors. Her knees were trembling so badly she was afraid she couldn't stand. In those days Disciple ministers didn't don robes to preach. Looking down she could see that the hem of her dress was not moving. Thus reassured she completed her speech.

Outgoing Dad on the other hand had studied elocution as a youth. All his life he could recite epic poems memorized for declamation programs in high school. We grew up listening to Longfellow's *Hiawatha*, *Evangeline*, and *Paul Revere's Ride* interspersed with the *Pied Piper* and other favorites. Addressing an audience was familiar territory for him.

Writing was a different medium, however. Mother shared the responsibility equally with Dad in describing their life at Mondombe. Her contributions tended to include anecdotes about the personalities on the station and family members:

> ... we find ourselves back in the old pleasant regime [with a baby], enjoying to the full the gradual unfolding of little girl personalities. Grace isn't yet a husky baby, but she is round and rosy and happy. Lauretta and Margaret vie with each other in showering her with attentions. Margaret is at last beginning to talk, and is so very pleased with her accomplishment. Lauretta understands her chatter better than the rest of us and they carry on extended conversations in spite of seeming handicaps. We are beginning to look forward to the time when they can have a year in the States with other children their own ages—"and catch all of the contagious diseases that they have missed in Africa," adds the family doctor. (General Letter 10-27-35)

Thoughts of furlough crept into my parents minds. While the first difficult term for new missionaries was supposed to last for three years, the shortness of Mission Board funds extended the length to four years. The Mission Advisory Committee (M.A.C.), which met on alternate years to the conferences at Bolenge, decided that Aunt Gertrude and we Bakers should leave for furlough in July 1936. That left another year to dig into the work to be done at Mondombe.

In a school composed almost completely of boys, the rare graduation of some girls merited mention in the next general letter:

> The end of the year brings with it the close of our school year. This year, among those graduating, there will be two girls, daughters of teachers, each of whom has finished the regular work of the school. They are about twelve years of age, can read and write, can sew some both by hand and with the machine, and of course, keep house in the native manner. You may be interested to know that they are both engaged to boys of the school and will probably be married after another year or two. They are so different from the girls of the back country. We regret that more of our mission-trained boys cannot find mates of the same quality. (General Letter 12-23-35)

Also, this last month of 1935 we girls got too boisterous pretending we were jack rabbits. We had never seen a jack rabbit, of course, but were hopping around the large bathroom, when I fell against the wooden shipping box used to hold sawdust and cut my forehead on the metal strapping band nailed around it. Mother grabbed a pair of clean, rolled up socks to use as a compress against the inch-long gash and sent the nearest African to the hospital to fetch the doctor. Dad admonished her for using *socks* for the compress. She always maintained it was not only handy but as close to sterile as she could find. White clothes in those days were boiled in wash water over the fire. The cut healed nicely with the help of stitches and left only a small scar under the eyebrow.

December also contained a visit of the *Commissaire* of the Province and his wife. The *Commissaire* was the ranking officer, or governor, of the Equator Province, one of six provinces in Congo. His wife had spent years in Britain and seemed almost more English than Belgian. There was little advance warning of their arrival, but with some behind-the-scenes scurrying to assemble people and prepare food, the missionaries managed to meet their guests debarking from the State boat. An inspection of the school as well as afternoon tea and an evening meal were most pleasant and enjoyed by all the station staff. The Governor recounted the following story from his generous collection:

> Both he and the *Commissaire* of the District—who had visited us a few weeks earlier—are large men. They are both very neat, well-dressed, and with hair well slicked down, and plenty of gold braid in evidence. The *Commissaire* of the Province told us of a motorcycle ride which he had made with the other, to visit a post of the State. The *Commissaire* of the District had not ridden very much on his new motorcycle which may account for the accident which befell them. We never think of the *Commissaire* of the Province but what we are reminded of his story.
>
> It seems that the whole post was lined up in review for their reception, native soldiers, citizens and all, waiting to welcome these two "big vegetables,"—as they were called in French. Just as they arrived before the assemblage, a dog ran in front of the motorcycle, stopped it, and they were both thrown over the handlebars, to fly into the town and finish the ride on the flat of their stomachs.
>
> Our natives couldn't get over the size and beauty of the *Commissaire's* dog. It looked like a cross between a German police and a Great Dane. The breed is used in Rhodesia to hunt lions and leopards, altho this individual did not seem very ferocious. The dogs

of Africa are such scrawny, miserable curs that the natives were properly awed by such a splendid specimen. As one of them said, "If he ever bites you, you will die dead!" (General Letter 12-23-35)

The "miserable curs" referred to here were the hunting dogs of Bantu Africa that never barked. They were not totally silent, however, and occasionally "yodeled." They had to fend for themselves as they were rarely fed, so it was inevitable that they were scrawny. When used in hunting, they were collared with wooden bells that resembled cowbells, the clappers wrapped and silent until the dogs flushed the prey. The hunters followed the mellow rattle of the bells once the chase began.

That they were loved at times by their owners is shown in one of my favorite photos taken of a young boy standing with legs braced holding a dog tucked under his arm to protect it from traffic going through the village. More than one motorcycle or bicycle fell over after hitting a dog sometimes causing harm or even death to cycle, rider and animal.

How these dogs were imported to New York as good bark-less apartment pets is related in a letter from Aunt Betty. In talking to the director of the nearby palm oil company, she found that he and his wife took responsibility for shipping the dogs overseas:

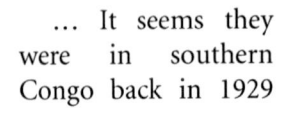

Boy with his dog

... It seems they were in southern Congo back in 1929

and were quite delighted with some native dogs they found there, evidently wild red dogs which had become domesticated. They purchased five and took them to England. Since then they have shipped dogs not only to England but to America and to Australia. They are known as BASENJI dogs, *basenji* meaning "of the bush or forest." (Letter from the Smiths 12-15-37)

The word *basenji* is found in both Lonkundo and Lingala, the trade language. This small, compact, shorthaired breed has a tail that curls tightly over its back. The dog is very popular in the United States.

And thus another year of singular experiences ended with my family happily immersed in the life at Mondombe.

CHAPTER 7

FETISHES OR MEDICINE

Witch doctors and fetishes—or physicians and medicine? The Africans wavered in their choice of treatment for illnesses during my parents' first term of service. Some patients from nearby villages gained enough confidence to come to the hospital or to one of the three outlying dispensaries staffed by mission-trained nurses.

Mondombe hospital stood surrounded by an area as large as the State of Indiana in which there was no other doctor or hospital. The people of the area equaled close to one tenth the population of the city of Cleveland, Ohio, at the time. One doctor would have been overwhelmed should everyone have used the hospital, but during the mid thirties most of them regarded the white man's medicine with great distrust. Wasn't illness caused by evil spirits? Local healers knew how to exorcize these specters. The mission's challenge was to prove the greater success of Western medicine. Dad employed many strategies to demonstrate this advantage.

These appeared in many letters, which described the work performed at the hospital by Dad and the nurses he had trained. He keenly felt responsibility for his patients; and his compassion brimmed over at times when support from the States lagged.

A drum call to waken the sleepers started the typical day before the sun topped the trees. Out of the hundred or so patients and their relatives, those able to work spilled out of the score of mud and thatch houses provided for their hospital stay. Hugging themselves in the cold mists of early morning and ignoring their aches and gaping ulcers, they made their way to the two brick hospital buildings to get their assignments. Without work there would be no food rations and salt distributed twice weekly.

Buena Stober buying food for the hospital patients

By nine o'clock the hot sun burned fiercely. Those at work had finished their stint at making bricks, searching for poles and vines in the forest or splitting and preparing the vines for use in repairing huts or building new ones. The women worked in planting and cultivating cassava, in the pineapple garden or in the fruit tree orchard.

Meanwhile, the nurses attended their school—the three R's, medicine, French, and so forth. Dad finished breakfast and returned to the hospital. He wrote:

> Bompoko has taken the little bronze bell in his hand, and called the sick folks to their treatments. The dispensary routine is well on its way. Those who have had previous treatments group themselves around the windows where their names will be called. Those who come for the first time line up to have their names written down.
> "Elanga."
> "Bekanga."
> "Nsongo."
> "Botsili."
> "Ekila."

One by one they advance and receive the little slips which indicate the treatment needed. Then they separate and pass to the drug room, the injection room, the fomentation room, or the ulcer or special treatment room.

Each new case is examined by the doctor, who indicates on the patient's history sheet his illness and the treatment to be followed. Many of the patients come for treatment of their sores. Bekita here has a horrible ulcer of his leg five inches in diameter, which he has tried in vain to heal at home during the last two years. Bokoto there, injured his leg, and two inches of dead bone are sticking out. Most of these folks have open cuts or scars where the witch doctors have tried to let out the evil witchery causing the sickness. Many of these cuts become infected.

Confidence is greatest in the power of the "needle" (injection of neosalvarasan) to cure. That is because of its miraculous healing of yaws or syphilis sores in a few days. Even the pains and aches which come in the later stages of yaws respond to these injections. Hence, the "needle" is asked for, no matter what the ailment. There will be a long line at the injection room. [Antibiotics were still in the future.]

Since most internal diseases such as pneumonia, are caused by witchcraft, it is unusual that help is sought for them, other than from the native witch doctor. Gradually, however, our folks are learning to ask for cough medicine for their coughs, and Epsom salts and worm medicine for pains near the waist line. Limambe is busy examining stool specimens for worm eggs with the microscope.

History taking is often difficult because of the naive ideas of anatomy and physiology. Sometimes one gives up in despair.

"What is your sickness?"

"It is like this," and the waving fingers start at the crown of her head and pass rapidly over her whole body to the tips of her toes "*kelele, kelele, kelele, kelele.*"

"Does your head ache?"

"It is like this," and again that all-inclusive hand waving with "*kelele, kelele, kelele, kelele.*"

"Does your stomach ache?" More of the same.

One makes as careful an examination as possible, writes the diagnosis "not determined," and calls in another patient.

Iyambe is busy sterilizing the linens and the instruments for an operation. Today it will be an operation for a ruptured hernia, tho in the course of the hundred operations per year many different kinds are undertaken. Ruptures are frequent, large, and disabling. Tomorrow, we shall operate a large tumor called elephantiasis. Yesterday we removed a large cyst or sack filled with water. A few months ago we removed one containing ten quarts of fluid, from a woman's abdomen.

Donald Baker returning arrow removed from patient's abdomen

Operations are performed with the curtains wide open and with an interested crowd of spectators on the outside of the windows. Perhaps it is just as mysterious to them as the "needles" to see us cut open a living human being, who lies on the table wide awake, without pain, and able to answer questions. But at least they can see what is done before their very own eyes as we take knife, forceps, needle and thread, and cut out the tumor masses. This is our front page publicity, our million-dollar radio hook-up.

Loola was a pathetic figure as he came with his rupture and foul, running fistulae. He had about resigned himself to his condition when one day he passed the surgery during an operation. He stayed to watch. When he came back later for his own operation, he said, "I saw you operate a man and he lived, so I want you to operate me."

Few women of this region, except those of the mission, have gained confidence enough to come to us for help at time of childbirth. Usually it is a place of last resort and the opportunity when help could have been given has been lost.

Each Saturday morning the babies and small children come for a baby clinic. Here they are weighed and examined. Here they and their mothers are taught hygiene, and new foods and their preparation. This work would be done best by a white nurse, but we have none at present. The possibilities of working with the women and children have never really been investigated. Both Miss Williams and Miss Stober did excellent work with them during their few years here. [These two American nurses were both in the States at this time awaiting funds for their return. Miss Williams finally resigned and stayed in the States.]

Ah! Here is Mata Bondo. She has but recently come to work with us. We are happy to have a woman in our group of nurses. Less than a year ago Mata was at Death's door. An abdominal hemorrhage emptied her veins and left her cold and pulse less. Her son-in-law and her sister-in-law gave blood transfusions and saved her life. Today she is learning the simple first rules of that science which made that miracle possible. She is learning to help others in their sickness and suffering.

These boys are in for supplies for Iyemo. Iyemo is running a rural dispensary after his three years of training in the hospital. He is bringing health to a new circle of folks back in the forest. Confidence in medicine will pave the way for an understanding of proper hygiene. Knowledge will replace ignorance. Witchcraft, fear, and superstition will be ended–tho O so slowly! Next week Iyambe Daniel will go to open another center of life and healing. The multiplication of these dispensaries will be limited only by the ability of the lone doctor to train helpers and to supervise them and their supplies. (DHB Mondombe Medical Report 11-35)

The medical miracle of Mata Bondo's recovery from an abdominal hemorrhage broke many rigid Bantu taboos. Its description was included in a general letter mailed early in 1935:

What would you do if you were all prepared to give a blood transfusion on the following morning to a patient whose blood coloring matter (hemoglobin) had dropped to 25%, and your only prospective donor took sick with a malarial chill and fever during the night? To give the malaria-infested blood would mean to inoculate the patient with malaria, a patient already so sick that she could hardly take liquids. It might mean a critical weakening of the donor of the blood. Not to give the blood might mean the death of the patient, who is the wife of one of our foremost young Christian leaders, a graduate of our Institute School at Bolenge. Well, we took a chance, waited, found and typed another donor and gave the blood transfusion later. The patient is improving.

The two blood transfusions which we gave her were the first of their kind at Mondombe, and perhaps the first in the Disciples of Christ Congo Mission. At the crises in our patient's condition, the house was filled with sorrowing women and surrounded by sympathetic men. We asked for volunteers who would have their blood examined before giving some to the sick woman. The crowd thinned immediately. Not that they did not want to help, but "What is this about giving blood to another person? Do they just take it out of your arm and give it to the other individual? They are saying that she is bewitched, her illness is so queer. Suppose she dies after I have given her my blood. Will they not say that it was I who killed her?"

The two who gave blood were the husband's niece, and the daughter's husband. When we searched for more volunteers they said, "We, the husband's people" (a daughter belongs to the father) "have given twice, it is now the turn of the sick woman's relatives." But they are heathen, and wanted only to carry her to their heathen witch doctors. No one outside of the family would volunteer.

This son-in-law, a nurse in the hospital, dared do this thing for a woman whom he would not look in the face. He objected to having his shirt removed, and his chest bared at the time of the transfusion, because, "Is she not my mother-in-law?" The two can have nothing in common according to the age-old customs. They must not even look at each other. Who knows what courage was required for this young lad to volunteer for this strange and unknown procedure? What a contrast! Life-saving blood transfusions in a land of pain, disease, superstition and death. How could they be possible except through a Christ-transfused society? (General Letter of 10-16-34 to 1-18-35)

As Dad headed into the back country for the annual census, the paddlers sang, "*Monganga aKoya kosigna mbuku. Docteur asigna mbuki.*" (The doctor is going to write in the medical books.) He sat in the canoe with his motorcycle as the long-handled paddles dipped into the brown Tshuapa River to the rhythmic beat of the drum. A snowy white heron flapped lazily across the water as the travelers slapped at the tsetse flies, carriers of sleeping sickness when infected.

This year, 1935, Dad found yaws almost exterminated among the 8,000 villagers examined, and no new cases of sleeping sickness. In over one hundred children tested the hemoglobin averaged only 53%, as compared with a normal for that age of 75%. Also this trip Dad came across a woman being treated in the local manner:

> On one trip I stumbled upon a native "doctor" treating a broken hip. The relatives and friends were grouped in a semicircle around the end of the hut where a smart fire of twigs was blazing.
> "Where is the woman?" I asked.
> "Over there," they replied, indicating the fire.
> I glanced again at the fire. That held me for a moment, until I remembered their habit of digging a hole in the ground for a broken limb, and of making a fire over it—somewhat like their method of firing their clay pots. Reasonable enough to do it for bones also!
> Examining more closely, I saw her feet sticking out of the earth at one end of the fire, and beyond a barrier of banana leaves and a native mat her shoulders and head. Soon she was screaming with pain, and the very real fear of being burned by the fire. At a signal from the "doctor" the fire was scraped away and the moist earth and leaves removed from the hip. At this point the "doctor" proceeded to massage vigorously at the place where the bone was broken, amidst the renewed screams of the woman. He was not at all pleased with the results of the first "firing," so the leaves, earth and fire were renewed. I watched the firing process three times, and each time the leaves became fewer and the earth drier and more scanty. I have often wondered what happened to the poor soul, treated by a method so barbarous. Perhaps she, too, like so many before her, emerged from the experience with some first rate burns in addition to her fracture. My plea to splint the leg and send her to the hospital went unheeded. (General Letter 4-5-36)

With the reductions of the mission budgets and the diminishing American personnel to staff the work, Dad worried constantly about the future of the medical work and how to pay for it. The stations where nurses ran the medical work received no recognition and no funding from the State. Their funding came out of the meager station appropriations. The stations with a doctor had State funding to support their medical work.

In January 1935 my parents were anticipating their approaching furlough and the absence of any white personnel on Mondombe Station for a time. Dad's concern for his hospital and the welfare of his patients spilled over in an unusual agonized and bitter appeal to the Christians of America for more compassion:

> We wish sometimes that we could have visit us, those complacent individuals who excuse themselves out of their opportunity and duty of missionary support, on the grounds that the heathen are happier let alone than they are after they have been interfered with by missionaries. We have all heard their specious arguments, which often sound very real and convincing. May God forgive them for their chiseling, and for their selfishly-turned theories! No dispensary at home could have the same proportion of pain, suffering and sickness as we see here, so much of it preventable. Yet we merely scratch the surface of what is present in this huge area....
>
> In this supposedly Arcadian picture, we must paint also, that before the white man came, might made right, and the strong man and the witch doctor ruled the land. Fear stalked man on every forest path, and no one ventured far from home. Intertribal wars were constant, slavery abounded, and death was just around the corner.
>
> And if we Christians should raise our thresholds of sensibility to their needs, and refuse them help, they will still be influenced by Western civilization, but largely by its commercial and sorrier aspects. Commercial traders are found in all parts of Congo, and commercial concerns already occupy vast areas of productive or valuable territory. Neither the government nor the commercial concerns can offer these people any method of inward control which can replace the rapidly disappearing taboos and fears by which their conduct was regulated in former times. (General Letter 10-16-34 to 1-17-35)

In his passionate appeal Dad went on to describe more of the miserliness of the life of the people that made such an impression on him. Health sagged for these people when two successive days of rain depleted the dry firewood. Without a fire, bodies chilled and no food could be cooked. How could they hunt food nakedly in the cold rain? Even at best their food lacked protein and variety. With no layer of fat or reserve strength, the first real sickness carried them off. Once little ones stopped nursing they grew stunted, pot-bellied and anemic for lack of easily digestible food and protein. Blankets and clothing came with the white men, but the villagers around Mondombe had few in 1934.

Dad mentioned the moral compass the church could teach and the help the hospital had been able to offer. Gaining the confidence of the people furnished his reward:

> We are happy that we can contribute to this change in so many ways at the hospital. Before one can be educated one must have a desire for other things, and before one can desire other ways, one must appreciate them and have confidence in them. Confidence in our ability to cure people is constantly increasing, and with that gain in confidence there is an equal loss for the old superstitions and the old ways. (General Letter 10-16-34 to 1-17-35)

The hospital saw one hundred operations completed that year, 10,000 injections for syphilis and yaws, and between forty and fifty thousand treatments. The enthusiasm for dressings of ulcers and sores was exceeded only by the popularity of the "needle." And the whole reception of the hospital (*l'hopital* in French) was expressed in the name of one baby born there. When asked what she called her baby, the mother said, "Lopitala."

Obstetrics held a large place in the medical work. Although it was hard to convince the women to come in for a birth, once things started going wrong, they were often saved at the hospital. Served best were those who lived close by. Many times the process had advanced too far to rectify by the time the mother found herself in trouble after two or three days of labor.

Hygiene lessons, the science of health, included another approach to upgrading the well-being of the Congolese—better nutrition. Dad's love of farming translated into a lifelong engagement in improving the agriculture of the area. By the midpoint of his first term he had already visited the colonial agronomy center down river and invited the Belgian agricultural agent to lecture the teacher/preachers on the topic of improved methods of gardening. The following report he titled "Feeding the Multitudes of the Congo":

One feature of the contribution which missionary work makes to the lives of Congo natives will not be found in any statistical or literary report. It is the constant, quiet introduction of new foods to their diets. At Mondombe, the furthest inland of our six Congo Stations, where the work is among a most backward primitive people, efforts are being continually made to increase the varieties of food and the manner in which they are eaten. For generations they have been accustomed to the simplest articles of food, which consisted largely of tough, sour bread made from manioc [cassava] roots, the pounded leaves of the same plant cooked with palm oil, and meat and fish when available. Bananas and fruits from the forest supplemented the diet at times. Corn was eaten on the cob but not otherwise. Few soft, easily-digested foods are available for the sick and the very young.

Demonstrations of new foods, such as rice, adlay grain, kaffir corn [sorghum], new leafy vegetables, tomatoes, peanuts, beans, cornmeal, and flours of various kinds suitable for mushes for children and the sick, are constantly made in hygiene classes and to the mothers at the weekly baby clinic.

Another way in which the diets of this whole Mondombe region are being changed is by the introduction of several excellent fruit trees which have been scattered thruout this area, largely thru the teacher/preachers. They have carried seeds and seedlings from the Mission Station with them as they went out to their posts in the back country. Oranges, mangoes, breadfruit trees and avocado pears have been distributed in this manner.

Unfortunately, many mango trees do not fruit in this section. Breadfruit trees must be started from slips, and so, tho their addition is a valuable one, their spread will be very slow for these people are poor agriculturalists. Orange trees require ten to fifteen years before fruiting unless cared for under favorable circumstances, so that their increase will also not be rapid. These trees, scattered as they are, already make itinerations easier for the whites who pass their way, and must gradually improve the diet for the natives.

Perhaps the most interesting, the most valuable, and the most revolutionary of all is the avocado or alligator pear. Avocado pears are quoted as containing, in the edible portion: 3.8% protein, 34% fat, and 7% sugar, (hardly a reducing diet), in addition to a rich supply of vitamins. The large hard seed in the center, thrown onto the rubbish pile, soon sprouts, and bears fruit in from four to five years. The trees bear abundantly, and almost thruout the year. It is rare that we are without them on the Station where there are hundreds of trees, and where they form a large part of the diet of our natives. With trees scattered thruout this region in strategic centers, the natives are carrying them everywhere, and in a generation they will revolutionize the meager diets of the natives of this region. This is an inexpensive, easy, and Christlike way of bringing them "a more abundant life." (DHB Article for Submission 3-2-36)

I have vivid memories of my father grafting improved oranges onto sturdy stock. (With my jackknife I tried the technique with hibiscus bushes, but mine had no success.) The grafted oranges bore sweet fruit, a contrast to the previous sour specimens. A shorter period to fruiting was another benefit. The shipments from the experimental agricultural stations brought new varieties of fruits from across the world, as well as thick-meated palm nut seedlings by the hundreds.

We had one tropical rough lemon bush that sprouted smooth lemons and tangerines on the same trunk after grafting. The dimpled lemon matured to sizes much larger than the store-bought varieties bought here in the States. It's thick, dark green rind left small space for its juicy interior. Grafting the spindly smooth lemon to the vigorous rough lemon tree successfully attempted to join the best of both types.

We sat eating a lemon pie one day during this time. "It's too bad the rough lemons are inedible. Then we could have this delicious pie more frequently," said my father.

Mother looked at him in surprise. "This *is* the rough lemon we're eating."

She used her skill and trial and error to develop recipes utilizing new and unfamiliar foods available locally. This experimentation extended to foods introduced to the Congolese in hygiene classes and the baby clinics, which she supervised during the absence of an American nurse. Thus she assisted Dad in his campaign to improve nutrition—one of his strategies for better health.

CHAPTER 8

TIME FOR FURLOUGH

To be three years away from the States seemed an interminable period for new missionaries arriving for the difficult adjustment to service in Congo. Working there required one to speak in Lonkundo, cook and eat strange food and fight attacks of malaria. One melted from the humidity. News from family and friends had aged two months by the time letters arrived. Missionaries anticipated furlough with relief by the end of the first term.

A year's respite in the States improved their health and allowed them to renew relationships with family members and supporters. During that year, refresher-training courses upgraded their professional skills. Disciple missionaries then returned to the field renewed for the longer four-year terms that followed. Term lengths differed from one mission board to another.

With the UCMS budget shortages in the mid 1930s, furloughs lagged and most missionaries were overdue. We Bakers were no exception. My parents had been in the Congo more than four years their first term. Their planning for the trip "home" was ongoing in early 1936. Along with her usual activities Mother wrote to her sister-in-law, Ruth Baker:

> ... Hope you and Mother weren't too disappointed over the postponement of our sailing date. We were going to ask permission to leave in April instead of February but because of the shortage of staff on so many stations the Missionary Advisory Comm. Asked several of us to stay over until July. It doesn't solve our problem, however, for Mondombe will have to close down until after our conference (proposed for September) if Gertrude and we leave in July. (LB Letter to Ruth 1-22-36, finished 2-3-36)

A letter to Mother's Aunt Cora thanked her for a recently arrived package. It contained items requested months before, in part for Lauretta's birthday and also clothes for the trip to the States. She mentioned hearing from her brother Grant that her father was seriously ill. "If it weren't for Papa's sickness, we should probably stay on here until September." Father Barber's health isn't mentioned again. He lived to be 93, so this ailment ended successfully. Perhaps their cablegram to UCMS asking them to see about medical aid for him helped.

Also in March, Mother wrote again to Ruth who, in addition to being her sister-in-law, had been one of her college roommates. Plans for furlough included sharing a house with Aunt Ruth in Cleveland. They asked that she go ahead and find one for them keeping in mind their small budget, laundry facilities and the quality of the local school.

The letter continued:

> We hope to spend four or five days with the Smiths on our way down river and take our language exam under their co-worker, Mr. Hobgood, who wrote the grammar. How I relish the thot! (LB Letter to Ruth 3-?-36)

Meanwhile, Dad was back from four weeks of medical census and had twenty-seven surgeries needing to be performed. In April my folks composed their last general letter before departure:

> If present plans carry, we leave Mondombe the last of June, and Congo the middle of July, arriving in the States by way of Belgium the last of August. We expect to have as companions, Miss Shoemaker and two grown girls, [missionary daughters]. We will take up residence in Cleveland, Ohio, after short visits with our relatives at Hiram and Beaverdam, Ohio.
>
> It looks probable that Miss Stober, our nurse at Wema [now back from the States], may be loaned to come and help Miss Mitchell at Mondombe for a month or two, which will take us up almost to Conference time in September. If so, the hospital and dispensaries can be continued in operation, and the general station work be kept going. That will be fishing season—the long dry one—and a vacation will be in order. If Miss Stober cannot come, we shall have to close the Station for three months.... (General Letter 4-5-36)

Because Lauretta fell ill with the chicken pox in London mid trip, the family was immediately quarantined, as was customary in those days. Dad moved the family into a guest house and out of the expensive hotel. While Lauretta recovered, Grace and I contracted the disease, broke out in spots and the quarantine continued for another two weeks. What a way to spend a month in England! Late September arrived before the family reached Ohio.

By October we had settled into a house on the west side of Cleveland with Aunt Ruth. Lauretta attended first grade at the nearby public school. One of my few memories of furlough was climbing up and down the high, black, coal-sooted steps that bridged the train tracks on the way to my sister's large city elementary school. Another vague memory recalls a paper plate art project she brought home. Paper plates were surely a novelty for us.

Dad was working with a Dr. Cole to sharpen his medical skills by learning the recent advances of American medicine. That fall he spoke at the national convention of the church describing the practice of medicine at Mondombe. The speech was well received. He was pleased by a commendation written by the head of the African Mission Division of the UCMS. "You did a splendid job of it in presenting your work to the International Convention," Dr. Yocum wrote. "I was exceedingly happy that you were able to attend and I know that everybody who heard you was stirred by your message."

During that winter we children lived up to predictions and contracted all the childhood diseases in one year, as well as ear infections and the usual colds. I alone escaped the mumps. Being only three years old I remember few activities of that year. The oft-told stories seem like memories, however. I do have a vague recollection of the doctor coming to the house as I lay on a velvety, wooden-legged couch suffering the pain of an infected ear. The doctor lanced it—a common treatment in those pre-antibiotic times. Despite the illnesses, there were many reunions with family and friends. One picnic on the bank of Lake Erie, aborted by rain, became confused in my mind with having taken place on the bank of our river at Mondombe.

A family reunion photo shows us children in snowsuits and wrapped in knitted scarves. The excitement of snow and seasons, automobiles and trolleys, department stores and large groups of American children brought new wonders into our lives. The African mahogany cutting boards in their hippo shapes, which my parents brought back as gifts, had been outmoded by the introduction of another wonder—sliced bread. No one had thought to mention this modern invention in letters to Congo. "As common as sliced bread" was just coming into vogue.

During our furlough the revenues for the mission board had not increased. In fact the UCMS again suffered some reduction in funds. Fortunately, it was able to maintain a budget that allowed all missionaries to travel home or return to the field. To the missionaries' surprise, the mission board also paid the month's salary that had been withheld in the spring of 1932. My parents were grateful that the imposed stay in London was accepted as a legitimate medical expense and reimbursed by headquarters. With the shortage of money no new personnel would be hired for the field. While expected, it was discouraging news.

The lengthy process for the return trip started less than four months after our arrival. The innumerable preparations included sailing reservations on the *Queen Mary*. In filling out forms for visas my parents had to obtain character certificates from the chief of police required by the Colony.

Baggage measurements demanded attention. Only fifteen cubic feet of luggage were allowed free of charge for each adult passenger. Could all the supplies be included?

By the end of July the flurry of departure ended as the *Queen Mary* pulled away from the dock. The Bakers again were traveling with Gertrude Shoemaker. Plans for our arrival on the mission field had been made. We were to travel up river to Mondombe on the *Oregon* with the representatives to the M.A.C. meeting.

Since Uncle Everton was Lotumbe's representative to the meeting, the Smiths, now including three boys and a girl, traveled up the river to enjoy a brief reunion with us. My parents recorded their happiness in returning and shared some of their memories of the trip out:

> It is good to be back! Our native friends have come to tell us so. We, for our part are possessed of a deep satisfaction. We had forgotten: How dark brown is the water of the river! How like Oklahoma heat 95 F. in the shade can be each day! How matted and mysterious are the forest walls of the river during the last two weeks of the inland journey! How terrifying the tropical thunder and lightning! How rhythmical the African activities!
>
> We are back in the land where people appreciate the miracles of everyday living; and their leisurely attitude gives them time and inclination to marvel. During our first visit with any of our co-workers, the native helper had succeeded beautifully in chopping some dried beef. It almost filled a quart saucepan.

He looked at it and then at the glass from which it had come, and queried with evident admiration, "How did they ever get it all in this one jar?"

The Atlantic crossing was enjoyable. The boat was steady and comfortable, and the trip short....

Ten days in Belgium gave us an opportunity to buy some suits for the tropics, metric measures, Belgian-made maps, and French books for school. Then there was a day's excursion in a rented car to picturesque Bruges and Ghent. We enjoyed, also, short visits with Belgian friends before August 13 arrived.

The *S.S. Albertville* (10,630 tons) had a friendly but not as intimate an atmosphere as the smaller *S.S. Elizabethville* on which we sailed home. We were impressed by the number of women and children on board—many more than when we came out in Feb. 1932. There was a large third class group of miners and their families, probably specialized workmen. The food was of the French cuisine variety—as usual, delicious, with fish, fowl and meat prominent on the menus. Grapefruit were not only on the menu but, much to our surprise, were eaten by many of the Belgian passengers. The chief steward told us that they call it the fruit of the "Stars" because they are eaten by the stars of the silver screen in Hollywood....

The biggest surprise of the trip came the night at the dinner table when a larger wave than usual reached our open porthole, and by doing a semicircle managed to hit Lelia on the back, and Doctor!– well, it showed no partiality to any part of him! (Oh! But it was chilly as it trickled down!) While handkerchiefs and napkins gathered up unabsorbed moisture, the steward removed the plates and silverware which had been liberally sprinkled with tasty saltwater. Someone suggested that it was more appropriate for us Disciples to have the baptism than for the Presbyterians across the table from us. (General Letter 11-21-37)

The trip across the Atlantic ended at Matadi. Again the Swedish missionaries provided lodging and assistance with baggage and customs. Their mission on top of a hill was restful and cool. It was a pleasure having safe food and water to consume.

The next day we boarded the train to Leopoldville. They made a stopover part way there at the American Baptist Mission at Sona Bata. One of the doctors and his wife most hospitably entertained the family and showed Dad their excellent training for nurses. This advanced school, certified by the government, required staffing by two doctors and an American nurse.

The extra staff available to the American Baptist Mission left Dad envious. At the DCCM just then the Bolenge hospital stood idle for lack of either a doctor or an American nurse. The hospital at Lotumbe shared the same shortage. It felt good to be returning to resume full service at the Mondombe hospital.

At Leopold we boarded the Otraco boat, run by the government, to reach Coquilhatville and nearby Bolenge. From there the *Oregon* paddled up river arriving September 26th.

The Bakers were launched into a second term of service.

CHAPTER 9

MONDOMBE'S STAFF AT WORK

During my parents' second term their letters reflected a decided change from the earlier years. They wrapped the Congolese in terms of friendship, appreciation of their culture, and happiness in rejoining them in the work. Gone was the emphasis on the pathetic, benighted primitive. Their use of the term "heathen" referred matter-of-factly to those who were pagan—non-Christian—and not to the alternate meaning of uncivilized or barbarous.

It grates on today's sensibilities that my parents used the old comparison of Africans to children, imbuing lightheartedness and joy in play to immaturity. Even there one senses their acceptance of a different culture with its leisurely time schedule, its wonder of daily miracles and enjoyment of little foibles in peoples' behavior. My parents were sincerely trying to understand a vastly different culture, a culture lacking much of the rigid attention to details, measurement and focus on logical progression that so defined work and responsibility for these descendants of the Puritans. Both missionary and Congolese needed flexibility and generosity in creating a community where success could be attained. The willingness was there, the knowledge and understanding increased yearly. The words occasionally evoke umbrage today.

My parents meant no disrespect either, when they referred to the single female missionaries as the "girls," though it puzzled my sisters and me. In the next breath, we heard ourselves so labeled. We regarded the term as age related. In those days, long before the women's movement, it would not have occurred to anyone to ask how Gertrude Shoemaker, Hattie Mitchell and Buena Stober felt about the designation. They didn't seem to take it amiss. My parents remained on the best of terms with all three. The American staff at Mondombe worked amicably and thoughtfully together. That didn't happen everywhere under the trying conditions and with the strong personalities found on the mission field.

The "three girls" and the Hurts staffed Mondombe when my parents returned from their furlough. They served as the missionary children's extended family, so we addressed them, and many other missionaries as "Aunt" and "Uncle."

Mr. Hurt, a minister, led the evangelical branch of the work with the able help of the Congolese pastor, Ntange Timothy. Tiny Mrs. Hurt taught at the school. Eight-year-old Virginia Hurt accompanied them on back country trips and joined in decorating the church and other projects.

Education, the second branch of the mission program, worked closely with the evangelistic, as demonstrated in the back country schools and chapels led by a single preacher/teacher in each village. Aunt Hattie and Aunt Gertrude supervised the different levels of schools, not only working together but also living in one house with separate bedroom/bath/sun porch units and a central living room and dining room in between. The kitchen stood separated by a porch from the dining room. Above was a wooden-floored attic, the spooky scene of the most successful Halloween party ever held at Mondombe.

Aunt Stobie headed the medical work while Dad furloughed in the States. Missionary nurses proved every day to be uncommonly resourceful and able practitioners. On some stations they never had a doctor to assist them. At others they filled in when the doctors traveled and helped in every aspect of the hospital. Aunt Stobie rescued orphan babies, saved our teeth, and even directed the Girl Guides (Congo's equivalent of Girl Scouts).

One early morning in August 1938 Mother called us to get up. "As a special treat you may go next door to the Hurts' for breakfast," she said.

I still remember that cool morning skipping over to the Hurts' house where we were served pancakes with Lyle's Golden Syrup. What a treat indeed! At home we just ate homemade brown sugar syrup.

After breakfast we transformed the Hurts' living room into a playhouse, upending chairs and a rocker and covering them with rugs. They made shadowy spaces in which to creep.

Around noon Mrs. Hurt sent us home with exciting news. "You have a baby brother."

"I knew that's what was happening," said Lauretta with her seven-year-old wisdom. We ran excitedly along the short path between houses. I was completely surprised. Obviously, I hadn't connected the fun of spending the morning away from home in any way with the approaching birth of a baby.

Mother had waited until well into her pregnancy before telling us a baby was on the way. Changing into our swimsuits one day to go to the sandbar seemed an appropriate time.

"What will it be—a boy or a girl?" Lauretta asked.

"When will it be born?" I asked in my turn.

Mother was most leery of Grace's question as she jumped up and down in her eagerness.

At last it was her turn. "WHEN are we going swimming?" she burst out.

We were entranced with our chubby baby brother. "So different from you girls," said Mother. He was named Maurice Wynne after an ancestor on Dad's side of the family. *Maulisi* was the Africanized pronunciation of his name. That became his Congolese name, too.

That summer the school break had provided the usual opportunity for the American minister and teachers with their African colleagues to travel in the back country for supervision and in-service training of the small school/churches with their teacher/preachers. After itinerating, the Hurts held an institute on the station, took another trip and then were transferred to Coquilhatville to serve as legal representative for the mission.

A new minister and his family just out from the States were assigned to Mondombe. With Ned and Jewell Roberts came their two tow-headed boys, one-and two-years old. From then until their mid teens the boys were my brother's inseparable companions. Usually where you'd see one little blonde head, there would be three.

Versatile Aunt Gertrude had assisted my father in Maurice's birth the year before. Now she added the Roberts' language training to her tasks of supervising the women's school, the advanced afternoon school and the boys' dormitory. Aunt Hattie led the rapidly expanding morning school, dealt with problems of the back country teacher/preachers and served as the station treasurer. And Aunt Stobie took on the twenty-three girls in the girls' dorm, baby clinic, dental clinic, the pharmacy with its provisions for the outlying dispensaries as well as her other nursing duties.

The missionary wives always helped professionally with the station activities, in addition to raising and home schooling their children. To release her time for missionary tasks, Mother always hired people to help with the housework. Having a cook was a necessity where not even potable water from the faucet was available. To purify the water it was boiled in a copper wash kettle on the stove for twenty minutes. Then a couple workmen carried the kettle with its soldered-on faucet to the end of the kitchen table. To wash clothes in big galvanized tubs, scrub them on a washboard and boil the white cotton sheets over the fire took a man's strength. The clothes dried on wire lines and a charcoal-filled iron smoothed out the creases.

With the time thus released, Mother taught one or two classes at the mission school. They were usually advanced classes in French, geography or mathematics, which demanded a higher level of academic training than was always available from the ever-improving African staff, especially in the early years.

She often taught a class for the women. What a chance to look into their lives! They carried heavy loads as they returned from their gardens with manioc roots in their woven baskets and firewood piled on top. Often two people would lift the seventy-or eighty-pound load while the woman adjusted the straps over her shoulders. Some of the baskets also had a head strap. There might be a baby on the hip as well.

To change their lives of servitude to their husbands into a more balanced partnership took years of teaching, modeling and working with both the wives and their spouses. Discussions in class about nutrition included the concept of serving food as the family ate together instead of the man eating first, for example.

Through the years Mother took her turn directing the girls' dormitory and baby clinic. Much later she assisted in language training and even became the station treasurer. Supervision of the staff at the house and in the yard and gardens fell mostly on her shoulders, especially when my father was gone for long periods. She wrote to her friends in 1938, just two and a half months before the birth of my brother, about her duties and daily activities:

> Doctor is gone now on census work. This is the fourth week and there will be one more. I've been busy with schoolwork for our girls, three classes of handwork per week for the women, and baby clinic on Saturday besides the regular routine of household tasks, garden, chickens and flowers. Of course I have native help, such as it is, but it takes a lot of supervision.
>
> I've also been supervising a so-called carpenter who is working here at our house repairing lids for the water tanks; making a chicken coop, tables for the girls' schoolroom, and stools; and putting shelves and legs on boxes so that they can be used as cupboards. He can't saw through a one-inch board without going slantwise. And it took us one whole week to roughly plane, saw and put in place boards for four shelves in the storeroom. I do all of the measuring and marking because I'm so much more accurate. My brains and his brawn never were meant for carpentry work. There are better carpenters in the country, but they seem to be located elsewhere at present. (LB Letter to Philathea Class 5-31-38)

Mother always said she contributed the most by example, as in demonstrating Christian family living. As a direct result of this belief she did not turn her children over to a Congolese nanny as many of the missionaries did. She felt confident that she had more skill and knowledge of raising Christian children than they did.

Supervising the young people who came to find additional education after they had finished the three years offered in the little backcountry schools was a valuable but time-consuming task. Many of these children were older than the nine to ten years one would assume in the States for that level of school. They didn't start school at any traditional age out there.

The boys who boarded on the station lived in a brick quadrangle dormitory built around a spare, grassy court. Arising in the foggy morning when the drumbeat wakened them at six o'clock, they received their work orders—grass cutting or pruning the palm trees, for instance. The latter job for the older boys sent them up a bamboo pole with a machete as their bare feet gripped the slight hold offered by a chopped off twig. There they hung by one hand, slashed away the older fronds and whacked loose a large bunch of palm nuts, which fell with a thud to the ground. The rich orange meat around the kernel of each nut furnished the delicious oil for many dishes.

Drumbeats released the toilers from work for a half hour before school started. Classes lasted for three hours; and then they had their one full meal of the day. They were free to make a few francs at odd jobs in the afternoon or gig for fish.

Mother hired Iyambe one Friday afternoon to make sixty toothbrushes for distribution at baby clinic the next day. He cut vines in the forest and divided them into six-inch lengths. Then he frayed them at one end. Mother called to him:

> "Did you hack the brushes with a knife, as I asked you to?"
> "No, Mama. I tried, and they split, so I chewed them loose."
> "'All sixty of them, Iyambe?"
> "Yes, Mama, except for the one I spoiled."
> "Iyambe, you've had hygiene in school. Don't you know about germs in your mouth that will get into the little children's mouths?"
> "Yes, Mama. I know about germs, but that is the way we make toothbrushes."
> At his suggestion, the toothbrushes were sterilized by boiling, altho it made him a bit late for his soccer. (General Letter 6-27-39)

Sending a daughter to advanced school at the station was rarely considered worthwhile by Congolese parents or even by a daughter herself. In a culture where most ten-year-old girls had already been promised in marriage by the exchange of bride-price, moneys between the grooms' and the brides' families, a formal education seemed irrelevant. The girls continued to live at home until reaching physical maturity.

Gertrude Shoemaker leading games with girls from the dormitory

By 1941, however, Mondombe was proud to have twenty-four girls between the ages of ten and fifteen in the boarding school. Aunt Gertrude expressed in an article her great empathy for the difficulty of being one of these rare students:

> This morning at girls' school four were absent. When we sent for them their excuse was that when they finished school they had no future except to 'cook manioc,' therefore they'd just learn to cook and let the reading go. Upon hearing that remark one of the teachers said, "Isn't that just like us Congo people. We don't appreciate the opportunities we have."

Being an upper grade school girl in Congo quite often means that you are the only girl in your class, because those that continue their schooling are rare. Our Sarah (called Sala in Lonkundo) is alone in the second grade of the second degree school. Her classmates are sixteen lively boys who love to laugh and tease as all boys do. She is the daughter of the assistant pastor of the church and is teaching a primary class in the children's school each morning. In her school she has been so very timid and reserved she has failed in arithmetic and French but finds hygiene, geography, Bible and composition easier.

At the end of the semester the general music examination for each student was to stand and sing the scale, up and down, in front of the entire school. When I called up Sala I wondered if the poor child would possibly get up the courage to stand in front of about sixty boys to sing alone. I saw her gulp twice, hang her head and twist her dress, but in a second she was on her feet and she sang the scale perfectly. She lives in the girls' dormitory. Being somewhat older she is naturally a leader there, and it is usually she who plans and leads the games. Many of the other girls are advancing rapidly in their first degree school, and we are happy that they shall be ready some day to help our trained young men in establishing Christian homes. (G. Shoemaker *Congo News Letter*, April 1941)

The mission raised one unfortunate girl when her parents abandoned her as a baby. While she was out in the village on a school vacation, her father forced her into marriage. The marriage was unsuitable from every standpoint as the husband didn't pay anything for his new wife and he had other wives. She fled back to the station when she became pregnant and supported herself by cooking for patients and helping Aunt Stobie in preparing milk for three orphans and another baby without a mother's milk. Her baby would lawfully belong to her father, since the husband hadn't paid money for his new wife. The husband finally sent one of his wives to care for Boola, the young wife, during her time of need, so the mission wouldn't take the problem of ownership to the State to be settled.

Women had few rights and fewer options in this culture. Gradually the awareness was increasing that educated young Christian men were going to need educated young Christian women as spouses to live successfully their chosen convictions in the new way.

When the Roberts arrived at Mondombe to replace the Hurts, they started language study immediately upon reaching Mondombe. Such were the demands upon the preacher that Uncle Ned jumped right into his work as an evangelist. Ntange Timothy, the native pastor at Mondombe, was pleased to hear an early sermon by Uncle Ned. "Now we have a real preacher!" he smiled.

Ntange Timothy and his wife Miliama

Whose authority commanded the respect to lead these eager Christians into the new era? Ntange Timothy, helped by his wife Miliama, became that courageous shepherd in 1936. He followed the down-river preacher Bokese Paul, who had led the Mondombe church since its establishment in 1920. In a letter to me, Ned Roberts described the difficulties Ntange overcame to reach the position of mission pastor at Mondombe. Through many years of working and itinerating together, Uncle Ned developed a "great love and respect for Ntange."

Although I, too, knew and respected Ntange throughout my childhood, I felt greatly moved by the following story written for me by Uncle Ned. Minor editing has left his story essentially unchanged:

> Eldest son of the chief of the Mbelo tribe Ntange sought permission from his father to go to Mondombe soon after the station opened. He was curious to learn the good news about the "Good Spirit." This request granted, the youth and his wife Miliama soon attracted the attention of the early missionaries. They saw great potential in the new students and started to tutor them. Ntange and Miliama learned quickly and were baptized into the Christian faith.

About four years later Ntange renounced his position to be chief in favor of his younger brother and became a preacher/teacher. He was determined to tell the story of his new faith in the "Good Spirit" to the heathen villagers where he was assigned. Three months passed and Ntange made progress in the school he set up. He found the heathen village elders and witch doctors so intimidating, however, that he had not spoken a word of his faith. Discouraged, he confided to Miliama his lack of courage and vowed either to break his silence or abandon his ministry and return to reclaim his chieftainship.

Another day passed at school with no mention from him of religion. Profoundly ashamed he walked into the jungle to confront his fear and lack of courage. [He told this story to Uncle Ned with tears in his eyes.] He prayed.

Along the path he impulsively turned to the grave of a sub chief recently dead and spit on it. This desecration of a burial mound would result in the immediate death of the disrespectful person according to the beliefs of the people. Terrified, Ntange in his great fear froze and couldn't move a muscle. He knew some villagers were watching and was sure he would die. Ntange began to pray. Gradually one joint and then another loosened. Eventually he could walk again. At that point he determined he would never again give in to fear or doubt his faith. He resolved to end the superstitions of his people.

Years later Ntange, a teacher from the seminary and I [Ned Roberts] were itinerating in the back country. As I approached after the other two had arrived, a huge crowd filled the center of the village. Curious, I was told to "come and see what Ntange is doing." There in the middle Ntange stood with a large knife seeming to be fighting with someone.

I couldn't believe what I was seeing, but everyone seemed to be having a good time. It turned out the witch doctor had come to the local pastor saying he wanted to become a Christian, but was fearful of all the witch doctor paraphernalia he had inherited from his father and grandfather who were witch doctors. He asked the local pastor to help him get rid of all this witch doctor material. [The local pastor] was afraid himself, but said to wait for Ntange, who was near, as he wasn't afraid of anything. When Ntange arrived he was told of the problem and agreed to help the witch doctor. He was cutting all the cords holding charms around the witch doctor's neck and taking off his anklets and bracelets that had superstitions attached to them.

The natives, while fearing the Evil Spirits, spent their time trying to outwit them. They didn't seem to have a very high opinion of the Spirit World.

Ntange finished removing the witch doctor's charms. Then he entered the witch doctor's little shed, in which he supposedly created all his charms, and tore it apart. He piled much of it in a heap and set it afire showing he had no fear of any of these things. He kept some of the many charms and tied them on his bicycle, the professor's, and my motorcycle, then hung some over the church door. To cap it all off he took a gourd from the shed, turned it up and drank from it, then stomped on it and threw it in the fire. The gourd supposedly held poison.

Ntange asked the people to come to the church for prayer. Remember the churches had low walls. The people poured into the church over the walls, but not through the door decorated with the witch doctor's charms. Ntange and the professor took the witch doctor with them and walked through the door, and I followed. The witch doctor was shaking like a leaf and would never have gone through the door without help from the two men.

Then Ntange preached a most powerful sermon about Christ's power over spirits.

The elders of the village came to me saying, "Ntange will die because of what he has done to this witch doctor and his charms." I assured them that the faith of Ntange was stronger than any evil spirits.

They went off and then came back and told me that if Ntange didn't die they would all like to learn about this "Good Spirit." We were traveling on for about a week and would be coming back. I assured them Ntange would be O.K.

I never prayed so hard in my life that nothing would happen to Ntange during those two weeks. Of course they kept informed by their drums that Ntange was all right.

When we returned after two weeks, the whole village had heard Ntange was coming and all went to the local pastor and signed up for classes to become Christians. Later I had the privilege to come back there the next year as we had a baptismal service of 887 converts at one service. It was all due to the faith, courage and life of Ntange. For some reason the Africans didn't seem to think we whites were under the control of the Evil Spirit World.

I watched Ntange through the years and realized his witness and fearlessness was a tremendous force far beyond anything we missionaries had. (Ned Roberts Letter to Author 6-22-03)

In 1942 my father reported in a general letter that the total number of baptisms in the Mondombe region alone had been over 1000 per year for the previous six years. There were 1308 baptisms in 1941. A number equal to one-tenth of the population of that area had been baptized in the twenty-two years of their work there.

Besides the three major aspects of Mondombe's work, as described in this chapter, erecting structures consumed a large part of the missionaries' time and effort. Dad expended much of his energy and planning in creating permanent buildings to house the work and the people. This deserves a chapter of its own.

CHAPTER 10

BUILDING FOR THE FUTURE

"Bongelemba. Bongelemba," an urgent voice called out of the black night. "The brick kiln is on fire." More than once the night sentry awakened Dad from deep sleep by calling his African name. Accidents at the brick kiln sometimes supplied the reason. Mishaps occurred, which then caused the thatch roof over the kiln to catch fire.

Pinning palm leaflets to make a sheet of thatch

Making and firing bricks continued most of the year in the ongoing building program at Mondombe. A decade later experienced builders arrived to oversee the construction, but in the late thirties any able missionaries supervised the erection of new buildings. These new buildings aided the total program of the mission.

My father was exceedingly pleased to find that Uncle Ned was experienced in building, having overseen the construction of a new church in the States before coming to the mission field. A practiced colleague was a happy addition when the tedious building process started with cutting down a tree. All the work was done by hand. Along with his wonderful chuckle and ministerial experience, Uncle Ned brought many practical skills to his work at Mondombe.

Lumber started with a felled tree. The log had to be floated down the river to the station where it was pulled up the bank by hand and positioned over the saw pit. With one sawyer above and another covered with sawdust below, the log was laboriously squared and then sawed into rather wavy planks. These never seemed to dry properly in the carpenter shop before they were planed, cut and nailed into frames or used as beams. Doors and windows needed constant adjusting to get them to fit in their frames as they continued to dry and warp.

Sand for mortar came from sandbars during the dry season. It, too, arrived by river transportation, usually in the large steel station canoe. It lay piled in a hill or contained in several 55-gallon drums until needed later in the year. Always in short supply, the cement arrived by bi-weekly river boat promptly, or often belatedly, after ordering. Sometimes a mud mortar helped to speed the building. Seams could be pointed later with cement to prevent leaching by the rains.

Thatched-roof brick kiln with tunnels for fires

Bricks completed the components necessary for building. A two-mold hand press served the laborious process of brick making. The only almost-pure clay to be found lay collected by ant colonies in conical hills sometimes ten to fifteen feet high. Skinned of their grass cover, the anthills provided the clay to make the rosy, fired bricks used at Mondombe. Although they were soft, as bricks go, they supplied a permanent material resistant to the onslaught of rain and termites.

Moistened with water the clay was compressed in the forms. Then the bricks were carefully turned out and moved to open, roofed, drying sheds. Thousands were made before they were evenly stacked many courses high for firing. Some of the unfired bricks crumbled during moving and stacking. Careful placement left cracks between them to allow the heat to rise easily from the log fires below. The fires burned in tunnels built through the lowest layers of brick. The flames were kept stoked for four to five days and nights with four-foot-long logs, which had to be hurled to reach the center. Each step of the manufacture took skill and could fail.

The most spectacular failure resulted in the collapse of one side of the kiln of red-hot bricks, when they shifted with the heat during firing. Usually the collapse set alight a column supporting the thatch roof in the middle of the night. Flames leapt twenty or more feet into the cool air brightening the night's darkness. Nothing else ever seemed to catch fire, so the damage remained the loss of many weeks of effort and hundreds of broken and misfired bricks.

A testament to the patience needed for Congo building is found in this article from the *Congo News Letter* written by *Is'ekanga*, the title of respect for Uncle Ned, meaning Father of Ekanga, the African name given to his eldest son:

> To come to Africa out of a civilization that has exact weights, measures and proportions in building construction is to prepare one to turn gray early.
>
> We at Mondombe are in the midst of a building program, using mission-made bricks, our only reasonably permanent building material. To find a mason who can and will lay a straight wall is our problem. Since no one here could qualify, we engaged a down-river mason, only to learn that he had been but a supervisor of masons, that is, one to keep them working! He had never laid a brick, but had seen them laid! We tolerated his feeble efforts for two months, then offered him free passage down river.
>
> Two others appeared whose (tax) books recorded that they had worked for the State for a short period. (Emphasize the short.) Results, tho slightly improved, left no chance for compliments. So many portions needed to be torn down and rebuilt, we ourselves could have done it more easily. The first completed building was marvelous in the eyes of natives who know to construct only with sticks and mud; we covet no inspection by an expert constructor.
>
> Ere our patience was completely exhausted we sent our two masons back to their fishing nets where they would be masters of their trade, and employed a man of more experience. This attempt proved considerably more encouraging. With only a six-inch bulge in a hundred foot wall, we were really becoming proud of our accomplishments until the carpenters began asking, "Is'ekanga, where should these roof timbers go on the brick columns?" To sight down that row of brick columns would make a snake dizzy, but we got a line through the centers of the two end ones, and followed the line.
>
> Wearied with the slow progress, I counted the bricks laid by the two masons and their two helpers in an eight and a half-hour day. The masons averaged a brick every five minutes. The main thing that is speeded up in Congo is the turning of missionaries' hair gray. (N. Roberts *Congo News Letter*, October 1941)

During this term the first brick ward building improved housing at the hospital. Additionally, Uncle Ned supervised the completion of the splendid new school with its quadrangle arrangement around a grassy center court. The three-sided classrooms opened to the inside to receive natural light. While this solved lighting problems, it created distractions for the students. A center wall was built bisecting the courtyard and reducing the visual diversions. Unfortunately the sounds multiplied, ricocheting off the wall. Finally, my mother planted brilliant blue morning glory vines. They beautifully blanketed the wall, providing natural sound control. A third construction project completed by Uncle Ned was a combined guest and storage house. With each project he learned more about the business.

One final lesson my parents included in their general letter:

> Early in his term, Mr. Roberts one day decided that he was losing too much time in supervising his workmen. The next day, he started his gang at their work, and settled down nearby to study. Absorbed in his books, he soon forgot about his men. When he came to, he looked up to find them all standing motionless, intently watching him work. (General Letter 3-23-43)

By 1943 the building campaign included brick houses for the African residents at Mondombe. The preacher, nurses and teachers welcomed their new houses. Cleaner and stronger in addition to being permanent, they offered safer, more spacious, and lighter rooms in which to live. The kitchens were still housed in mud huts out behind.

The subject of safety in housing was not an academic exercise in the Congo where at night leopards frequently roamed both the native village and the yards around the missionary houses. The Belgians experienced trouble, too, when they were lax to the danger, as my parents wrote:

> Four weeks ago, a white man was brought to the hospital for medical care. He had been wakened in the early morning by a terrific blow on his face, as he lay asleep in his bed, by an open window. He awoke to see something going out thru the window and to feel blood running from his face. Besides numerous cuts, his upper jaw was broken right across the hard palate. Leopard tracks were found outside his window. The beast then killed two calves of the only herd of cattle in this region, several sheep, and several goats. A hunt was made, and he was killed by encircling him with hunting nets, and with spears. The man is recovering. (General Letter, 6-17-39)

The patient lived in our guest room eating only liquids until his wired-shut jaw healed. In another leopard story from Lotumbe Aunt Betty wrote:

> Everton left the night of the 21st and the night of the 23rd the leopard paid us a visit. I had been sure our stock was safe but our largest rooster and a hen were missing and we found the leopard had raised one corner of the tin roof and reached in to help himself to a good meal. Dr. Horton [the doctor from the days at Kennedy School of Missions] nailed the roof down again and tacked on a couple of boards where there were large cracks in the coop. The next night the leopard again visited us. He couldn't get into the chicken coop but he tried hard to get a rabbit and we found one of them had a couple of toenails missing. I put iodine on the raw spots. The following morning the rabbit died and Inyongo said of course I had killed it because it licked off the iodine. I attempted to do an autopsy, with Dr. Horton looking on, and he decided it had died of a ruptured heart, frightened to death. (EBS Letter to Family 7-1-39)

Few slept in the village when a leopard patrolled, gruffly snorting. With only a thatch roof and a lightweight door propped over the doorway, the Congolese stoked up the fire and huddled inside waiting for morning. Once Congolese hunters started using wire snares, they became more successful at trapping leopards in the jungle.

The missionaries used either a gun or a box trap in fighting leopards. I never heard of an effective shot on the station, but the leopards were scared away from our rabbit hutches with the sound of a gun's discharge. The box trap was more successful and caught at least two of the cats during the nineteen thirties.

We Bakers lived on the second floor of our brick house until the expanding family needed another bedroom after World War II. Grace and I never felt as safe downstairs with our large screened windows as we had felt upstairs. Psychologically, the mosquito net made a secure cocoon to burrow into for the night, but realistically we knew it wouldn't stop a leopard. I was never completely confident that the reinforced screen would do that either. Scorpions posed the real hazard. The two-inch-long insects matched the color of the cement floor making them hard to see. To this day I still shake out my gardening shoes before putting them on from a habit started in childhood.

All this emphasizes that brick houses with sturdy hinged and latched doors offered a security not available in the native construction. The owners' pride in their new sturdy homes showed clearly in their planting of bright flowers and colorful leaves around them.

CHAPTER 11

HYGIENE, LEPERS AND A LITTLE FROG

Iyambe wanted to become a nurse. He approached my dad with the idea and, because he was a good student and of good character, his request was approved. Almost all of the nurses in the thirties and early forties were men.

The first step in training was to work for my mother while he finished school. Iyambe came to our house to assist the cook. He served company meals when Belgians were present. He learned Western standards of cleanliness and hygiene, like washing his hands before working with food. He practiced precision measuring with kitchen utensils. He gained assurance in decoding white people's communication. Their use of Lonkundo rarely exactly matched the way the Africans talked. These were some of the skills Iyambe learned. They prepared him for training at the hospital, where he attended classes directly related to nursing at the same time he started working with patients. The nurses Dad trained eventually served proficiently as surgical assistants, as directors of outlying dispensaries, and as attendants in the daily activities of the hospital.

Several years passed before any Mondombe students qualified to enroll in the State accredited nurses' training schools to become certified professionals. The State then paid them more adequate salaries than the mission could afford. Although Iyambe never became certified by the State, he became a dedicated nurse and served at the Mondombe hospital all of his life.

My father's work during his second term encompassed an increasingly demanding medical practice. Two days a week he performed scheduled operations. Strangulated hernias and emergency Cesarean sections came up more suddenly. Patient examinations took place daily at the hospital.

One approached the hospital complex from the main road on a soft dirt path flanked by colorful poinsettia bushes growing four to six feet tall. First on the left stood the small brick surgery building with its pharmacy and operating room. The windows in the back wall of the operating room faced the treatment building across an open weedy courtyard thronged with patients early in the day waiting for diagnosis and treatment. The long brick treatment building stretched back to the swamp hidden under the forest trees. Off to the left were The patients' thatched huts. Later, to the right, new brick ward buildings were erected.

Chief nurse examines patient in "Congo ambulance"

A very rare sight was a patient carried to the hospital in a "Congo ambulance." One had to have broken a leg or be on the verge of death to lie in a blanket slung hammock style on a pole for deliverance to the white doctor's care. One patient walked a couple hundred miles with advanced pneumonia to receive care. This was notable only in the distance he came, not that he came under his own locomotion.

The brick treatment building with its cement tile roof was completed a year after my father first arrived at Mondombe. Here blood samples could be examined under the microscope for the ubiquitous malarial spirochetes or the rarer sleeping sickness trypanosomes. Large windows provided the necessary illumination in the absence of artificial light. Injections to cure the lesions of yaws were administered twice weekly. Examining rooms and treatment rooms included the dental chair presided over by Aunt Stobie. With no electricity, a steam autoclave sterilized linens and instruments for surgeries.

One larger room was used as a classroom for training nurses during the week. On Saturdays mothers with their infants crowded in to have their children weighed on the baby scales and to learn more about their care. In good weather the clinic might be set up outside.

A path from the rear door of the treatment building led directly across the swamp to the hospital manioc gardens. Sitting in the dental chair for cleanings or fillings, one looked out the back window across the swamp for distraction. Perhaps birds were flying or monkeys were jumping across the branches of the tall trees.

Always, the hospital complex included a cluster of indigenous mud and pole huts roofed with sheets of the swamp palm thatch of our area. Patients from out of town, accompanied by family members to care for them, stayed there for the duration of their treatment. In later years ward buildings provided beds where patients could be housed in less primitive quarters.

Dad wrote about tropical medicine:

> "Boluku, what on earth is the matter with you?"
>
> "*Njobika Nk'aeyoko.*" (I have only just now gotten well.)
>
> Boluku is convalescing from a serious attack of pneumonia. Of course, he didn't know that it was that. He has a pretty vague notion that he has a heart and lungs in his chest, but just where they are or how they work, he isn't sure. As to their diseases, he hasn't the least idea. He called it *iyonga* or sorcery.
>
> He did know that with the pneumonia, something was seriously wrong. How it hurt to draw his breath! He just had to cough, but what agony it gave him! He couldn't get breath enough. What could he do, a hundred miles from the nearest hospital or dispensary? In becoming a Christian, he had torn from around his neck, and thrust from his house, all of the witch doctor's medicine. But now, with this frightful thing within him, what was there to do? It was killing him, that he knew.
>
> The neighbors and relatives all crowded around. "Let them make just a little cut," they pleaded. The witch doctors seemed so sure of their ability to help him and to suck out the sorcery with their heated gourds. Surely it would do no harm to try. The pain was awful, and he felt so weak. Where else to seek help? It was the witch doctor or nothing. What would you do?

> It is not enough for us to take away the charms and magic medicines from our Congo converts. We must offer them, in a positive way, something to replace these things. Nothing else can so quickly convince them of their inefficacy and deceit, as can ready access to scientific methods of curing disease. (DHB, *Congo News Letter* October 1942)

Later the Africans began to recognize the symptoms of pneumonia as a disease that could be cured by the white man's medicine. Access to a distant hospital, however, remained a problem. Travel over the forest paths was difficult and accomplished best with a bicycle or by motorcycle, but the Congolese could afford only their feet. That made travel by canoe appealing where that was possible.

When he could get away, Dad rode his new Belgian motorcycle into the neighboring counties over deep ruts and around barking dogs to bring medicines and supervision to five outlying dispensaries. In each little clinic he conferred with the nurse, examined patients and offered more extensive assistance than the first level of help available for dispensation by the brave and solitary aide.

Health care of the workers on nearby coffee and rubber plantations also lay on the doctors' shoulders. Every-day illnesses of these men, such as malaria, were treated locally. Emergency action usually demanded that the patient be brought to the hospital. In between, the visiting doctor examined the workers at intervals of several months. During these stops he cared for the Belgian plantation directors and their families, too.

Those early years included continued medical census-taking required by the government, which wanted to know the condition of the population and the distribution of certain diseases. Thousands of villagers met the doctor as he fulfilled this demand. The census provided opportunities for teaching large groups of people some of the basics of disease prevention.

The motorcycle my father used this second term improved his back country travel, but it had its drawbacks when rain turned the roads into slick mud. He wrote more descriptions of his census experiences in 1938:

> Will you join us on a trip thru the back country? A trip over equatorial Africa's forest and swamp roads? Rough dirt roads baked by the boiling sun, furrowed by the tropical downpours, and pockmarked in places by the heavy tread of ivoried pachyderms! But roads bordered again by stately palms, leafy bananas, and the mud-walled, thatch-

roofed homes of dusky Africans. We shall examine over ten thousand of them in an annual medical census....

On a trip to the swamp for butterflies, saw a recent grave of a small child, and near it were a bunch of bananas and some short sticks of sugar cane. Asked why, those with me replied, "His mother put them there because he liked those foods."

Bononga, a former boy of the Mission boarding school, was brought in for examination today. He had been injured about five days earlier, in a fall. His father, and others, impressed by his serious condition, urged taking the lad to the Mission hospital. On the way, a witch doctor saw the lad carried in the hunting net hammock, and stopped them. He persuaded them to let him treat the boy, and they returned home after the treatment. When they came to me, in their village, it was too late to help, and he died the next morning.

Great interest in our hygiene teachings:

Once upon a time, a huge spreading forest tree got into an argument with the tiny white ants, or termites, almost lost in their smallness and softness, as they moved over the ground at its roots. Said the big tree proudly, "Who are you, and what strength do you possess? Look at me, who can stand so straight and tall thru sunshine, rain and storm. You have to hide from every living thing, hidden from sight in your tiny underground tunnels."

The termites only answered in chorus with the noise which gave them their name, "*Nye le liya, nye le liya, nye le liya.*"

But they went to work with all of their strength and might at the roots of the big tree, tunneling and eating, eating and tunneling. The proud tree did not realize what was happening, as down underneath it the tiny miners multiplied by the thousand, but they worked ceaselessly away, night and day, eating and tunneling, tunneling and eating. And then, finally, a big windstorm came one day, with rain and thunder and lightning. The great tree trembled and shook, and with a mighty crash, tumbled to the ground. The swarming termites built their tunnels all over it, and through it, and ate up all of its leaves, then all of its small branches, and then even its trunk. As they ate, they said. "*Nye le liya, nye le liya, nye le liya.*"

It was as if they asked, "Who's mighty now? Who's mighty now? Who's mighty now?" (A murmur of assent from the crowd.)

With this native story we begin our daily hygiene lesson to the several hundred folk grouped on the ground before us in the native village. They have come for their annual medical examination. But before we examine them we experiment a little in mass education.

The native nurse continues, "The big tree is a human body; the termites are the tiny insects (germs) which cause our diseases."

We pause to choose out of the crowd an individual with marked anemia. It is not difficult. One can always find markedly anemic babies, and generally children and adults. It is more difficult to find someone with good rich red blood for comparison. For a better contrast, the doctor often sticks his own finger for a drop of blood.

"You see this baby? How pale it is? Look at its eyes. There is no color there! They are white, like the white clay of the swamp. Look at its tongue."

A drop of blood is obtained from a finger and absorbed on white paper. The color scale reads it as 40 per cent. One wonders how the poor child can live. A drop of good blood is obtained for contrast and the two passed thru the crowd. Bottles of intestinal worms and mosquito larvae are next shown, as we proceed with our lesson on hookworm and malaria, the two chief causes of anemia, weakness and death. Hands are silently clapped in wonder and assent as the story continues.

"Your witch doctors tell you that you are bewitched, or that your ancestors are plaguing you, but what is really wrong, is that your blood is as thin as water."

[At one stop] the nurses and others constructed the first latrine in this village today, part of our instruction in the avoidance of infection with hookworm....

Slippery hillsides after the rain. Motorcycle first on one side and then on the other, going down the steep grades to the swamps. At one place I was stopped by a man in the road, signaling me to stop. "One of your men is coming, wait," he said. I noticed that the drums were beating furiously in the direction from which I had come.

"What does he want?" I asked.

He went to his drum and beat out a message, then listened to the reply. "He is bringing something of rubber, for your feet. There!" and he indicated the pedal. Sure enough, the rubber cover was missing from that side. I waited ten or fifteen minutes until the bearer came. Thanks for African telegraphy!

Before retiring, went out on the verandah to close a window, and almost stepped on a four and a half foot snake, which I at first mistook for a crack between the wall and the floor.

A gray morning and a late start. Last clan finished and then rain until 3:00. Off with baggage. Motorcycle carried over a swollen stream, and then I showed them how to make a chair by joining hands, and was carried also. They greatly enjoyed the new manner of carrying. Dinner with the State agent, and to bed in the same house (one room). He had just finished nailing up sign posts, indicating the name of the village and the directions. Civilization arrives! Now if we can just teach them to read!

Rain till noon. Worked till four. Then a late start home. Carriers arrived well after dark. Wife says, "Thank the powers that be, that work is finished for another year!" (DHB General Letter 4-10-38)

A decade after arriving in the Congo my father wrote an article for the *Congo News Letter*, which seems appropriate to repeat here as I tell of his medical work. In it he spells out his appreciation for American nurses and particularly for Aunt Stobie:

> It is now ten years since we arrived at Mondombe, the farthest inland of our Congo Mission stations. During these ten years, it has been my privilege for five years, to have associated with me in the medical work a nurse, Miss Buena R. Stober, who was also in charge of the medical work during my absence.
>
> No other station has been so fortunate. Bolenge and Wema have each had one whole year without nurse or doctor, and eight more years without a doctor. The other three stations have each had a doctor for nine years, and one year with only a nurse. At Monieka and Mondombe only, during these ten years, have doctor and nurse been present simultaneously; at Monieka for one year, and at Mondombe for five years.
>
> It is natural that a doctor can do his best work associated with a nurse, and a nurse associated with a doctor. And when I say nurse, I

mean a nurse from home, not a native hospital assistant, often called a nurse. The [Congolese] aides help make our work possible, and I should like to pay them a high tribute. They are lads with less than an eighth grade education, trained to perform certain tasks, but still superstitious Africans, one generation out of the forest, and believing, at least subconsciously, in witchcraft and the power of the spirits of the deceased to harm the living.

Great are the demands placed upon our [American] nurses when on a station alone, where they are required to assume the responsibilities of a physician. Few of you will ever realize the serious emergencies which have been met by these courageous and resourceful women.... (DHB *Congo News Letter*, October 1942)

Capable Aunt Stobie came from an Oklahoman family of very modest means. Her sturdy nature and generous character tackled whatever problem appeared. With Cappy, her tan and white short-haired dog, I picture her feeding a baby on her porch or playing with a girl from the dormitory. An earlier newsletter article by Dad praised his admirable colleague and explained how she came to have and use a dental chair:

... Mondombe considers herself extremely fortunate to have Miss Stober located here. During her last furlough, with the generous aid of an experienced dentist at home, Miss Stober learned to clean

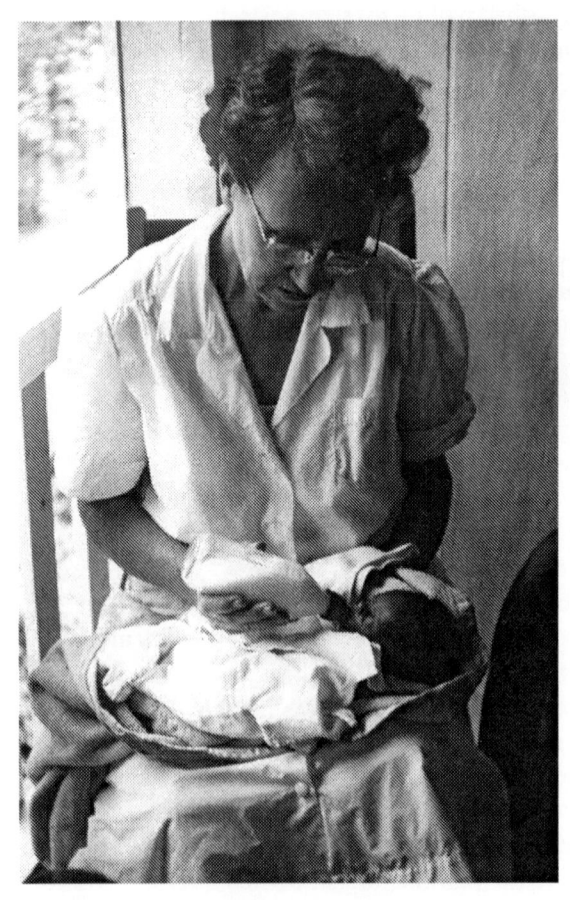

Buena Stober feeding motherless newborn

teeth, and to do simple fillings and extractions. Returning to Congo with a portable chair and a foot power drill, she has been blessing this area with her foresight and generous service. Already, she has cleaned teeth and done fillings and extractions for over thirty whites—more than half the number in our region, and for over two hundred and twenty natives. The native boys and girls in our schools are becoming tooth-conscious and are taking better care of their teeth.

Many natives have large, strong, beautiful teeth. Among the older generation however, numerous front ones were chipped and pointed, rendering the teeth early victims of decay. Many others, contrary to the popular idea of an aborigine, have, besides halitosis and pink toothbrush, very poor teeth. Since every human being is supposed to have thirty-two permanent teeth, it is not surprising that many have at least one or two to decay during the lifetime of the individual. One cannot even estimate the amount of such suffering undergone by the Congolese. We frequently see dental abscesses draining through the cheeks, and not long ago removed a piece of dead jaw bone, from one of these sufferers....

Miss Stober was kept very busy during the recent upriver trip of the *Oregon*, in filling teeth for the junior missionaries and their mothers, who had come from other stations. Unfortunately, the *Oregon* travels the river to Mondombe very infrequently, and the other boats are too expensive. Our thanks to Miss Stober for this splendid aid. (DHB *Congo News Letter*, December 1940)

Even that long ago, Aunt Stobie knew to paint our teeth with fluoride. Fillings that she tamped into cavities, which formed despite her valiant efforts, are still performing well after sixty years. Her unique dental practice included, at times, ridding teeth of antelope hairs along with tartar and plaque. The next closest dentist lived in Leopoldville.

Malaria stood even higher than dental problems at the top of the list of medical scourges in the Congo. No matter what illness one contracted, malaria immediately struck, too. With the anemia caused by this and parasites, curing sickness always required a multi-pronged strategy.

Leprosy remained the most repellent disease from Biblical days to the present. While improvement could be obtained by treatment with chaulmoogra oil in the early days, it was after World War II that the disease finally could be stopped. Patients suffering from Hansen's disease, the medical term for leprosy, needed to live close to the mission station in order to receive treatment. Later, that treatment could be offered in their home villages.

During our second term trees came down, a school, a church and a group of dwellings rose near Mondombe—homes for these afflicted and handicapped people. The medical effort at Mondombe addressing the plight of the lepers appeared in a *Congo News Letter* article:

> His face was deformed, his body covered with huge brown spots, his feet and hands rotting away. Bosilama looked forward to an early and gradual death from leprosy. It was certainly a misfortune for him to be born into an infected family. First he saw his father's painful and lingering death. Then the telltale spots appeared on his mother's back. Finally, his own skin lost its uniform shiny black, as the light brown spots spread over it.
>
> In the leper colony at Mondombe, he has found his first help. He and his mother have had a house built for them; a garden has been cut in the forest for them; they have had their ulcers dressed and their leprosy treated.
>
> Of the six provinces of Belgian Congo, Equator Province, where the Disciples of Christ are ministering, contains one-third of the total number of lepers. In Tshuapa District four out of a hundred inhabitants are infected with leprosy.
>
> Congo natives have little fear of lepers and make no attempt to segregate them. Quite frequently the skin spots are tattooed or a bit of cloth is worn to cover them, so that the disease remains well hidden during the earlier years when it is mild. For these and other reasons it is not always easy to separate the lepers into special colonies for treatment. At Mondombe we are happy to have made a small beginning by establishing, with the help of the government, an agricultural colony with a dozen resident lepers receiving constant treatment. Over two acres have been set with trees which produce the chaulmoogra oil used in the treatment of these poor unfortunates. (DHB *Congo News Letter*, April 1941)

The doctor as teacher appeared almost as often as the doctor as healer. One of my father's science lessons sixty years ago has always embodied for me the multiple facets of his character. Suffused as he was with biology and science, he sparked in those around him a keen interest in natural phenomena. The night sky became a lesson about the stars and constellations. Caterpillars were fed in a jar and allowed to progress through their stages to emerge in due time as beautiful butterflies. Growing fruits and vegetables not only fed the family and others but engendered demonstrations in grafting, fertilization and transplantation. Dad was moved by great compassion, a need to nurture, a drive to better whatever condition he found amenable to improvement and always a desire to teach. The lesson on circulation that he describes in the following letter was one more of his attempts at providing knowledge to dispel ignorance:

> At school this week, we demonstrated the circulation of blood in the tiny capillaries and venules of the foot of a frog. It is a simple but beautiful demonstration, seen easily with the low power magnifying lens of the microscope. The natives marveled as they saw the red blood corpuscles scurrying over the tiny pathways like continuous streams of driver ants. We shall link it up with hygiene talks on the circulation, and on the ever present anemias caused by hookworms and malaria. (General Letter 1-24-42)

The sun shone on the small table holding the microscope, which was moved outside the school building to take advantage of the bright natural light. The little green tree peeper lay alive, its webbed foot strapped precisely under the lens. Expectation rippled through the line of respectful students eager to see what the doctor was displaying today. What a memorable lesson in the ongoing campaign to improve everyone's health.

CHAPTER 12

NATIONAL GEOGRAPHIC WONDERS

When asked where she wished to be sent for her Peace Corps tour of duty, a young friend replied, "I'd like a *National Geographic* posting." What a picturesque response! It struck me as the perfect description of my childhood experience.

My birth at Mondombe put me as far into the interior as one could go. The people in our area seemed little affected by Western civilization at the time of my birth. They utilized the jungle abundance to meet their needs. Raffia from the swamp palm provided the threads woven for the loincloths they wore. Intricate basketry furnished not only containers big and small but also sieves, dust mats, rattles for the witch doctors and other household items like trays. Fired clay decorated with simple lines or zigzags yielded pots in which to steam manioc. The women boiled manioc roots, which they then mashed in wooden mortars and shaped into the staple, sour carbohydrate "loaves" akin to Hawaiian poi. The men hewed large tree trunks into canoes, the largest of which could hold a hundred men; the smallest, maneuvered by a single paddler.

Hollowed logs from carefully selected trees became drums. The round cylindrical tom-tom covered at one end with skin was beaten by the hand for entertainment and ceremonies. The famous "talking" drum of Africa was a hollowed log left with a mere slit at the top. The edges along the opening in differing thicknesses provided four different tones when struck with firm mallets. The four tones plus a double note obtained by striking both lips at once provided the five notes necessary to convey a message, as would five vowels. Very few foreigners knew the drum language, but most Congolese understood it.

These tribes didn't know the use of the wheel except to place poles as rollers under the finished canoes to aid in pulling them to the river. The blacksmiths did know the smelting of iron and the smithing of copper and bronze rods obtained in trade. In 1940 a village just five miles from the station set up an old-style iron smelter. My father was delighted.

Sitting in the sidecar traveling to the smelting site at the age of six thrilled me as much as seeing the molten iron run in to a little clay hollow and cool into a filigree of impure metal. The blacksmith's two assistants pumped air rapidly into the hot charcoal fire as the smith himself sprinkled the crushed red ore over the coals, and someone accompanied the proceedings on a *bonjimba*, the local guitar. The dim interior under a low roof created quite a mysterious setting.

A blacksmith shaped the metal jewelry worn by the tribesmen and women. Copper, bronze and even iron bracelets and anklets ringed the wrists and ankles of both genders. Especially wealthy men could afford to buy large anklets for their wives. These were sometimes sand cast flat and then curved by the blacksmith to encircle a woman's ankle. What the blacksmith put on usually needed

Village elder with tattooed face, leopard skin hat, fetish and medal around neck, many bracelets and a wristwatch leaning on his spear

a blacksmith to remove. These larger anklets weighed seven to ten or more pounds and were cushioned with a padding of woven leaves to prevent abrasion of the skin. They shone brightly from frequent polishing with sand. My father offered a prize one time to the winner of a race by a lineup of women so burdened. He was amazed at how quickly they could cover the allotted distance weighted down as they were.

Bright commercial beads, intricate string necklaces and fetishes adorned the necks of the natives. Chiefs and important elders wore conspicuous leopard tooth necklaces, symbols of their authority. Occasionally a boar's tusk could be seen suspended around a neck. A monkey skin cap and a swatch of small animal skins attached to an impala skin belt holding up the loincloth usually completed the outfit of one of these tribal elders. These older citizens displayed the scarification and chipped, pointed teeth, which were considered desirable embellishments.

Although all people in those early days showed the identifying tribal cheek scars, some tribes—prominently the Topoke—tattooed the whole face, the back, the chest and, sometimes, even the abdomen. A 16-mm. movie of the process, taken and described by my father, reveals an impassive client being nicked with a sharp African razor in symmetrical swirls and lines. The cuts were rubbed with powdered charcoal. During healing, the powder both raised a scar and darkened it. Today none of those old ornamentations still exist. They were truly National Geographic wonders.

One of my mother's favorite stories told of the arrival at the house one afternoon of a village woman to sell some garden produce. She had a particularly intricate hairdo. My fascinated mother peered closely at the upswept, waxed creation decorated with brass tacks when she realized the African was regarding her with the same rapt attention. It was a Saturday and my mother had just completed her weekly shampoo. She was setting a wave in her short hair, in the mode of the time, with the help of teethed aluminum-crimpers placed in rows all over her head. She had a wonderful sense of humor and laughed the rest of her life about the sight each made for the other.

In 1940 Dad described a local village rite, which was a combination clan gathering and inauguration of new leaders:

> An African family reunion was recently witnessed at Mondombe. About a thousand natives were present, all dressed in their best. A few had clothes. The rest, in addition to their loincloths, wore cat skins, anklets, bracelets or necklaces, and were daubed with clay or powdered camwood [a bright red powder from the decayed camwood tree]. The men carried shields, spears and knives. They looked most formidable, massed in groups, threatening each other with their spears from behind their shields, at one part of the afternoon's activities.

Sham battle with decorative spears (Note horn blown on left)

This celebration, called *Bokeke*, is the one big, planned social event of this region. It takes place some months after the death of an elder in the family. It honors the memory of the dead man, flatters the egos of the living descendants, and offers variety to the monotonous lives of these forest-bound primitives.

The young people dance folk dances, and the others gossip. Each clan enters the village as a group, and snake dances back and forth thru it, finally massing in a corner to unite with the other clans which form the long stretched-out village. Each and all, of course, trace their ancestry to a common origin more or less distant....

The climax of the affair comes with the final exchange of chickens, hoes and axes from the widow's family, for knives, spears and anklets from the family of the deceased. The redivision of these among the different members of the families must certainly be a ticklish problem. Truly, the social customs of these folk are bewilderingly intricate to us of another culture. (DHB, *Congo News Letter*, October 1940)

Another "bewilderingly intricate" custom in Congo was the paying of the bride price. Moneys paid by the promised husband might be started as early as the age of ten or younger for a girl. When the bride reached marriageable age, elaborate negotiations would determine the final payment collected and paid by the husband's family to the wife's family. When the first child was born, more compensation was expected. As the following anecdote from my father indicates, there could be many other demands made upon the husband:

> Perhaps you are familiar with the good old Congo custom whereby the son-in-law makes payments upon his wife, whenever demanded by his father-in-law. Several days ago, I was out in the native row and ran into Isekalompoko, one of the big men here when Mondombe was first opened. His village has since been moved a long ways off, but many of the children are still among our finest workers. Isekalompoko's daughter is the wife of my first assistant in surgery, who is responsible for all of the sterilization and preparations there. "Have you come?" I greeted him.
>
> "Yes. Are you there?" he answered. And to my assent, he stated the reason of his visit—collecting money from his son-in-law with which to pay the State tax on his four wives.
>
> I said, "We should be ashamed in my country, to ask the young folks for money. In fact, we might even help them with some."
>
> "Oh," he replied, "I am not working; I do not have any money."
>
> The next morning as we scrubbed up for an operation, Iyambe said to me, "I should like fifteen francs advance on my pay. My father-in-law is here collecting money for his tax and I want to get rid of him as soon as possible. I told my wife, Clara, to cook up a lot of food, and if I give him the money I hope that he will move on to another son-in-law further down river."
>
> I said, "Iyambe, you're a wise man. Here's your money." (General Letter 1-24-42)

When Mother went into the back country for an institute with Aunt Stobie, she found the informal discussions with the women formed her richest experiences. The problems that troubled them revealed that many of them did not support the old customs:

> "Our families regard us as property on which they can collect money from our husbands anytime that they need some. We don't think it is right, but they make us come home where they punish us if we don't help them. How can we change it? A husband's older relatives can ask him for anything they wish and custom demands that he give it to them. How can we ever get a flock of chickens, a mos-

quito net, and the household equipment you have taught us to use? How does one care for a sick child when it takes almost a week to get to the mission doctor?"

These questions will not be settled by us or in our generation. (General Letter 7-12-41)

The colonial government required the payment of annual taxes. Finding cash to pay them was so difficult as to cause some to be imprisoned for non-payment. Those living out in the villages without any paying work and few products for sale found this particularly true. One of the methods of finding the money was to gig with a long, slender, pointed iron spear for copal, a resin that fell in solid chunks from trees into the swamps. In appearance it resembles the fossil resin called amber, which is so treasured in Europe. Copal, used for making shellac and varnishes, sold well.

In addition to taxes the villagers were required by the government to do road maintenance in our area. During the forties, the State gradually straightened, widened and improved the roads, even to the point of moving some of the villages, in preparation for the passage of trucks and automobiles. The log and plank bridges were strengthened over the small streams. Large canoes tied together with planks across them provided the ferries for crossing the larger streams. Most of these elementary ferries provided no barriers on the sides at either end of the vehicle. More than one imprudently driven or brakeless truck rolled off the far side into the water.

Traveling these roads revealed interesting aspects of Bantu life. One day returning from an inspection of a plantation dispensary, Dad observed several recent graves by the side of the road:

> The trees at the road edge of the little clearings had been smeared with clay. "Why did they do that?" he asked.
>
> "Oh, that is to prevent the spirits from leaving the grave and coming back up the road to the village," the carriers replied. "We don't have any cement to fasten them in as you white people do." (General Letter 1-18-44)

In the same letter my father tells of missing some of the mission Congolese staff when he went visiting one New Year's Day:

> Several of the nurses were gone to help bury a stranger. They explained later that he had come to the hospital for treatment, then

had run off to friends in the middle of his treatment. These friends, seeing him gradually getting worse, would have nothing to do with him. He died practically alone. So the Mission folks had gone to bury him. It sounds like a small thing to do but many an African refuses to go near a sick or dead person for fear of being accused of having caused his death. We were pleased that in this instance some of our Christians could forget the old fear. (General Letter 1-18-44)

In describing the beliefs of the Congolese, an early missionary named E.R. Moon wrote, "The dominant impulse of the Bantu religion is fear ... If a man is feared here, his spirit is to be more intensely feared when he is dead." These people paid much time, wealth, and attention to appeasing the spirits of the dead whose spirits were much more to be feared than the spirits of the river, swamps, forests, and everything around them. The *nkanga* interpreted signs of the spirits with his occult vision. He was more than simply a witch doctor being also shaman, wizard and sorcerer. The *nkangas* were astute at deceiving the people and turning them against anyone who challenged their authority. The witch doctor created the fetishes worn by all and placed everywhere. Mr. Moon made the following observations:

> Fetishes are the means employed by the living to get in touch with the spirits by whom the Congo people believe they are constantly surrounded. By means of fetishes they attempt to get the spirits to act in their behalf, to bring them good luck, good health, and prosperity. They also try to influence the spirits to act against their enemies, causing misfortune, disease, or death. Every house, every garden, every individual is protected by some fetish, and one must be constantly on guard lest he come into contact with some destructive fetish placed by an enemy to bring him harm. (Moon, p. 124)

With this belief system came fear, which could only be conquered by a higher control, which is love, explained Mr. Moon. A dawning belief in the strength of a higher power gave the new Christians the courage to pull off the fetishes and believe in the teachings of the missionaries, not only about God, but also about science, geography and natural consequences undetermined by the spirits. The courage of Ntange, the preacher, in confronting these fears confirmed his leadership.

A visiting Belgian commented on the smiles of the mission folk at Mondombe and said he had never seen a happier group of Africans. They no longer believed that the angry spirit of a relative, for instance, caused disease. A germ could be treated.

Most people today hesitate to negatively compare the level of one civilization with another. The adjectives "advanced," "primitive" or "simple" carry emotional bias when used to define a culture. They are assumed to measure the worth of a people instead of the intricacy of their knowledge, religion, even science. At the turn of the twentieth century the people in the Mondombe area knew nothing of the organisms that caused malaria and other diseases. Their scientific knowledge at the station by mid-century was advancing but still had not reached the level of the Western world. This in no way diminished the worth or intelligence of these people.

The Congolese at Mondombe were skilled mimics, storytellers and eloquent speakers. By means of oral folklore they passed their history and wisdom from generation to generation. The lead paddler singing in the canoe would tell of the days' events. He was answered in rhythm after each verse with a chorus by the other paddlers. Stories around the fire on a moonlit night recalled the origins of the earth and its animals.

To honor an elder one greeted him with a request for his *losako*, his wise saying. The elder then replied with his favorite proverb. The Congolese proverb we children heard most frequently from our parents was, "A wise child needs only one teaching." There were hundreds of *losakos*.

The African customs of naming children and changing names of adults was puzzling and revealing. The missionaries and their children were given African names when I was growing up. A new missionary was usually named after an illustrious person of the region who had passed away. These customs caught my parents' attention. They wrote them down:

> Names are interesting—and numerous for each individual. Frequently a baby has a name which is discarded after the family decides that he will live—a sad commentary on the infant mortality in Africa. Then he is given a name which is his "name of the path." It is written in his tax book and is used by any acquaintance or passerby. In addition, he has a name or several names used by his family and intimate friends. As he grows older, he sometimes changes his name because of a whim, or a new age grouping. A more formal name is to address a father as "Father of So-and-So." When a man's father or older brother dies, he may and often does assume the name as well as the new responsibilities.

Recently in children's clinic one of the mothers from the back country districts told me the name of her child. I looked for it in the files where it had been placed when they lived on the station, and was startled and puzzled to find "dead" written on the record. The nurse reminded me that this was a younger brother of the child whom I had known. It makes records and statistics difficult and unreliable.

When they want to give the names of two ancestors, they avoid jealousies in a clever manner by calling the child *Bahe* (Two) or *Iyafe* (Both of them). Wouldn't you chuckle to yourself if you asked a mother the name of her child and heard *Mpea* (I don't know)? It is fairly common. One child who by right should have been given any of several names was called *Baobunga* (They have forgotten) because all of these relatives were dead. One wonders what superstitious fear prompted that.

The Smiths—*Botuli* (Blacksmith)—of this region are as numerous as at home. The boy's name *Iyambe* is as common as John is at home. Doctor says that when he needs a nurse quickly he can call *Iyambe* and be sure that there will be one of them within call. One man is called *Lofompengole* (Don't scold me). *Ekila* (Taboo) is the most common name for women in this region. Another ordinary individual bears the heavy title of *Lokumo* (Fame). Animal names are numerous: *Njoku* (Elephant), *Nkoi* (Leopard), as are also the names of things, *Botamba* (Tree) and *Ntange* (Bed). It pleases our fancy not a little to call our poky night sentry *Lokake* (Lightning). (General Letter, 7-18-38)

My father was introduced as *Ise'a Ngando* (Father of Lauretta) for formal occasions, such as in church before preaching. Mostly he was called Bongelemba, his African name. I can remember being awakened at night hearing "Bongelemba" repeated softly but insistently until Dad awoke, dressed and went to the hospital, or the brick kiln, to attend to some emergency. The name "Bongelemba" was well known over the whole region.

Mama Nsombo was Mother's address. The other women missionaries also were honored with the respectful title "Mama" preceding their African name. Formally Mother was addressed as *Nyang'ea Ngando* (Mother of Lauretta).

Blindness was not uncommon in the Equator Province, but cataract operations were rare. In 1932 Dad successfully performed one. The patient claimed to "be able to see his eight wives" after the operation. Six years later the same man returned for an operation in the other eye. Injuries causing blindness resulted from the hardships of their life and beliefs. In an article about native life that my father wrote for the *Congo News Letter,* he told about some of the troubles that beset their eyesight:

> Longomo, one of the promising young lads in our Mondombe station school, has had a most distressing accident. Running along the path at night, without any light, he bumped suddenly into a bundle of firewood carried on the shoulder of a man coming from the opposite direction. A sharp stick pierced and destroyed his right eyeball. In addition to the pain, he suffers the irreparable loss of his eye.
>
> In any medical census of these people, living so close to nature, one is repeatedly struck with the frequency of blindness in at least one eye. Over fifty persons per ten thousand of population have lost the sight of one or both eyes. Many of these eyes were destroyed in accidents. Many are injured by flying sticks and branches when they are working with their crude tools in the jungle. We marvel constantly that they leave their houses at night without lights.
>
> Still another former cause of injury to the eye was in testing for the innocence or guilt of someone accused of stealing. When thus accused, the individual concerned could defend himself by putting a bit of medicine in an eye to prove his innocence. Or, the accuser could insist that the accused do so. In the first instance, the accused hunted the medicine, and in the second, the man making the accusation. The medicine was prepared by removing a generous chunk of the bark of a certain tree. From this, the soft innermost bark was taken and soaked in a little water in a large leaf used as a cup. A drop of the solution was placed in the eye. If the accused actually stole the article, the eye would be destroyed; if he were innocent, no harm resulted to the eye—or so they thought.
>
> Freedom from superstition is bringing more and clearer vision to these primitive folk. Christian medicine is preventing blindness both by healing and by teaching. (DHB, *Congo News Letter,* December 1939)

The joys and necessity of fishing for the Congolese have been mentioned already. No account of their life would be complete without a full description of this cross between a happy throng attending a county fair and the useful efforts of a barn raising. During the dry summer months when little rain fell, the waters of the streams and rivers dropped, exposing long strips of gray-brown banks between water and trees. The water levels in the lakes also receded. That was the time to go catch fish, as described by my parents:

> Such low waters mean fishing season, for the swamps and small streams back through the forests are nearly dried up. The natives, especially the women, spend their days fishing out these spots. Perhaps two, three or four women choose their location, then build two dams across the stream. Their next task is to bail out with their baskets over the lower dam, all of the water caught between the two dams. Then they search around with their hands in the stream bed of sand, mud and leaves until they are satisfied that the fish have been caught. This done, they build another dam higher upstream and repeat the procedure. It appears to us tedious and often disappointing. They leave at five-thirty in the morning carrying a bit of firewood to protect their thinly clad (if clad) bodies from the dew and fog so characteristic of the dry season. They return at dusk with those fish which must yet be cooked. One wonders what they eat on those days when there is no catch. But dawn of the next day finds them on their way laughing and chattering like carefree children.
>
> Fishing out a lake seems to appeal even more to their play instincts. When the waters begin to go down, the outlet of the lake into the river is closed with mats which permit the water to recede but hold the fish in the lake. After the water reaches the proper low level, the tribe that owns the lake invites in to help as many neighbors as necessary to "fish it out." There may be 100 to 600 people depending on the size of the lake. The spirit is that of a picnic—gay, sportive and expectant. They line up near the mats in rows with their large fishing nets or baskets, those behind placed so as to catch the fish which pass between the front nets. Then they advance across the lake amid a din of excited talking, yelling and laughing. Some get many fish, some practically none. The invited neighbors must pay a part of their catch as tribute to the owners of the lake. Nighttime finds them on their homeward way with the best part of the fishing season behind them—in their baskets. (General Letter, 7-18-38)

On more than one occasion the Americans on the station hired some paddlers, packed a picnic lunch, and joined the crowd heading toward a fishing holiday. The large steel canoe of the station sported a flag stuck in the front, a drum to keep time and energetic, singing paddlers rhythmically and in unison dipping deep into the water to make the canoe fly. On particularly joyous occasions the paddlers even tipped the paddles through the water arcing sprays of droplets in sunlit-prismed rainbows. After arriving and tying safely up to the shore out of the way, we had a ringside view of the six-foot-wide nets dipping into the water—the men's nets held open by a loop of vine. The women almost submerged as they slipped their hands down through their funnel-shaped, open-ended baskets plunged to the bottom of the lake to catch anything inside.

Frantically the fish swam, invisible in the muddy water, driven by the horde of advancing people. The narrower the distance to the end of the lake, the more desperate became the fish. Some simply swam into the large traps in the fence belonging to the lake owners. Others took to the air jumping into people's arms, into our canoe or uselessly back into the water. Nothing equaled fishing out a lake for excitement!

As I grew up, the people increasingly adopted Western culture as their knowledge, beliefs and finances permitted. The changes surged most in the cities and down-river areas. On the station, as the natives donned shirts, shorts and trousers, the missionaries taught them how to keep the cotton clothes clean and mended. Long bars of soap shipped in wooden boxes arrived in fifteen-to eighteen-inch lengths. Cut into small rectangles, the mottled blue and cream cakes of soap were distributed for both laundry and personal use.

The natural beauty of unchipped teeth shone in the younger generation. They had learned the benefits of protecting the integrity of dental enamel. Scarification went out of favor. Intricate feminine hairdos swept the region at intervals as the latest fashions penetrated the interior.

These outward manifestations covered even more remarkable inner transformations in spiritual understandings. The change in religious convictions altered beliefs in causation, such as the culprits in disease. Knowledge of the universe and interpersonal relationships differed widely in the younger generation from that of their parents. The old lines of authority, held by the village elders, weakened among the young, newly-educated men. Weren't they better educated? Then didn't they know better? They now lived far from the elders.

Not all people could adjust to such earthshaking quakes. One elderly man sent his child to fill her head with the new learning, because, as he said, "My head is too hard." Thus beliefs were scattered all along the continuum from old to new and often in the same person.

CHAPTER 13

HOME ON THE STATION

The erection of my family's two-story brick home during the establishment of Mondombe Station in 1920, brought the natives from far villages to view and marvel at the wonder. Nothing comparable had ever been seen before. It claimed the honor of being the first in the region of such size.

The Baker house at Mondombe

The large airy house, shaded by encircling porches, had been conceived as a place for both business and residence. Combining the two functions turned out to be very unsatisfactory. Soon our family occupied the second floor. The ground floor was converted to include storage, a guest apartment, a classroom and, later, an overflow bedroom.

By the time my parents arrived in 1932 with one-year-old Lauretta, the completed building still lacked a few necessities. A railing for the upstairs porches became the first priority. After I was born, a corrugated iron roof replaced the thatch. "Rain on the roof" drummed a comfortable lullaby all of my childhood.

The view out the large screened living room windows showed a two-mile stretch of the mirror-dark river to its upper bend. If one turned right to face the main path to the front, the house looked toward the down-river curve past the boat beach to the next disappearance of the river. It spanned a quarter of a mile in width. These magnificent panoramas were framed by palm fronds.

At the boat beach the current flowed swiftly and deeply allowing steamboats to pull right up to the bank to moor. A back current helped an experienced captain swing his craft snugly into its berth against the grassy river's edge.

Swamps flanked both sides of the station. The spit of land between lay about a third of a mile wide. A sandy path bisected the station lengthwise starting at the twenty-foot high riverbank next to our house and running straight inland for a mile to the next village. The path was lined with palm trees planted at thirty-foot intervals by the first missionaries. The fronds arched to form a wide, shady tunnel that rested the eyes from the glaring sun. The palm nuts provided ample amounts of useful oil for the station's inhabitants.

Although Aunt Betty described an extraordinary palm tree on her station as being eighty feet to the crown of fronds, I think these were probably one fourth of that. Ferns and rank-smelling little brown and yellow orchids soon grew in the axils of the cut fronds, draping the trunks in green. The central mission buildings along this dirt path connected the missionary residences at the river to the African cottages at the other end. Through the years these native clay and thatch dwellings were replaced with substantial, simple brick houses. In between were the church, the school, the boys' dormitory and the hospital complex.

The spacious rooms of our house seemed even grander because of their thirteen-foot-high ceilings and large picture windows typical of the architecture in the tropics. All features encouraged the movement of air and any gentle breezes to cool the hanging humidity. Across the back porch lay the kitchen, the heat of its wood-burning stove isolated from the central rooms.

While this open style of construction served comfortably during the typical day, it could be cool during the driving rainstorms that whipped the station during the rainy season. Then we scurried to the narrow porches to drop the split-vine mats that partially screened the windows and kept the sweep of water from drenching the living and dining rooms.

I remember watching the dramatic advance of many a storm down the river under darkening skies. Lightning flared and thunder resounded off the clouds. The palms writhed and swayed in the wind seconds before the house was engulfed in a wall of water. Then the yards flooded and drained in swift rivulets. The sudden drop in temperature sent us shivering in search of sweaters. A palm flared one evening when lightning struck close to the house setting the tree afire. Rain quickly doused the flames.

Such moisture supported the profuse tropical flowers carefully planted and nurtured by the missionaries: flaming lantana, red double hibiscus globes and highly perfumed gardenia hedges. The delicate, deliciously-scented tea roses, the bushes of enormous yellow alamanda bells—blossoms too numerous to mention, even if I knew all the names. Half a dozen vases of blooms brightened the house every day.

While flowers painted the front and side grounds, gardens, rabbit pens and a large chicken yard occupied the generous backyards. Spiky pineapple and broad-leafed banana patches stretched to the forest behind.

Each member of the family had responsibilities for the gardens and animals. Even as young as three, five and seven years of age we girls spent hours grinding corn, carrying water and watching the chickens. Hawks were only too happy to swoop in for a quick catch, so the fuzzy little hatchlings spent most of their time surrounded by wire coops.

Chickens provided us with both eggs and meat, although eggs were always in short supply. Mother extended the quantity by using one-egg cake recipes. No one begrudged two eggs for a batch of ice cream.

Our flock of chickens varied from large, beautiful Rhode Island Reds to scrappy bantams. Half the flock of three dozen carried names for their distinctive physical characteristics, such as the regal King and Queen, the dominating Dictator or the comical Jester.

To furnish meat for one conference, Dad carefully chose a handful of young roosters and old hens past their laying days and caged them for the long trip down the river on the *Oregon*. Once started and away from home we children were horrified to discover Judith, a favorite plump red hen, among the doomed. Because of our entreaties, lucky Judith became the only chicken to travel both down and up the river and back to the chicken yard over a month later.

The difficult task of finding enough food for the family included not only the growing of food locally, but, also, the planning a year in advance to place orders for staples such as flour, canned oatmeal, tinned butter and powdered whole milk. The orders included canned hot dogs for birthday parties anticipated months ahead. Coarse, moist sugar was obtainable in the colony.

Managing the food was enormously facilitated after the first furlough by the gift from Dad's brother of a kerosene refrigerator. We depended on Aunt Ruth to mail the parts Dad needed to keep it running. Mother referred to it in a letter to her sister-in-law:

> The Electrolux, which worked perfectly from the time it arrived until we went to conference, has been out of order for a couple of months. Don didn't find time to work on it until recently. Now he has it working again and we think will be able to bring it back to par. We bought a new drum of kerosene at conference time which had dirt and water in it. Either or both got into the machinery and "jimmied" things. It was supposed to be good Texaco oil, too. We certainly enjoy having it in working order. The cold water and ice creams and Jellos taste so good. The wild meats have a better flavor if I put them in and chill them before cooking. Then, too, foods keep so much better. (LB Letter to Ruth 7-4-38)

Although chicken or wild meat served as a welcome change of pace, rabbits remained the staple meat for the table. They reproduced rapidly and fell victim to fewer ailments than chickens. Rows of wire pens a couple feet off the ground housed solitary breeding does and bucks. The young ones could be accommodated in more crowded circumstances until they reached about two pounds and their allotted time was up. Two rabbits per week doesn't sound like much protein, but it was supplemented with fish in season and milk made double strength from the tinned, whole powdered milk. In a general letter my parents extolled the raising of rabbits:

> Our rabbits continue to be a splendid food resource, and their rapid multiplication is a thing of wonder and envy to these meat-hungry natives. We have been gradually giving pairs of young rabbits to the natives on the station, and they must have over a hundred in the little hutches built back of their houses. We were a bit fearful for them last week, when a leopard visited us and the nearby villages. He got a big dog, a goat, and some chickens, but seems to have moved

on. Driver ants are almost as dangerous for chickens and rabbits, and they are present almost constantly. (General Letter 1-24-42)

Although the posts holding up the hutches were painted with turpentine to discourage insects from crawling up into the pens, driver ants, a kind of army ant, marched in such numbers that sterner measures were necessary to discourage their ravaging invasions. Because so many people have been deliciously shocked to hear that army ants will eat up an animal leaving only a pile bones, be reassured that would happen only if the victim were caged and unable to escape. I quote from *I Saw Congo*:

> The army ants are of medium size, are dark red in color, and have no eyes, working entirely by scent. There are two classes, the workers and the warriors. The warriors are much larger than the workers and have large black mandibles. When they take hold, you can pull them in two before they will let loose. The army ants usually travel in runways one and a half or two inches wide. If their path lies across an open roadway it is guarded on each side by a line of soldiers facing outward, with mandibles raised. If you stamp your foot within three or four feet of them, they all march forward to find the cause of the disturbance. When disturbed very much they call enough soldiers to form a living tunnel, by locking themselves together, under which the workers pass to and fro, entirely hidden from view. The narrow runways are connecting paths between their nesting place and their feeding ground. As they advance, they scatter out over considerable territory, capturing and killing and carrying back to the nest.
> When driver ants come into a house, which they do occasionally, every living creature—rat, bat, or insect—gets out or they take it out. Every house in Africa needs such a cleaning periodically, so when they come in, the human occupants leave and let them have their way. They will finish in two or three hours. It is sometimes inconvenient when they come at night, which time they usually choose. However, if one has a good mosquito net, well tucked in, he is perfectly safe, for they never cut through. (Moon, p. 50.)

Driver ant incursions around the rabbit hutches were fought with fire. Dozens of rabbits thumping danger signals were enough to awaken one from a deep sleep, to rush out and light a match to a trickle of kerosene.

Termites were another scourge of the tropics. These soft, white, grub-like ants seemed defenseless, but the damage they did was unbelievable. They worked in the dark or inside as they devoured poles, beams, even books. If undisturbed, they might eat away everything but a thin outside skin before being discovered. Houses could be built with a layer of concrete and tarpaper near the foundation, which was impenetrable for the termites. They had to form clay tunnels outside allowing them to climb in darkness over the outside of the building until they found some timber in which to bore. Regular inspections revealed the tunnels, which were scraped away.

Books stored in trunks or boxes were not immune. My parents found such damage when returning from a furlough. The book suffering the most harm was aptly titled *Reading I Have Liked*. My sister remembers this damage perpetrated by cockroaches. Certainly either insect caused untold destruction.

The termites in the forest survived on dead trees and built charcoal gray, rock-like turrets out of clay mixed with their own secretions. These stood many feet tall. When crumbled with a severe beating they made solid gravel-like coatings for paths, which otherwise became muddy trails after it rained. The chickens liked to eat the termites thus exposed. However, we found eggs laid thereafter were disagreeably scented and unappetizing.

On the subject of ants, other types existed in abundant numbers, sizes and colors. Their levels of venom ranged from unnoticeable to extremely painful. The tiniest ants were invasive, as was displayed by their silhouettes on film when they took up residence in Dad's camera. Slightly larger kinds invaded every shelf, cupboard and table utilized for food preparation and storage. Although setting table legs in tins of water created safety moats, the ants were known to bridge even those with chains of ants, if the tins were not sufficiently large. A strand of hair sufficed as a slender bridge.

Climbing trees was more adventurous when stinging ants were present, and they lived in our favorite breadfruit tree. Fortunately, those inch-long red hazards lived in sparse numbers. We maintained an alert watch at all times ready to flick them off the branch as soon as they appeared. The half-inch, plump black variety in the frangipani (plumeria) tree crawled in multitudes and stank when crushed. We loved to loll on the low branches at comfortable angles but were kept busy brushing away the little pests.

Though opportunities for creative play abounded, our childhood was not one of constant recreation. Mother taught us the excellent Calvert School correspondence course curriculum in a room set aside for desks and learning. Each lesson plan book listed the day's tasks for an eight-month year. We carefully worked through the assignments, asking for help from Mother when we got stuck. The responsibility lay on our shoulders and was not completed until we had finished the day's assignments.

Mother used to say that what we lacked in the multiple talents of many teachers, she would try to make up for by thoroughness. I can remember memorizing and reproducing verbatim three complete pages of dates and their significance to satisfy a fourth-grade requirement in world history. The list has served me as history's time line ever since, but it was difficult to memorize at the time—*4000 BC Bronze Age begins; 202 BC Zama, Carthage falls to the Romans.*

Unlike the oft-heard theory espoused today, such rote exercises did not turn me against the topic. History became the subject I chose in college for my major field.

Without physical education, choral music, reading circles or art, we whizzed through the school day in three hours and finished by noon. Not until the greater demands of ninth grade did I ever study in the afternoon. Calvert introduced us to art history, but the applied arts were experienced in daily activities later in the day to a greater or lesser extent. Our music education was acquired mostly in the same unstructured way.

Our piano had a stubborn tendency to stay silent when the keys were struck. Humidity swelled the hammers. An hour of heat from two small lanterns placed in the back were required to dry out the piano's works sufficiently for them to resume operating. This doubled the aggravation children usually experience with piano practice. I preferred playing our beautiful oak pump organ, but playing it couldn't develop in me the touch one needs for piano proficiency.

Daily class began when Mother called us into session. If she and Jewell Roberts fell into neighborly chatter over the side yard gate, we children disappeared out of hearing range. We had learned not to provide a reminder of passing time. Why Mother didn't just establish the starting time for us to be in class, I don't know, but we loved every minute after nine o'clock spent in surreptitious play.

One type of occurrence frequently interrupted our class session. When visitors arrived at the station, they usually came to see the doctor. Then Mother would get a note delivered from the hospital that there would be company for dinner, served at noon in the European fashion. Off she would go to make changes in the menu with Bosumbe, our African cook. (His presence allowed her to teach in both the African school and ours.) Between them they would concoct a soup course, the main course, a salad and a dessert with as many dishes as possible that would appeal to the Belgian palate. The visitors were almost always Belgian government administrators or commercial plantation managers.

With enough advance warning an African student would be scheduled to serve as waiter. Otherwise, the meal was served in the American "family style." The Belgians, unfamiliar with passing food, would usually help themselves when offered a serving dish and leave one holding the bowl. It became a family epithet among us children, as in, "Hey, Belgian, pass the gravy!" Conversation flowed around the table in French, the governmental language of the colony, and was always spirited and wide-ranging. In later years, we children learned enough French to follow the conversation, but in our shyness we never gained the fluency to join in easily. Later still the Belgians eagerly practiced English, their newly acquired language after World War II.

Facile use of French challenged Mother in the earliest years. Panic struck her the first time Dad took a Belgian husband off to the hospital. She was left with the wife for a period she knew would stretch to a couple of hours. What could she do to fill the time? She resourcefully picked up a *Ladies Home Journal*, sat down beside her guest and explored the mutual interests of women set forth in its articles. Fluency and ease came with practice. In later years she taught some of the advanced courses in French at the African school.

Other guests came one day with their small boy. After the boy's third or fourth polite request to use the bathroom, Mother inquired with concern if he was having trouble or was ill. Embarrassed, the mother admitted that he only was fascinated with our flush toilet. Such was a rare device in an area where wooden seats over buckets with the accompanying box of sawdust were universal.

Dad had installed the modern convenience along with plumbing and a hot water system. Rainwater from the roof drained into an above-ground tank. The water was hand-pumped daily upstairs to a 55-gallon barrel set at attic height to furnish pressure to circulate the flow through the pipes. One pipe, which encircled the wash fire out back, moved the water into an insulated barrel to provide hot water. (This was the era when a laundry fire was needed to boil cotton sheets on washday.) American ingenuity and know-how certainly made life more comfortable.

In reading letters exchanged by my mother and Aunt Betty, I was struck by how many were filled with detailed accounts of the menus assembled for company dinners, picnics and special occasions. The explanation for this focus on food was probably the skill, effort and advanced planning required to produce nutritious, varied, and essentially American-style meals. A dessert of ice cream with berries can serve as an example.

The only berry that would grow in our tropical climate was the mulberry—one to two inches long, plump and juicy. By pruning the bushes six weeks in advance, Dad could harvest mulberries for ice cream on a specific date. He usually tried to keep them available all the time. Dad compared them to those he had known as a child:

> We are now enjoying fresh berries—mulberries. As a child, all the mulberries I knew were pretty insipid, and grew on trees. I never quite understood the song about "Here we go round the mulberry bush." These are real bushes, and the berries are very gratefully accepted by us, since we can't have strawberries or others so welcome at home. (DHB General Letter 1-24-42)

We all learned at a young age to whip up ice cream from eggs, sugar, water, Klim and vanilla. It hardened in the freezer pans and tasted delicious—like ice milk.

Bananas and pineapples grew in a longer cycle, bore once and then had to be replanted.

All the missionaries at Mondombe cultivated vegetable gardens. Preparing the soil, which was badly leached by the rains, required many applications of forest leaf mold and other compost to provide enough humus to produce anything tasty in adequate amounts. Students were paid to bring the rich, decomposed material from the forest carried in wide baskets hung from both ends of a pole. The gardens were fenced with chicken wire and posts from the jungle. They required frequent maintenance, because the wire quickly rusted and the posts tended to send up shoots and grow.

On stations where pigs and goats were allowed to roam freely there was much friction between the gardeners and the animal owners. The pigs rooted up everything and the goats ate indiscriminately showing no distinction as to owner. At Mondombe my dad autocratically banned such animals at our end of the station to prevent destruction not only to gardens but also to all unfenced growth of young fruit trees, flowers and other flora. There were some goats at the African end of the station, but they were not allowed near the river.

Admirably, my eldest cousin Bryce Smith at the young age of eight years could butcher chickens and rabbits. At our house the adults—our cook Bosumbe or my parents—did the meat preparation. The shriek of a scared rabbit unnerved me. The "rabbit punch" behind the ears quickly knocked the animal into oblivion. The skinning was as neat as pulling off a glove. We children played only with the "Easter bunny" little ones or named the brood does knowing that we didn't want to get attached to the meat animals.

Mother purchased delicious catfish and some kind of silvery trout from the fishermen in season. A licensed hunter for the mission stalked the antelope and wild boar. As the station matured, the nearby wild game became scarce. The hunter searched more distant areas of the jungle for meat. In later years the kill smelled too rank to appeal to the Americans by the time it reached the station, perhaps two or even three days later. The Africans usually still welcomed it to their pots.

This was a land that distinguished with different words between the hunger for protein and the hunger for food in general. Congolese in our area couldn't afford powdered milk for their children, many of whom showed the protuberant abdomens of malnutrition, especially off the station. Obtaining enough protein was a constant problem for them.

Although the needs of work and daily living demanded long hours of attention, play and relaxation were not ignored by the missionaries. Birthdays and holidays found *"les douze Disciples"*—as the Belgians playfully called the dozen Americans—gathered for grilled hot dogs and buns at side yard picnics or fried chicken dinners with all the side dishes. The joyous festivals of fishing out a lake have already been described.

Another beloved dry season activity was swimming at the sandbar. As the water level fell, white sandbars were exposed along the river banks. The one nearest us appeared each year one mile up river. Great excitement and flurry of preparation occurred when Dad came home early from work and announced that we had a paddler and should get into our suits to go swimming. Dad and Mother had old-fashioned wool suits their first term, which covered them to the knees just as in early historical pictures. Dressed and ready, each with our own pointed-blade paddle made to size, we soon pulled vigorously against the strong current to reach the sandbar. Lauretta described the adventure in a Calvert School composition assignment at the age of nine:

> We live on the bank of a river. Not far up this river is a sandbar. In the dry season it stretches out quite far, but in the wet season the water covers it. This is where we like to go swimming.
>
> We go to the sandbar in a dugout canoe. Daddy calls the paddlers. Most of us children like to paddle at the front end. Everybody has his own paddle. Along the way we pass by a little lake. The natives like to catch fish in it. A tree, we call potato tree, has enlarged roots like big potatoes.
>
> The minute the canoe touches the sandbar we are out with a splash. We race across the sandbar. Often a water deer or crane has

been there before us and left its tracks. We go swimming at the upper end. There is a log from which we pancake dive. Another thing we do is to make sand castles by letting wet sand drip off our fingers.

Once a band of monkeys came to watch us play. We were in the zoo that time. One day Daddy came shouting out of the water, "I have a leech on me." He finally pulled it off. We were quite excited.

We have never seen crocodiles near our sandbar. However, we do see a hippo once in awhile. One liked to eat the grass on the bank by our sandbar. As we were swimming one afternoon, he very politely waited in the river for us to finish. He kept bobbing his ugly head out of the water. We all decided that if he were in a hurry we would not stop to argue with him. (Lauretta 1940)

Not having crocodiles in our stretch of the river was truly a boon. Eleven pairs of anklets filled the stomach of one murderous animal killed down river.

The hippo foraged on the station at night occasionally. Mother surprised it between our house and the Roberts' as she returned from a meeting one dark evening. The weak light of the flashlight played upon a large, noisy mass, which fortunately headed away from her and ran heavily toward the river. The hippo acted as startled as she. There wasn't time to be scared until after the incident had ended.

On leaving the sandbar one day we spotted the zigzag ripples in the water caused by a two-inch something sticking out of the river. Soon we could tell it was approaching us. A pink water snake's head barely cleared the water as it swam directly toward our canoe. The native in the prow stood rigidly clutching his paddle transfixed with fear. He believed the folklore that the snake would enter the front of the dugout and poison everyone along its way to exiting at the rear. Somehow my dad's voice from behind finally unlocked his muscles. He reached out with his paddle and drove the snake under the surface as we came up to and passed it.

Another day as we were swimming, the African paddlers cocked their heads and called our attention to the talking drums from the station. "Mama Besau (Aunt Hattie) has had trouble," they said. "She has fallen and something is broken." We knew that she was on an itineration in the backcountry traveling by motorized bicycle, but the drums were not specific about the injury. Quickly we gathered our towels and headed back home full of alarm and hoping that it was the bicycle that was affected.

Unfortunately, a fall on a particularly rough bit of road fractured the outer bone of her left forearm at the elbow. She was solicitously cared for by the

Africans, but the painful, injured arm was tremendously swollen and discolored by the next morning. She set out by jogging *tepoy*, or sedan chair, for the station thirty miles away. Her assistant in the meantime, after a long hard day, returned by bicycle to the station to alert my father—a message by the African drums preceding him. Dad set out on his motorcycle the next morning to give help.

Buena Stober in a tepoy

With her arm stabilized by a splint and placed in a sling, Aunt Hattie made the larger part of the return trip on the back seat of the motorcycle. Holding on with one hand over the very rough roads, she was unable to cradle the throbbing injured arm. The trip had to have been a nightmare.

Eventually the bone healed, and Aunt Hattie resumed her activities, but the elbow never completely regained its previous mobility. She was forever grateful to the loyal villagers who came to her aid with warm water, food and clean linens. The incident never deterred her from subsequent trips.

A happier excursion by *tepoy* took place in June of 1941. Our family spent six days on a trip that was just a vacation—the only one I can remember at Mondombe. Perhaps that is why it is still vivid in my memory. Porters carried four tepoys holding the two adults and four excited children. Additional porters handled the "chop" boxes of food and the other bundles of cots, linens and clothes. Dad disliked the monotonous riding in a *tepoy* and spent most of the trip trotting along side the porters at the swift pace they set.

We slept in "state houses" provided by the villages at the requirement of the State. These one-room hostels had covered front porches. Under these simple conditions even the creamed onions served the first night tasted delicious.

To celebrate Grace's birthday, which fell during the week of the trip, we children received fancy animal-shaped balloons. Mine was a bright sky-blue monkey that attracted large black butterflies with matching blue stripes. They fluttered around the balloon adding a bit of brilliant color.

Our destination was a forty-foot waterfall far into the shadowy forest. As we carefully avoided tree roots along the shaded last mile of a narrow mossy, jungle path, we saw pale blue violets, the only African violets I ever glimpsed in their natural setting. At the time I didn't know they were a popular houseplant in the States. I just remember their beauty.

We sat on damp rocks close to the cloud of spray admiring the falls while eating our boiled eggs and bread and butter sandwiches. I found the following description in a general letter:

> The falls are deep in the forest, where a narrow swath through the trees has been cut by the turbulent waters. They plunge with a roar to the rocks below, and dash on over huge stone formations in a series of little rapids. The rocks, trees, and ground close by are covered with a lush growth of moss, ferns, and creeping vines. It is not a large stream, nor are the falls high, but well proportioned, and fascinating. (General Letter 7-12-41)

Two years later I came to death's door. I had succumbed to the aches and fever of malaria, a not unusual illness out there at that time before the advent of new anti-malarial drugs developed during World War II to treat American soldiers in the Pacific. Somehow this time was different.

As my mother told the story, she stayed up late with me and went to bed very worried. With ill-defined dread she started to cry, muffling her sobs so as not to waken her sleeping husband. He nevertheless awakened. Taking her in his arms he asked gently what was the matter. "It's Margaret." She replied, "She doesn't smell right. I know something is seriously wrong."

Dad lay there a moment, then rolled out of bed and started getting dressed. "What are you doing?" Mother asked.

"I've learned to heed a mother's instincts," he answered. "If we need to treat Margaret more aggressively, then we may as well start now and not wait until morning. I am going to the hospital for supplies."

I still remember being moved to my parents' high, full-sized bed in the middle of the night. The regimen of intravenous feedings with glucose and quinine commenced. This was to be my invalid bed for the next six weeks as my parents fought to keep me alive through the ravages of blackwater fever. Blackwater fever—a diagnosis of almost inevitable death.

The malaria had progressed rapidly into the secondary stage as the kidneys stopped functioning unnoticed amid the myriad more obvious symptoms of a malarial attack. My parents later sent this report to their general readership:

> Already a quarter of a year since our last letter. What changes has it made in your lives? In occupation? In grief? Or happiness? To us, it brought near-tragedy. Hardly had we gotten our last letter off, when malignant malaria, that curse of this otherwise fruitful, kindly, tropical climate, struck our second girl, Margaret. Down deep in the Valley of Death she went, as, for a week and a half, her kidneys refused to function. Kind Belgian neighbors went by motorcycle and by truck to Wema, and returned the following day with Dr. Howard Horner, having traveled all night. What days of careful administration of medicines, solutions and blood transfusions, as we plied the little body with all the resources available! What nights of discouraged vigil as all efforts failed. She seemed to be following the fatal course of another anuric patient treated some two years earlier. The constant nausea made it necessary to give all liquids and nourishment by other routes. Just after the kidneys started to function, a violent chill and fever followed an intravenous injection, while chest signs indicated a broncho-pneumonia. Fortunately, she was able to take the necessary tablets of sulfathiazole, and her temperature shortly returned to normal. Margaret was grand, and accepted almost without a murmur, the many injections and the hours of lying absolutely quiet in her bed. She has now resumed her usual activities, and we are all most thankful for our unbroken family circle. (General Letter 6-23-43)

Some time after recovery started, I heard laughing and talking in the side yard. I slid off the bed to go to the window to see what was transpiring. To my shock I could hardly stand. Climbing back into the high bed required several attempts and all my feeble strength. I spent many days gaining energy and skill to walk again; many weeks passed before I resumed feeding the chickens and going to class.

After the illness I felt much loved from the attention showered on me. My sisters whispered that Dad had actually had tears in his eyes with the first evidence that function had returned to my kidneys. None of us had ever seen him cry. A distant Belgian, upon hearing that I had a thirst for grenadine and none was to be had locally, sent a bottle from his personal store by special carrier "for the little ill one." Everywhere we went for the next year my parents were asked, "Which is the child who was sick?" Word had spread over the whole province.

Life returned to normal and school began again. Feeding our black cat and the wonderful gray parrot with the red tail as well as the chickens could be tasks shared once again.

Polly was a big part of our life. She lived between the beams supporting the upstairs porch on the large spikes downstairs suspending the wooden box that was her house. By pulling herself up the wire with her strong beak she slept perched on one of the nails. Her fruit, sunflower seeds and palm nuts were placed on the top of her "penthouse" where she scattered the pieces happily in all directions over the ground below. Daily she practiced her vocabulary in three languages, her calls and whistles and her instructions to the animals. "Shoo. Shoo," she admonished the chickens freed from the chicken yard for the afternoon. She learned that she could make the visiting male turkey gobble by whistling shrilly and kept him going for minutes at a time.

As Mother wrote in a letter home, "Much to our delight, she is able to squeak like a water bucket carried on a pole. Of her many accomplishments that seems to be most enviable." Also, Polly had learned to say our children's names. Adults, both Mother and Africans, anticipated the day with dread when they would humiliate themselves in answering a call, only to find it was the parrot in perfect imitation of a family voice.

Perhaps most surprising was her ability to whistle a tune. Dad always descended the stairs before retiring at night to bid Polly goodnight. He would whistle a line from his favorite song *Souvenir*. Polly would reply with the next line. Then, "Good night, Polly" from Dad and "Good night, Polly" from Polly. The mimicking skills of African parrots are legendary and unexcelled by any other bird.

As on other typical Saturday afternoons, one day we were occupied in cutting and shampooing hair, polishing shoes and other preparations for Sunday. The action and activity on the porch above her head proved too tempting to miss. Polly abandoned her home in the usual awkward, trimmed-wing mode of half fall, half flight off her platform to the concrete floor below. She often sported a scab on her breast from this ungainly action. Up the stairs she hoisted herself with claws and beak until she could mount the porch railing and join the family bustle.

That day we children had found we could make a raspy sound by blowing through the tube of the almost leek-size onion leaves from the garden and were joyously making a nuisance of ourselves with the discovery. Polly enthusiastically joined right in, bobbing her head in her little dance with wings akimbo. She experimented vocally until she reproduced the harsh buzzing sound and joined the hubbub.

One year Grace got a pet monkey, which also joined in the ruckus of busy Saturday afternoons. Let out of its six-foot-tall wire cage Kiki would race along the porch swatting Purr, the black cat, in the face with its tail, grabbing bites of the bananas from bunches hanging from the ceiling, and jumping into Grace's arms to be held. Grace never let Kiki roam very far when uncaged. She called her back to keep her from running off to the nearby forest.

More exotic than the parrot or the monkey were the brief times Dad accepted first a leopard kitten into the family, and then a wild piglet. The parent animals had been killed and the Africans, knowing of Dad's interest in wildlife, brought him the babies to gain a small fee. The kitten's eyes had hardly opened when he was brought to us. Spotty showed up in a general letter:

> Would you like a little African pussy cat for a pet? The latest addition to our family is a little spotted baby which the natives call *nkoi*. It is a leopard. It is harmless enough now, but when it gets larger we shall have to kill it or send it to a zoo. Its front feet and front legs are large. Its claws are already as big as those of a cat. The natives ask us if we shall cut off its claws and pull out its teeth. They greatly fear leopards. And rightly so. (General Letter 6-17-39)

Spotty grew rapidly soon equaling the size of a house cat. Mother never trusted him and kept my baby brother off the floor whenever the leopard was out of his cage. With Maurice beginning to crawl, they moved at about the same level. A swipe of the claws could put Maurice's eyes in danger, she thought.

The leopard was much stronger than any house cat. While still a kitten he grabbed a duck around the neck. It took two men to pry his jaws apart and free the frightened duck. Spotty sported the characteristics of the full-grown breed, slinking on his belly among the alarmed chickens from the earliest age. Most of the time Dad confined him to his cage. By September he rode the *Oregon* with us to Conference where the following incident took place:

Last evening, Spotty, the young leopard which we raised and brought down river with us, got out of his cage, and Mr. Roberts with whom we are living at Bolenge, had a leopard hunt. Don was gone at the time. Spotty is now bigger than a house cat and very strong. He is not yet nasty, but no one forgets that he is a leopard. He is going down on the State boat to Leopoldville, the capital, to the Zoo. (General Letter 9-12-39)

Traveling through Leopoldville five years later we went to the zoo to see Spotty. To our disappointment, however, he was not there. We never learned whether he died or had been shipped somewhere else, perhaps to another zoo.

Pioneer life demands the use of every talent and skill a person has—even those previously undiscovered. It thrills one with challenges more elemental and far different from those found in modern surroundings. When I'm asked how I felt about growing up in Congo, it seems a strange question. Who thinks about how one loves home?

CHAPTER 14

CRUISING ON THE S.S. OREGON

Cruising down the river on the *Oregon* sounds enticing—and it was to us. I enjoyed six happy months on the boat in increments of one to two weeks. My family added up the journeys once and settled on the six-month figure as the total time for all the trips taken up and down the river from Mondombe. Memory has selectively erased the crowded cabins, the monotonous hours, and the hot, humid nights spent moored at the bank of the river with not a breath of air stirring.

The S.S. Oregon

I recall crocodiles slipping stealthily into the water from almost invisible perches on gray logs; the bathtub filled luxuriously to the brim with cool, tea-colored river water; the sight of the massive paddlewheel splashing and turning as I lay prone on the cinder-pitted deck peering through a small square opening. More thrilling yet were the few times we were allowed to accompany Dad, stepping carefully across the slippery, narrow, steel catwalk over the paddlewheel misted with spray, to the shelf holding flats of fresh lettuce for salads brought from our garden at home and needed for the next meal.

Occasionally the *Oregon* traveled by the light of the moon to make up some lost time. Without electricity there were no spotlights to illuminate the current or highlight submerged logs and sandbars. The captain's infallible memory kept us safe. No mosquitoes tormented us in the middle of the river as we sat squeezed onto the three upright chairs in front of the first cabin or perched on the platform supporting the barrel of drinking water snugly pushed into the prow of our passenger deck. Then we sang in the dark *I've Been Working on the Railroad* as the water swished by and the engine chugged along with its comforting monotone.

Long before most of these trips my parents described the boat to their friends in the States:

> The *Oregon*, with its deep-throated, characteristic whistle, has a personality little short of living, all up and down this river. So a resounding cry arose from the throats of all of us on October the sixteenth, at two in the afternoon, as we heard its whistle at the State beach one hour's travel further down river. Not quite an hour later we were assembled at the river bank to see it round the bend, close to our beach. But this time it was a new and beautiful boat which met our eyes. The rotten upper deck had been entirely replaced with large new cabins, lounge room and dining room, all in rich cherry-colored Congo wood, and the steering wheel had been raised to a small third deck in front of a nice new cabin for the captain. Actually, the *Oregon* is starting its second quarter of a century in better condition than its first. All of which may mean little to you but is of tremendous psychological stimulus to us, both white and black. (General Letter 10-27-35)

Known to the Africans as *Nsang'ea ndoci,* the *Oregon* was indeed "good news." The African title was apt, as it was also the African word for "gospel." For forty years the *Oregon* spread the gospel along the river.

Its birth was conceived in 1908 when the Disciples of the State of Oregon met in summer convention in Turner, Oregon, to hear Dr. Royal J. Dye and his wife recount stories of their work at Bolenge. They had arrived on the field in April 1899 carrying the legal documents that transferred Bolenge to the Disciples from the Baptists who were over extended. Dr. Dye immediately set about establishing his hospital and Mrs. Dye worked with the women and children. At the convention the Dyes appealed for support, more missionaries and a steamboat to carry their work up river. Their stirring speeches aroused the convention goers to promise to raise $15,000 for a boat to be named the *Oregon*.

E.R. Moon and his new bride Bessie, honeymooning in a tent on the grounds, heard the call and came forward to volunteer their lives to the Congo mission. Within the year they arrived at Bolenge. Twelve years later they helped open the new station at Mondombe. Ten years before that, E.R. Moon agreed to the challenge of assembling the *Oregon* when it arrived in its 1200 packages.

Herbert Smith tells the story in *Fifty Years in the Congo* that when the shipbuilders at James Rees & Sons in Pittsburgh learned the purpose of the boat they had been commissioned to build, they deemed it inappropriate to swear while they were at work.

By the following year the UCMS had raised the $6,000 to ship the now completed *Oregon* to Africa. The boat was assembled for dedication on October 13, 1909, at the Disciple Centennial Convention in Pittsburgh. It deeply impressed a twelve-year-old boy attending the convention who later went to Congo and became my father.

After the convention ended, the boat was disassembled and shipped to the Congo. In Leopoldville the British Baptist Missionary Society generously offered their shipyards and beach along the Congo River for the *Oregon*'s assembly. There, two Disciple missionaries "pooled our ignorance," as one of them said, and undertook the task of riveting it together for actual use. They did a splendid job even being foresighted enough to bring soft soap with them to grease the skids to ease the boat down into the water off the launch ways. In his book *I Saw Congo* Mr. Moon, one of the two men supervising the job, described the task:

> The *Oregon* was a shallow-draught, stern-wheel river steamer, with eighteen-foot beam and ninety feet over-all in length. The hull and lower deck were steel. The frame was put together with one-half- and three-quarter-inch hot rivets, and the plates double-riveted with three-eighths-inch cold rivets. It took about twenty thousand rivets for the hull. These were put in by hand by the native crew we brought down from Bolenge. They had never seen a rivet hammer or a dolly-bar until we put them in their hands and showed them their use. (Moon, p. 25)

After launching the hull, the boat builders installed the boiler, machinery, upper deck and cabins. Almost six months passed by the time they took their maiden voyage up river and arrived safely at Bolenge. In those days there were few refueling sites. The crew had to have sufficient members to chop wood for the next day's travel after completing the day's run.

The early years of the *Oregon* included training whites and blacks to crew the engine and to navigate. According to Mr. Moon, an early captain named Edwards had as his assistant an African named Inkima Jean (or John in English). Mr. Edwards had come to the DCCM after serving with the British Balolo Mission for one term. Soon Inkima John merited the position of captain and replaced Mr. Edwards.

The inspiring story of Captain John was written down for us MKs (missionary "kids") by Ned Roberts and printed in a 1995 newsletter. Although I had heard much of the legend before, Uncle Ned's story included many details that were new to me:

> I first met Inkima Jean, Captain of the Disciples of Christ river steamer, the *Oregon*, in the month of July 1939. He was an elder in the church and an ordained minister along with his responsibilities of being captain of the *Oregon*. He was a tall, slender man—one of the tallest of the Nkundo men that I knew. He was very quiet and seldom spoke unless spoken to or to carry out his responsibilities. He seldom spoke of his past, but stories were numerous about him....
>
> Inkima was born in the region of Lotumbe on the Momboyo River. His people had suffered under the rule of King Leopold of Belgium in the infamous rubber war days. He had been told never to trust a

Captain John Inkima

white man as they were all devils. A number of the men of his village had lost a hand, foot, ear or nose because of their failure to produce the required 10 kilos of raw rubber. This was the penalty for such failure. Later the village was to rebel and refuse to go for rubber and it is estimated 175 were murdered in cold blood for such rebellion.

At a young age, possibly eight or nine, he went with his village to the river where neighboring tribal fishermen were selling fish. He climbed a nearby tree to watch the proceedings. After the sale was completed and the villagers had gone home, the fishermen were still there. Jean was also still in the tree. They urged him to come down, which he did, and they kidnapped him and fled to sell him to a slave trader from Zanzibar. He was chained in the line of slaves and they began their long march across to the slave market on the East Coast of Africa. [Historical records show that four out of five died on the marches to Zanzibar.]

In their march they passed through an area then occupied by the Congo Balolo Mission. There one of the missionaries, who had hated and fought the slave trade, lived. I couldn't find the exact time, but it was in the late 1890s. I have lost the name of the missionary, but he bargained with the slave traders for Inkima. At first, the trader laughed at him, as he knew his hatred of the business, but eventually they agreed on an extremely high price. The missionary had to borrow to raise the money, but he bought Inkima to set him free. He was certain that Inkima, as a boy, could never live through the rigors of the long journey overland. Probably the slave trader realized this also so was willing to bargain with the missionary.

Inkima was horrified that he had been purchased by a white devil to be his slave. He felt he would rather die than to be such. He was taken to the missionary's home but only cowered in fear. He refused to cooperate in any way to eat or drink. The missionary's wife tried to care for his already acquired wounds, but he had to be held down. The natives, who could converse with him, tried to tell him that the white man had bought him to set him free. He couldn't believe it, as his fear of the white people was so great. After a few days, during which he needed to be fettered and guarded to prevent his running off into the jungle, he began to cooperate slowly and cautiously, but still fearful of the worst. Gradually, seeing the other natives were not treated as slaves, but were students, workmen and were not afraid of the white man, he began to trust them, but still carefully.

He was treated as a son and soon attended school. They knew he was from the Nkundo people, but he couldn't tell them from whence he had been kidnapped. His mentor soon became his trusted friend and adopted father.

The missionary was captain of the mission boat. Before long, Inkima was going with his white "father" on the boat. He seemed to be a born mechanic, so was encouraged to learn all he could about the boat and other machinery. He was thrilled with the faith he found among all at the mission and soon became a follower of the Christ. He was given the Christian name of Jean, French for John.

Before long his missionary rescuer died and another missionary, William (Bill) Edwards took over as captain of their steamer and along with it, Inkima Jean. Years passed and Inkima grew to manhood and worked as a mechanic on the steamer. About this time, Bill Edwards became interested in a single missionary who was with the Disciples of Christ Mission. They were married and Bill agreed to become a part of the Disciples Mission. Soon he was called upon to serve as a captain of the steamer *Oregon* and when he did he induced Inkima Jean to join him and work with him on his new steamer. Inkima proved to be so good as a mechanic and so trustworthy that he was soon asked to take Mr. Edwards' place and set him free for other work. This he did.

In the meantime Inkima had become an ordained minister and a very good preacher. Wherever they stopped, he gathered the people together and preached to them. Soon crowds just had to hear the *Oregon* was coming and they came to hear Inkima Jean preach. By the time I arrived it was taken for granted that when the steamer was in port at any station Inkima Jean would be the preacher.

On one trip up the Momboyo River he was asked to speak in the Lotumbe church. This he did and on that occasion he told of his life; how he had been kidnapped; how he had been bought and set free by a missionary. At the close of the service a little old nearly blind woman came forward and greeted Inkima and asked him to open his shirt and let her feel the cicatrices cut into his chest as a small child. He obliged and she carefully traced the scars and cried, "Inkima, you're my son. You're my son." Thus a life-long mystery was solved for Inkima Jean.

Inkima Jean continued as captain of the *Oregon* until it was sold to some Indian merchants expecting to use it on the rivers in controlling their many stores. For some reason they never refurbished it, and before long it deteriorated and sank in the Congo River.

Inkima Jean had a stroke after retirement but regained his physical well-being and learned to drive a car. One of the last times I saw him he was driving a jeep for a company near Bolenge. I understand that he retired in Bolenge and like another famous John of the New Testament times, he kept his house open for visitors with one simple message for all, "Love ye one another." God took him home at a ripe old age following a bout with pneumonia. God works for good through all things, even kidnapping. (Roberts, *Lokole*, October 1995)

Climbing to the top half-deck of the *Oregon* awed us children, assuring our most polite behavior. Captain John's tall, venerable presence permeated the bridge where the highest honor was pulling the wooden handle that blew the three-tone whistle unique on the river. From this elevated platform Captain John directed the helmsman to steer around every submerged tree and sandbar with an uncanny memory of the length of more than one river.

One day he was down supervising some work on the engine when the steersman's attention was distracted. The *Oregon* veered into the bank, plowing full steam ahead into the soft mud at the edge of the river. Captain John looked thunderous as he raced up the two flights of stairs to the bridge to deal with the inattentive helmsman. Fortunately nothing was seriously damaged and we were able to pull away and continue on our way.

A typical morning on the *Oregon* began before dawn with the firing of the boiler and the rousing of the crew for brief devotions led by Captain John. The scripture passage and prayers were inaudible to the middle deck, but passengers might be roused by the singing of the hymn "Awake My Soul, Awake" floating up from the bottom deck in beautiful harmony. The hymn still brings me the warm sensation of turning over for a few more winks of sleep as the paddle wheel began to turn, the boat got under way and darkness retreated before daylight.

Many cooks feeding the one to two dozen passengers from a tiny galley not much bigger than the wood stove, and with an outdoor table serving as the preparation surface, demanded diplomacy of the highest order. As the farthest up-river group the Mondombe missionary women took general charge of menu planning and cooking. Sometimes the daily fare was augmented by a local catch. The only time I ever ate the flaky meat of the crocodile was on the *Oregon*. It resembled a chunk of albacore. Likewise, that was my only experience with monkey meat, a soft, dark, meat—"The closest to human flesh," one elderly African was quoted as saying in the early years, when they undoubtedly knew. I didn't care for its sweetness.

Shortly after World War II the age of the mission steamer ended. Improved roads and vehicles for the stations made faster travel possible. Mondombe's truck arrived in 1947:

> Which will it be–auto or steamer? The race is on. Heretofore, our travel to and from Conference has been by steamer. This year, coming home with our truck, part of our staff took the road from Wema, and drove on to Mondombe in one day. The rest of us, sweating it out on the good ship *Oregon*, swung the long curves of the river and arrived two days later. Transportation and strategy are changing. (General Letter 11-8-47)

I heard that the *Oregon* was sold shortly after I left Congo in 1948, but the details of the transfer of ownership were skimpy until I read about it in the *Congo Centennial*, a recent history of the mission written by Dr. Gene Johnson. He wrote that it was sold in 1950 to a commercial outfit. The sale stipulated that the new owners should renovate the boat so as to change its profile making it unrecognizable as it traveled the river. The mission kept the matchless whistle, bell and name plates.

Dr. Johnson quoted from a sermon given by Captain John to his crew about the unique purpose of the boat in transporting missionaries, evangelists and good will:

> And as her purpose is different from that of other boats so must her crew differ. I expect every man to live as best he can in accord with that higher purpose. If our lives belie the message that the teachers bring to the people, do you suppose the people will believe? Unless our lives conform to the message, then the evangelists are carrying water in baskets. (Johnson, p. 27)

Later, when the mission moved to air travel, it was fitting that the pilot of the new Cessna mission plane received Captain John's name as his African designation.

A retired missionary who visited the field in 1964 was thrilled to visit Captain John in his retirement at Bolenge. She wrote:

As the airplane moves from station to station, isolation will no longer be a problem in Congo. Life will be geared to a different pace, but lest we think we have all the answers, perhaps we will do well to remember the proverb which Captain John gave us, "No matter how you look at life, death is inevitable...."

I recall the lovely proverb of Rose, the Captain's deceased wife, "We are all flowers—here to make life as beautiful as possible and then to pass on." (Johnson, p. 90)

Those who traveled on the mission after the era of the *Oregon* missed one of the most nostalgia-inducing experiences of life out there. When the "old-timers" begin to reminisce about their trips on the river, the more recent arrivals say somewhat wistfully, "Yes, I've heard much about Captain John and the *Oregon*, but it was before my time."

CHAPTER 15

SHADOWS OF WAR IN THE CONGO

Shadows of the approaching conflict, to be named World War II, filtered into even the remote jungles of central Africa. Although mail took three months to deliver the written and printed news, word of mouth quickly spread the latest reports from those favored with radios. By the fall of 1939, as they traveled down river on the *Oregon* to Conference, my parents wrote of the serious direct impact some of the Belgians were experiencing:

> War news over a radio at Boende tonight. The fortunate owner (a commercial man) has one of the few radios in the region that is really receiving. All of the rest need batteries or bulbs or a mechanical genius. This particular man and his wife are happier than many another Belgian in the Congo, for their lovely little ten-year-old girl has just arrived after making the four-day trip from Belgium to Coquilhatville by plane, unaccompanied. We understand that it was the last plane to arrive before the service was discontinued. Boats coming from Belgium are crowded with women and children coming to be with husbands and parents in Congo. The Administrator and his wife at Boende have cabled for their two sons aged seven and nine years, but know of no one who can help the boys along the way. The mother's one desire is to get them out of the country before they may be separated from relatives and completely lost. Her husband reminded her that the children wear plaques bearing their names and addresses—an attempt of the government to avert tragedies of lost identities such as occurred during World War I. But in spite of her calm, gracious manner, a great fear lay in the depths of her mother eyes. (General Letter 9-12-39)

The onset of war in Europe immediately affected the colony and all who lived there, as this letter affirms:

> Because of the difficulty in purchasing and shipping medicines and surgical supplies from Belgium, it has been decided to economize to the uttermost in their use here in Congo. In some places dispensaries are being closed, and we fear that ours may soon share that fate, since their supplies are furnished by the government. This reminds us that some of you may not be familiar with the List of Service Gifts prepared by the UCMS. Some churches may care to send some of these supplies to us.
>
> So far, we have suffered no great privations because of the war. Our grocery order from New York was on an unfortunate vessel in crossing the Atlantic, but we still hope for a replacement of what were largely supplemental provisions. The ordinary staples are still available here. Mail has been irregular, and we keep wondering if the letters which we haven't received have gone to Davy Jones' locker. (General Letter 1-20-40)

The German army overran Belgium on May 10, 1940. Many ships were torpedoed and sank in the Atlantic that year. By September my parents wrote of more deterioration in the colony:

> We are happy to receive your letters, even three months old. Some certainly have been lost, so if we don't reply—write again. Commerce has been zero, and mailboats monthly. When the stores stop buying resin, palm oil and nuts, the natives in turn have little money to buy clothes, pay tax, or put in the offering. Even the tranquil jungle is turned upside down.
>
> What a privilege in these days of destruction, to be engaged in construction! Would that we could match the dollars put into destroying life and property, with a like number less prodigally spent in saving and creating them!
>
> Work at the hospital has been interrupted by the difficulties in obtaining supplies, the absence of several government officers from their posts in the backcountry, and the general uncertainty of the times. Our dispensaries are still open, but the government has withdrawn its help. They double the service we render and we are working hard to keep them going. (General Letter 9-16-40)

The DCCM churches in compassionate concern started taking special offerings to assist other missions. Mondombe church sent three hundred francs (over eight dollars) to China Relief. The Bolenge church took up a collection for missionaries of the British churches and another for Belgian refugees. The April 1941 *Congo News Letter* reported that this church for several months past had set aside the third Sunday of each month to make "offerings of love" for special work away from Bolenge. "The pastor and elders seem happier over that type of work than anything they have undertaken."

In the back country the Africans collected the sap from the latex-bearing vines of the jungle. They pressed it into thin sheets, which they dried over the fire, and then sold at special markets to help the war effort. Over twenty-eight tons of rubber was purchased in one week at the store near Mondombe.

Disciple missionary travel across the North Atlantic came to a complete halt in 1941. The Edwardses from Bolenge had survived the sinking of their ship in 1939 as they made their way home for furlough only to be torpedoed again on their return to Africa in 1941 on the *ZamZam*. The *ZamZam*, an Egyptian ship, sank with the loss of only two of the 142 Americans on board. The surviving passengers were rescued from the icy water by a boat from the German warship.

Because the United States had not yet entered the war, the Edwardses were sent back to the States, but the Hendersons, a young Canadian couple traveling with them for their first term with our mission, were interned in Germany. Eventually Mrs. Henderson was able to return to Canada in a prisoner-of-war exchange. Much later Dr. Henderson escaped from a German prison camp to Switzerland. He remained there until the end of the war.

After rejoining his wife the Hendersons traveled out to Congo to the Monieka hospital. Dr. Jaggard stayed at his post long past retirement age waiting for his hospital to get a new doctor. He finally had to retire and leave his hospital to the care of a nurse. The Hendersons' sacrifices in coming to replace him were much appreciated on the field.

The Smiths and others had returned to Congo safely by the roundabout route across the South Atlantic to Capetown and up through South Africa. Now furloughs were canceled for those, including us, who had completed their terms; the sailings of those already on furlough were thrown into doubt; and only prayers could be offered up for those en route (who fortunately safely arrived at their destinations).

Lauretta anticipated the dry season when the sandbar would appear. She wanted to learn to swim "just in case our boat should be torpedoed like the

ZamZam." By the end of January the report from Mondombe showed everyone had settled into an adjusted routine:

> Everyone inquires about how the war is affecting us. It has limited our staff, as many who were home have not come back on time. Our two new missionaries are still in Germany. Those of us who are here, are taking short vacations at Capetown when it seems necessary to rest and to get out of the tropics. Prices are higher, 50% or more, cutting down our buying power terrifically. Foodstuffs come in from the States and Capetown instead of Belgium, Holland, France and England. That, of course, isn't a hardship for us Americans who prefer well-known brands. However, they would keep better in tin instead of cardboard cartons. We try to keep our work and our spirits normal. The most of our mail arrives fairly regularly....
>
> Great excitement has been created among our natives by the occasional passage of an airplane. We never saw one at Mondombe previous to September past. Many have been the questions asked. "Isn't it a thing of awe itself?" they demand. On one particular day they were more than usually excited. In geography class they asked for time at the end of the hour to discuss its significance.
>
> "We've become somewhat used to seeing these airplanes passing overhead, but today we're truly alarmed. Is the war getting so close? This airplane today went in the opposite direction from all of the others."
>
> We remind them that their fathers felt the same fear and awe when the first little steamers plowed up these rivers. To which they agree. (General Letter 1-24-42)

After many arrangements, it was our turn for a short vacation in South Africa. We left in July traveling overland with Dr. and Mrs. Jaggard. Kind missionaries from other missions ferried us by truck from one to another station and then to the train. My parents chose to spend only part of the respite in temperate Johannesburg. We spent the last month of vacation at Lotumbe with the Smiths, so the cousins could get reacquainted.

After re-passing Victoria Falls and Elizabethville in southern Congo we took the State boat down the Kwa River. My parents wrote about our vacation:

> ... At the Congo River, where we changed from the big passenger steamer, *Kigoma*, to our own *Oregon*, we met a French missionary

family of the country near Dr.[Albert] Schweitzer's mission. They had stirring tales of Vichyist and Free French fighting on their very own mission station.

We were heartily welcomed by the [staff of Bolenge and the Congo Christian Institute] and my three Mondombe nurses in school there. It is still most difficult to get used to seeing this once beautiful Bolenge with its big schools and local population, and its huge backcountry field, so inadequately staffed. Or to see the unoccupied houses, monuments to a happier and more fruitful past. Or the big shop building surrounded by rusting mechanical equipment. How small a fraction of the war expense would bring this plant back to maximum productivity in enriching human life!

Here also, we learned more details of the recent serious illness of my sister, Mrs. Everton B. Smith, taken with pneumonia, at her station of Lotumbe, without any resident doctor or nurse. By great good fortune, a passing missionary family with some knowledge of nursing, was staying there, awaiting passage on a boat. By as great or greater good fortune, Mrs. Smith's rugged constitution fought off a fatal outcome to this great killing disease.... This near-tragedy does re-emphasize the great shortage of our personnel and the necessity of closing one or more of our stations, unless adequate staff can soon be provided....

We are back again in the land of aching joints and limbs and backs, we find, as we spend a few hours each day at the hospital helping Lotumbe's only medical worker, Miss Alumbaugh, a nurse. Miss Alumbaugh was promised, early in her missionary career, that she would never be stationed alone without a doctor. Yet for the many years of her Congo service, she has needed to act in the capacity of a doctor, responsible for the lives of white and black of her station.

Hardly had we arrived at Lotumbe, when a young lad of perhaps twelve years was brought in gasping with a big hole in his chest. It had been made by an arrow, shot at him by a fighting playmate. Every breath was labored, since the left lung could be seen, collapsed, inside. Fortunately, the heart had just escaped. He had a temperature already of 104 degrees. Believe it or not, but we inserted a funnel into the chest cavity, and rammed in ten powdered tablets of sulfapyradine. [There were no antibiotics yet in Congo.] Then we stitched the wound shut and dressed it. With the oral administration of more tablets of the same drug, and rest in bed for a few days, the temperature dropped, the wound healed, and the lung expanded. He has already returned home, apparently well. (General Letter 1-16-43)

My memories of our stay at Lotumbe include games played after supper outside in the pitch black, the yard lit in one bright spot with a resin torch. Scaring oneself and others playing "Witch in the Graveyard" took little effort in that atmosphere. This was the same yard where the leopard caught a chicken and scared a rabbit to death.

Imagine our dining table for twelve. The circle of extended family surrounding it teased and joshed. Too soon the *Oregon* arrived to transport us up river.

When we returned to our station, the five Robertses were to leave for their vacation. (A daughter had been born since their arrival at Mondombe.) Following their stay in South Africa they were to be loaned temporarily to Bolenge. Since we didn't know how long they would be away, Lauretta and I asked our much-loved Uncle Ned if he would baptize us before he left. He agreed.

The lovely immersion service was held up the river in the shallow waters at the sandbar. My parents noted it in their general letter:

> We are happy over the baptism of Lauretta and Margaret, in a beautiful service conducted by the Rev. N.M. Roberts just before his departure in February. It was held at the edge of the Tshuapa River, attended only by the missionary staff, Capt. John of the *SS Oregon*, Ntange Timothy, our native pastor, and two other natives chosen by the girls. It took place in the late afternoon of a beautiful day, and the long rays from the setting sun across the forest wall on the opposite bank of the river enriched the beauty of the scene. Our Congo friends and we were pleased by the solemnity and peace of the ceremony. Capt. John said afterwards, "It was quietness itself." (General Letter 3-23-43)

This contrasted sharply with the village baptisms, which took place for hundreds. The new Christians sang enthusiastically on their way down the bank of streams for immersion in successive groups of four or five.

Symbolically, baptism in a river has always appealed to me as being closest to Biblical immersion and acceptance into the church. The service remains to this day the loveliest and most moving baptism I have ever attended.

Coinciding with the war came an emphasis by the government on improving the roads to bring faster travel and communication. My father wrote two articles published in the *Congo News Letter* in 1941 describing the changes. They are combined here:

> Long distance travel in tropical Congo is necessarily by water, since the rivers alone offer continuous stretches of the same element. By land every few miles swamps or rivers require a change in conveyance. Such breaks have rendered roads in the Lotumbe region especially primitive and difficult. On our other mission stations as well, one could rarely go very far in any direction on paths other than by foot or bicycle. The auto road past Bolenge has been a single exception to this.
>
> Lately, however, great attention has been paid by the government to the construction of motor highways in these parts of the Belgian Congo, also. Probably in the near future autos may travel from Mondombe to Bolenge, the entire length of our river. The Mondombe end of this highway, over 300 miles long, is nearly completed. Branch roads are being improved, many already permitting the use of motorcycles, and even autos. Local transportation soon will be completely changed. Near Mondombe alone there are now seven trucks and three autos.
>
> Motorcycle travel is now infinitely less time-consuming, and less fatiguing on highways. Recent emergency trips were made by me in three days from one end of my region to the other, a distance by road of two hundred and twenty miles....
>
> But the personality of the villages is gone. This impersonal road stretches on and on, the same in one place as in another. Gone are the individual "thank-you's," the sharp dips and rises, the curves that meant this or that village. The painful swamps as well where one surged through mud holes, or sank through dirt-covered bridges of rotten sticks; the swamps that marked the end of each little clan or the limits of a village. I race over these smooth dikes and plank bridges; forgetful of the boundaries they used to mark so distinctly. The villages, too, bear an unusual likeness one to each other now, torn up by this stranger that leaves ditches and piles of raw earth on either side.
>
> Gone, too, are the friendly faces running beside me with words of greeting as, slowly and carefully, I dodged the goats and dogs and holes in the old road. The villages now seem more deserted. Perhaps the natives are hunting, or it may just seem emptier as I pass more rapidly. The old houses close to the road are torn down, and all must

be built new farther back. This highway underlines anew the contrast between the primitive forest culture and the speed of modern civilization. Can the people bridge the gap to greater knowledge and higher training? They built the road under the white man's supervision. Will they receive from his hands, the more prolonged and detailed training necessary to follow the highway, and what it symbolizes, to happier richer life?

Faster communications are here to stay. (The new highway permits speeds of 30 miles an hour.) What changes they will bring in the development of these jungle regions it is hard to prophesy. (DHB in *Congo News Letter*—October 1941)

The missionaries carried on through 1943 with an abbreviated staff. The Hurts returned to Mondombe to oversee the evangelistic work. Aunt Stobie left for her vacation in South Africa. Hattie Mitchell left for her furlough in the States. The Bakers summed up the year:

The monthly mail boat has come and gone, and we breathe a sigh of relief that the annual reports are finished and sent in. Here are some of the Mondombe figures for the year:

Hospital:		
	New cases	8,400
	Treatments	82,600
	Major operations	83
	Students in schools	1,400
	Baptisms	1,257

Interpreted, these mean that all station activities are continuing at around the usual figure. The number of students has decreased, due to the war effort of rubber gathering. Our church membership is enlarging at the astounding rate of a thousand new members per year, though its supervision and shepherding are only very slowly and slightly increasing, as to native leadership, and unchanged or decreased for the moment, as to missionary direction ... (General Letter 1-18-44)

Plans for our approaching furlough had been percolating for five years. Aunt Betty proposed their getting a car during their leave in 1939 and our having the use of it for our stay. Perhaps grandmother's house in Hiram could serve both families as a furlough home and as home base as we children stayed in the States to finish school. Furloughs could be staggered and extended.

How to manage this meshing of children's education and work in the field challenged all missionaries. Some missionaries simply resigned and stayed home with their offspring at that crucial time in their lives. Others had family members with whom to leave their children, or even, in the British manner, boarding schools.

The war changed the timing, but our departure in April or May seemed assured in 1944. The Smiths decided that Bryce, now almost fourteen, would travel home with us. We would attempt to find passage on a neutral Portuguese liner from the mouth of the Congo River. The *Oregon* would carry us down river detouring by way of Lotumbe. From Coquilhatville we would board the State boat to go to Leopoldville.

Because Gertrude Shoemaker was traveling home with us for furlough, only three missionaries remained at Mondombe. This depleted staff was echoed at the other stations. Some had only two missionaries. None had doctors.

The nurse from Bolenge closed her hospital, which had the largest obstetrical service of the DCCM, and moved to Monieka to replace Dr. Jaggard. He could wait no longer for Dr. Henderson, still isolated in Switzerland until the war ended. Dr. Horner at Wema had no nurse to head his hospital and had to close the work in his huge field.

Closures in education and evangelism weren't as drastic or as apparent, but they were almost equally serious and depressing. The few missionaries restricted the work to their capacities for supervision and accomplishment with the help of the African staff.

Even though Dad's hospital could stay open with the supervision of Aunt Stobie, leaving it was a wrenching experience for my father. There were going to be many occasions when she simply could not fill in for him. He expressed some of his emotions to his friends and supporters:

> ... Just before leaving our station it became necessary to reduce our work, and no more operations were performed except really acute and serious cases. The others, some of them come from long distances, were told to come back again some time in the future, when again there might be a surgeon on hand to relieve them of their tumors, their ruptures, their bladder stones, and their abscesses.
>
> "But Doctor, here are the francs to pay for my operation," they said.
>
> "I am sorry, but I have no more time to do it," I replied.
>
> "Who will help us when you are gone?" they asked.
>
> "Oh, Mama Mputshu (Miss Stober) will be here."

"We are glad to have Mama Mputshu, but when an operation must be done, who will do it?" I had no answer.

Two cases, we were happy to relieve, even at the last moment. One was a little three-year-old who had had a palm kernel up one nostril for over a year. It yielded in two minutes after the child fell asleep with the anesthetic. The other was a young lad whose nose had been completely obstructed for over two years by nasal polyps growing down from the nose into the throat. His "Thank you, Doctor, thank you!" will stay with me for many a day, as the tumors dropped out and he found himself with an open nose, able again to close his mouth and yet breathe.

We are planning to be with Mother Baker in her home in Hiram. (General Letter 7-20-44)

Six months after leaving Mondombe our little band finally reached Hiram by train from Philadelphia on November the eleventh. Grandmother had happily answered all the questions asked her by the FBI agent who came to her door. She realized this meant we were close to landing. Her eager cooperation was somewhat deflated when the agent said, "Yup. That agrees with the information we already have."

Our odyssey kept us in Leopoldville six full weeks. While we were there awaiting a place on a Portuguese liner, the inn hosted some passengers rescued from a ship sunk on its way to Africa. I remember wondering why these passengers were "saved by God's hand," as they believed, and God had declined to save the others. At eleven years old I found it difficult to believe the loving God I revered would interfere to save some and condemn other passengers to death. Surely there must be some other explanation for the outcome of this intervention.

The Bakers in 1945—Lelia, Donald, Margaret, Grace, Maurice and Lauretta

The women awaiting passage hid their fears of war travel from the children. I remember hearing discussions by them about whether they should be investing in slacks. Skirts and dresses were the attire of that day, but pants would be warmer and more practical in lifeboats. Even neutral ships were known to have been stopped by the Germans to remove passengers.

From Leopoldville we descended the rest of the way to the coast to embark on a neutral Portuguese passenger ship bound for Lisbon. What beauty of etched glass, snowy table linens, red roses and gleaming silver appeared before our astounded eyes as we boarded the liner and passed the first-class dining room on our way to the lower decks!

We had just spent a weekend at a newly created loading point, an island in the mouth of the Congo River. Our housing comprised of a shell of a new hotel being erected to accommodate the passengers at the newly scheduled stop of the liner. The building lacked window sashes, hot water and other amenities. Two women and eight children slept in three single beds and one baby crib in one room. Only two mosquito nets were furnished. Mother tacked one over the open window frame and the other hung over the heads of the six children sleeping across two of the beds pushed together.

Cold, greasy water without a bubble of suds in half of a fifty-five-gallon barrel served for washing dishes in the wide doorway of the dining room, which displayed wine-stained, dirty tablecloths. Mother always said "our weekend at Cesare" sounded romantic. The reality left her hoping fervently we would escape without any serious consequences.

Reaching Portugal accomplished half the sea trip. Lisbon in October was dreary, cold and gray. For a month we stayed in a chilly hotel awaiting passage to the States. Only those whose blood has been thinned in the tropics can appreciate the cold that creeps into the bones in a high-ceilinged hotel room without any heat.

The beauty of churches and castles failed to move us children in the shivering dark, stone halls. We enjoyed the bins of sugary raisins and fresh green grapes sold on the streets. I marveled that Dad could use his knowledge of Latin, French and German to decipher the daily news spelled out in Portuguese in lights across a downtown marquee. The US was in the last month of a historic presidential election. Would Roosevelt win a fourth term?

Daily, hand-washed laundry dried on lines strung across our hotel suite. Breakfasts of hard rolls and cocoa were brought to our rooms. We learned the first day after an hour-long wait that the hotel didn't encourage serving breakfast in the dining room. Lunch and dinner we ate in the hotel dining hall. The bright pink, boiled shrimp on the hors d'oeuvre cart met our quick approval. We let Dad try the squid dish. "Tastes like the boiled lower lip of a cow," was his graphic judgment. With lessons from the school texts brought along, the time finally arrived to embark on another ship for the States.

The trip across the Atlantic in steerage proved to be the least pleasant of all our crossings. Our queasy stomachs felt no appetite for the daily fare of boiled potatoes, boiled fish and highly garlicky meat. The powdered milk was so ancient it separated in the glass into water and chalky sediment. After listening to our constant complaints Dad brought a bottle of iodine to the table. He tested a glassful thinking the milk might possibly be chalk. The test turned out negative, but we were no longer required to drink it. We lived for afternoon tea out on deck with its Ritz crackers topped with butter and sugar. It was wartime, we understood, and we were lucky to get safe passage home.

Fortunately, we children were spared the fear of being stopped by a submarine. In those days some information was considered improper for young people to hear. Meanwhile our parents worried for us all. A brightly lit Portuguese flag painted the length of the ship announced its neutral nationality.

One day some Allied ships were spotted on the horizon. Immediately our ship veered away from the convoy hidden behind the curvature of the earth. At last our trip ended without incident.

We disembarked in Philadelphia on November 9, 1944, a Saturday. Because of Dad's inability to cash traveler's checks along the way, he was short of funds. In those days no banks were open on weekends. Taxis were out of the question. The last of Dad's money sufficed only for seven trolley car tickets. Fortunately, trolley cars had large empty spaces that accommodated our mound of luggage. Also, fortunately, Dad had relatives in Philadelphia. We set off for their place and astonished his elderly spinster aunts in their tall, tidy home. What a flurry to settle seven guests in a small row house with three floors! Hotdogs had never tasted so good. And real milk!

When Dad found out that the banks would not open on Monday because of the Armistice Day holiday, he prevailed upon a banker in Aunt Ida's and Aunt Alice's church to open his bank on Sunday and cash the traveler's checks. My parents considered it too great a strain on their loving eighty-year-old aunts' hospitality to stay more than two days. Monday we boarded the train for Ohio.

The day after we arrived in Hiram Mother led us to the small local school and enrolled each of us in the appropriate class. The sea of faces floored me as I entered my combination fifth/sixth grade room. Forty-four faces swiveling toward me seemed akin to facing a full arena. I couldn't run away, so, stiffening my spine, I entered sixth grade.

Although I was well prepared academically, nothing had equipped me for the regimentation of American classrooms. Desks of scarred wood and black wrought iron clung to the floor in rigid rows. We turned in our seats, stood and marched in a straight line to the count of three. The teacher allowed no whispering or talking without being recognized. The rambunctious son of the college president sat right next to the teacher's desk at the front of the room amid the small students despite his tall stature. Only English was spoken, although I often had no clue to what was said in the jumble of slang expressions.

In a small college town such as Hiram everyone knew who we were. We quickly made friends and adapted to our new environment. With its maple tree shaded streets and friendly people Hiram offered a lovely setting in which to sink our American roots.

CHAPTER 16

PROPITIOUS TIMES

During our memorable furlough the Smiths' arrival back in the States the following summer filled the house in Hiram to the attic. Grandmother died the following Thanksgiving weekend of leukemia after experiencing the joy of reuniting with her two long-absent children and getting to know her eight "African" grandchildren. I picture her sitting alertly in her rocker, her white hair in a neat bun, with my brother beside her after school as she listened to him practice his reading. Probity and enlightenment had characterized her eighty-seven years as English teacher, wife, mother, and grandmother.

After we returned to Congo, Aunt Betty and Uncle Everton assumed the duties of house parents for Lauretta who stayed in the States to finish school. I was returning for two years before rejoining Lauretta to complete my education. My parents planned on a short term of three years. They would come back the year after I did to take their turn as house parents for all eight children. There would be a two-year hiatus between the end of the Smiths' furlough and my parents' return.

We left New York in January on the *M.S. Gripsholm*. The dark swimming pool deep in the dingy interior of the ship remains my clearest memory of the trip across the Atlantic in 1946. I'd describe the steamer as functional, rather than beautiful or luxurious, but it justly earned its fame as a "mercy" ship during World War II. Under Red Cross auspices the *Gripsholm* with its Swedish crew made twelve round trips from New York to various ports returning Japanese and German nationals or POW's to their home countries and picking up European and American diplomats, missionaries and nurses. The January we shipped out from New York marked the ship's return to commercial travel.

In two, long general letters my parents described the trip to Congo through the Mediterranean Sea to Alexandria. Up the Nile River (down the map of Africa) we crossed Egypt and the Sudan and passed into Congo by chauffeur-driven car. The contrasts we viewed couldn't have been more stark: empty brown desert to lushly green, irrigated Nile Valley; ancient pyramids and brightly painted King Tut's tomb to the busy, drab modern city of Cairo overflowing with traffic and beggars; wealthy landowners to poor peasants with little more than an acre of land to support a family; camels everywhere ferrying people in flowing robes to swift trains whose colored window glass shaded the eyes from glaring sand.

The war seemed very recently ended in Cairo. Military personnel were much in evidence. We did our sightseeing riding on hard wooden benches under canvas canopies in the backs of army trucks—trips organized by the Red Cross for uniformed soldiers and nurses with other Americans allowed to join the group. Museum's artifacts had returned only recently to their shelves from safekeeping deep in the caverns of underground burial sites for the royal horses.

Our 8,000-mile journey took us past the Great Temple of Abu Simbel with its immense statues of Ramses II about twenty years before a seventeen-million-dollar project relocated it to higher ground and out of the bed of Lake Nasser behind the modern Aswan Dam. In one span up the Nile, our small boat zigzagged for five days through papyrus swamps. The long green stalks stood eight to twelve feet high, topped by huge pompoms. The land of the Dinkas rolled past us in southern Sudan, where the tall, proud men stood totally naked, foot against knee, leaning on their spears. And just before crossing into Congo we added a miniature dinosaur-looking chameleon to our menagerie. Googleeyes traveled with us to Mondombe fantastically changing color to match his background from bright green to yellow to dark brown—even adding stripes at times.

We found an exhausted Aunt Stobie ready to leave on her furlough to the States having led the medical work heroically for almost two years. Ending the second general letter my parents wrote:

> There is a better, happier spirit among the native workers. The increased proportion of Institute-trained men has stabilized and strengthened our work tremendously. The desire for an education is constantly growing. The work of the hospital is heavy. The mass Christianity continues. Never were the times more propitious for an energetic expansion of our work. (General Letter 4-3-46)

Modernized transportation had reached the deep interior. By summer, airmail letters from Hiram arrived in seventeen days; sea mail still took three months. One missionary reached Bolenge from New York by plane in less than three days, whereas our trip took seventy-five days. Cultural development showed equally dramatic advances as reviewed in July:

> This arrival gave us a special thrill. Previously, we were predominantly aware of the contrasts between the Christians and the people of their home villages. This time we notice the progress made by individual Christians. When we went home, war was ruining our backcountry work; the schools and churches were feebly struggling or, sometimes, closed down. The teachers were discouraged and constantly asking, "When are you white people going to stop your war?"
>
> Now, the Congolese is released from war work and free to resume normal village life. The children are attending school and new chapels are going up. There is a new happiness on the faces of the teacher/preachers.
>
> On the station, several more potential leaders have returned from the Institute at Bolenge. Just this extra few makes a big difference in station schools, hospital routine, and church services. Their children are clean, bright eyed, and responsive. They are much petted by the men and women on the station who were in the dormitories with their fathers and mothers. How much farther removed from the old heathen fears and restrictions will be these children than are their parents!
>
> There has been an amazing increase in attendance in our station schools. The first-degree school (two year), which numbered over two hundred students when we left, now averages three hundred. Since brick walls don't stretch, the pupils must bulge out under the shade trees.
>
> Two more years have been added to the curriculum, soon to become three more and now a new school building is a <u>must</u> for the full eight years of schooling. We have a splendid plan made, to fit it into our present buildings harmoniously and efficiently. We are a bit like the man who said, "I have the taste to cut a dash [bribe]; the thing that's lacking most—is cash."
>
> Mondombe mission station is indeed a park, and looks especially beautiful at this moment. It has been well cared for. Now we are again helping in its improvement. The two mission-trained masons have been cementing floors in our most recent school building, and have foundations in for two duplex cottages for nurses and teachers. The walls of one of these are now rising. We are making bricks, getting in

sand from the river during the dry season, and laboriously sawing planks and boards by hand from big logs supported over a pit. Our one trained carpenter is making new benches for the church, shelving for the hospital, offering boxes for the rural evangelists, and repairs to school desks and building.

At the hospital, sick folks have been pouring in from all directions. The volume of work is so much greater, the facilities for treatment and the quality of care so much better than when we arrived in 1932. Our one small ward building, used also for obstetrics, is most inadequate. It and some twenty-five two-room mud and thatch huts, rebuilt during our furlough, are overcrowded, and we are overflowing into the station workmen's homes. Our prayer is for a new ward building—an essential, if we are to provide proper medical care. It is the next big step. (General Letter 7-11-46)

The letter included a wish for an X-ray machine to help in diagnosing the increase in pulmonary tuberculosis cases. Blood transfusions could aid the patients made severely anemic by the witch doctors' practice of blood letting, but where could blood be obtained? New medicines developed during the war now helped cure malaria. Opportunities abounded. Additional staff was sorely needed.

The *Oregon* made three trips to Mondombe in 1946. After one arrival, Mondombe rejoiced at the return of the Roberts. Each visit of the steamer brought new missionaries to visit the upriver station. Twelve new missionaries invigorated and thrilled the older staff members who had anticipated their arrival for a long time, but twelve was all the new staff they could expect for the near future.

At the end of the year the six American staff took stock of their year and laid plans for the year ahead. They felt an urgency about their work and the challenge of the large area they had not yet reached with its population of 140,000 and distances of one hundred to two hundred miles. A dozen large plantations producing coffee and rubber were situated in the area. Stores and traders increased rapidly. These commercial interests along with the government were introducing Western patterns of life avidly adopted by the natives.

As my parents wrote, "While we get some small support in our work from these agencies, they are, by and large, completely amoral and secular. Only from the mission schools, churches, hospitals and their outreach can these people get the moral, spiritual values that will make their progress real and worthwhile." Old mores were failing. What would fill their place? A story told by the native pastor after returning from a trip to a distant forest village illustrates the pain of change:

> An *nkanga ea nyama* (witch doctor of hunting) had lived there, whom all believed could indicate to them when and where to do their hunting. Without his help, they could not hope for success. At his death, his duties naturally passed on to his son. The son refused, saying, "I am a Christian and don't intend to go around with dead men's bones in my *ntombe* (shoulder bag)." He probably knew his father's occupation for the charlatanism that it was.
>
> Seeking approval of their choice, the villagers said, "Let us go into the forest hunting, calling upon the name of Loya, the son, and praying in his name." So they did, and were rewarded with two pigs—a lot of meat. Then they were convinced that Loya must accept the position of *nkanga ea nyama*.
>
> Still he refused. The chief was finally appealed to. The chief put him in prison for his stubbornness.
>
> About that time, Ntange, the native pastor, and Mr. Roberts arrived in the village. They and the village elders discussed Loya's first loyalty as a Christian. At last the elders agreed to let him go free and to molest him no longer. (General Letter 2-15-48)

While the station work proceeded, Mother was busy teaching her own children and Paul Roberts. As Paul advanced in age, his mother no longer felt confident in supervising his class work. She wanted him taught by a certified teacher, so Paul joined our class. My studies required more time now, which often stretched into the afternoon.

That spring Lauretta wrote that the Smiths were planning on leaving the States to return to Congo in the summer of 1947. To replace them, a young couple named Dade agreed to be house parents and moved into the house in Hiram. It would be to their care that I would travel in a year.

A medical consultation at the nearest mission station allowed a couple of us to accompany Dad in April in a plantation vehicle for a welcome break in the routine. What comfort to ride in an automobile and let the chauffeur struggle to jack up the rear tire when it slipped between logs on an old bridge.

Aunt Hattie discussed teaching arithmetic and new texts with the educationalist at Wema. Dad conferred with Dr. Horner about a very sick plantation manager. On the way home we stopped at a rubber plantation where the manager introduced us to his new Piper Cub airplane, the travel mode of the future.

The Belgian regretted the scarcity of landing fields and weather reports. He later buzzed our station on his way to a place with an airstrip. At the time there seemed no practical way to clear and maintain a landing field. No one saw even a glimmer of the future that later would make a landing field not only practical but vitally necessary.

The government doctor in charge of the medical work of the province visited Mondombe for a day. Although he was very critical of the deficiencies under which the hospital labored, he increased the government's contribution of both drugs and money. He clearly stated the need for new buildings and equipment.

The building program in 1947 completed a brick cottage for Ntange and Miliama, his wife. It needed only some cement work, but unfortunately, no cement had been available for several months. Supplies for the hospital ordered in the States in January 1946 had not arrived either. Dad eagerly awaited a new electric generator. The tiny one previously used broke down during a Caesarean operation at midnight. Coleman lanterns lit the operating table to successfully finish the surgery. The mother, who had lost all four previous children at birth, delivered a healthy boy. Work continued. More bricks were burned. The masons moved to repair jobs that could be made without cement.

By 1947 all the schools were trying to meet the requirements that would make them eligible for government subsidies. The State had always subsidized the Catholic schools, but Protestant school subsidies started after World War II. Although the missionaries clearly understood what was needed, their inspection of the problems revealed little they could change to meet the demands—limited as they were by financial and personnel resources.

School break was extended in 1947 to accommodate the missionaries' conference in September. The conference transferred Aunt Gertrude to meet a greater shortage at the Institute next to Bolenge

The Disciples of Christ in the US had instituted a campaign to raise money and re-consecrate the Brotherhood to its support of missions. With that in mind my parents' next letter described the great needs of the Congo mission as discussed at Conference:

> ... This Conference, more than any other, emphasized the increasing demand on our Mission to raise the standards of its work....
>
> How to give instruction to the upper grade classes by missionaries, with only one educationalist on the station? How can she properly supervise the native teachers of the other classes? How teach French when our own knowledge of that language is but rudimen-

tary? The [government] inspector insists that all native teachers of third, fourth, fifth and sixth years should have had at least nine years of school (Institute graduate). That seems little enough, to ask that a grade school teacher have finished grade school. But teachers of that quality and development are still very, very few. Even our Institute faculty is as much native as missionary. The inspector says that all of the staff should be missionaries.

Starting with 100% illiteracy, we have given the Africans of our area a lot. We realize the progress made as we look back. But in the eyes of a school inspector fresh from a literate country with a highly developed educational system, our schools seem very primitive and inadequate. Most of his criticism could be met with a greatly enlarged missionary staff. Never before had we so realized the inadequacy of our educational work, even though we know that it compares favorably with that done by most of our neighboring missions! ...

Every station is in need of new school buildings. Few of them have persons qualified for this work, and none of them have personnel free to do it. Nowhere is it possible to have this work done by a contractor. How we need builders! We must also erect churches, ward buildings and surgeries....

Important in our thinking too, were those large areas on the borders of our field, where the Gospel message has never yet been taken. If our workers cannot be increased to the number necessary for our present areas, can we dare hope to go on beyond? Since these areas have been assigned to us by the various church groups working in Congo, we have a virtual monopoly upon their Protestant instruction and evangelization. Do we have the right any longer to restrict the entry of other Protestant church groups into these areas, if we do not do so ourselves? Ought we not immediately, seek out other evangelizing agencies willing and able to preach the Gospel to these folk? (General Letter 11-8-47)

So great the needs; so inadequate the means.

CHAPTER 17

THE END OF MY CHILDHOOD IN CONGO

The second busy year of my parents' third term meant that my stay in Congo was soon to end. Schoolwork and reading filled the greater part of my day. No longer could I complete the day's assigned tasks in a morning.

I spent siesta reading. A collection of donated books left by previous missionaries stood shelved in the classroom next to my bedroom. Some of the books had never been read by my parents, I'm sure, or *Forever Amber* and some of the other somewhat risqué novels would have been removed from my ready access. Wonderful historical novels, such as the classic *Northwest Passage*, developed in me a taste for history.

Playing with the younger set no longer appealed to me. Games of Cops and Robbers, Hide and Seek or playhouse had lost their charm. An occasional trip such as the one to Wema or another when I accompanied my father on his motorcycle on a day's inspection of an outlying dispensary was more stimulating. We took our lunch and stopped in a cool bamboo grove to eat our sandwiches. Suddenly Dad came hopping out to the path stamping his feet. He had stirred up a trail of driver ants hidden under the dried leaves. They were swarming up his legs. Time for a hasty exit.

I began to crave friends my own age and a return to the States. While I never felt the typical teenagers' desire to lose self-identity in mimicking the fashions of the moment, I did want to join the activities of an older, more mature group. Separation from the field looked more and more attractive. With the truck we would be able to drive overland to Stanleyville. There I could catch the riverboat and travel the thousand miles down the full navigable length of the Congo River, joining my traveling companions midway at Coquilhatville.

In the next three months plans and contingency plans for my trip to Hiram were made. Mother made lists of food and bedding to take in the truck. These were assembled. The mail order of clothes arrived. Stitching more clothes to complete my wardrobe for a temperate climate seemed to take forever. Dad and Uncle Ned worked on the truck as vehicle maintenance also seemed unending. The truck needed to complete the trek over miles of rutted dirt roads without garages along the way. Dad wrote to Lauretta just before we left:

> We are all excited because we leave here day after tomorrow for Stanleyville to put Margaret on the *Kigoma* for Leopoldville. The B.M.S. missionaries there, the Chestertons, are going that way also, and have promised to keep an eye on her. It seems like such a big undertaking across country, and we have had so much trouble with broken springs and worn inner tubes. What next? Gas isn't too plentiful out here, but so far we have not been restricted. Hotel accommodations have been pretty tight also. Hope that the boat will not be crowded.
>
> We had feared that Mother might have to go through to Coquilhatville [on the State boat with Margaret] and come back on the *S.S. Oregon*. It will leave two days after the *Kigoma* leaves Coquilhatville, on its way up to Wema for the M.A.C. meeting....
>
> Aunt Hattie, Aunt Jewell, and Mother have been working hard on the sewing today, and it is not yet finished. It has been a real task for Mother to get the sewing done, on top of the schoolwork, and just nip and tuck to meet the deadline. Margaret is completing some of her last exams, and Mother sews while she helps Margaret. Margaret is going to have some really nice clothes and looks like a million in them. She should have a jolly trip home with the Cobble girls and the Byerlees. (DHB Letter to Lauretta 7-5-48)

I had forgotten the back-up plan for reaching Coquilhatville. As it was, the vehicle sufficed. My parents described the trip:

> In early July, we Bakers drove to Stanleyville, a two-day trip each way. There we said goodbye to Margaret. We hear that she, the Byerlees, and the two older Cobble girls didn't get away from the mouth of the Congo for New York until August 9th.
>
> Our trip was made in the station's new Ford delivery. In addition to Margaret's trunk and suitcase, we took along a couple of boxes

of "chop," a camp bed and bedding apiece, a pressure lamp, a one-burner oil stove, and extra gasoline for the truck. We stopped each night at one of the mud and thatch houses put up by the state officials for their use when traveling "circuit." One of them was full of fleas, and in the morning we looked like the measles. Doctor and the children set up the beds and hung the nets, while Lelia cooked supper. Early the next morning we filled the gas tank, ate breakfast, and packed ourselves and baggage into the little truck.

The roads are much better than formerly. However, the government is badly handicapped by lack of machinery and skilled labor. On the way over and again on the way back, we had the misfortune of breaking a spring in a stretch of bad road. There was nothing to do in this land of no garages and no springs for sale but to creep along and hope luck grew no worse. Only one new leaf could be obtained at Stanleyville. (General Letter 8-29-48)

I occupied a nice, airy cabin on the *Kigoma*, which left at daybreak the following morning. As the boat pulled away from the pier, I roused enough to realize a new day was dawning both literally and figuratively. An overwhelming sense of liberty and self-sufficiency filled me before I turned over and fell back to sleep. Thus buoyed, time passed quickly for the four days it took to churn down the Congo to Coquilhatville. I amused myself, joined the Chestertons for meals and tried out my few words of Lingala in conversation with the cabin steward. At Coquilhatville the Byerlee family with their handsome son and the Cobble girls, my age, joined me for the rest of the trip to Leopoldville and on to the States. I felt relieved to have Mr. Byerlee handling the technicalities of customs and shipping for me.

Independence, which previously I had never known I lacked, felt wonderful. I credit my parents for ably preparing me for life greatly under my own direction from then on. Years later in conversation I queried Mother about the freedom from parentally imposed rules, curfews and regulations she allowed us as teenagers. Mother said she never felt she should lay down such laws once we lived together again, since she had expected us to set them for ourselves during the interim. In fact, she thought we were sometimes more restrictive on ourselves than she would have been.

My trip across the Atlantic proved to be two weeks of endless fun. The *Vingt*, a freighter carrying only twenty-three passengers, allowed us almost free run of the ship. Half the group was between the ages of nine and twenty-one. This young set amused itself with a great variety of activities from looking down the anchor chain hole at the foamy water, to helping the crew make ice cream. We fried the flying fish that landed on the deck and played innumerable games. Tours of the engine room or the bridge could be arranged at mealtime with the captain or chief engineer who shared our small dining room. I highly recommend the informality of freighter travel.

My homecoming this time happily differed greatly from four years before. My sister greeted me in a house I knew well in a familiar town with schoolmates unchanged from two years before. The Dades, the young house parents, with their two-year-old son Vaughn, lived in harmony with five teenagers: the two Bakers, the two Smith cousins and a school friend needing a home to finish his last year of high school. Barbara Dade's warm, accepting personality resembled my mother's to a remarkable degree, making home a comfortable, familiar place.

Fitting into school proved to be a mixture of the familiar, the novel and the unknown. In two years there had been only one change of my fifteen classmates in this stable, college community. Teachers, too, were familiar. I found I understood the words people spoke, but the meaning was far from clear, especially with the teenagers. They, on their part, thought my speech amusing and stilted, devoid as it was of all slang and idiom. Far more than just slang clouded my understanding, however. Names, titles and proper nouns left me completely in the dark wondering whether the conversation revolved around a popular band, current affairs or a movie. The easy humor of both teachers and students left me far on the outside of most punch lines. For years I despaired of truly comprehending the communication going on around me.

Strange, too, were the fads to which everyone adhered—the Gibson girl look was back in style in 1948 with its full sleeves and demure neckline. This uniformity of dress seemed quite juvenile to me. I didn't care for any particular style of clothing. I was just glad Mother had gotten me a nice wardrobe to bring with me. In Congo we dressed very simply and were greatly aware we had a lot more than the Africans could hope to own. I was fortunate. The Hiram High School students accepted me with friendly good humor and included me in their activities without demanding that I join the latest fashion.

Academically I was well prepared. With half of my class going on to college from this little high school of less than one hundred students, I was challenged with excellent teachers and a conscientious student body. Everyone joined in all activities to make possible the extra curricular functions—music, sports, drama, and social clubs. I played Mary, the maid, in the senior play and guard on the girl's basketball team. But I was definitely a "third culture kid" from central Africa. Even in the nurturing environment at Hiram High I often felt out of place.

It seems appropriate to insert here that when my parents returned to the States a year later, they were as impressed by the Dades as we teenagers were. Our "house parents" not only unselfishly and lovingly monitored their five charges, but Edgar Dade was a meticulous and skilled builder. My father set about persuading the mission board to create a new category of staff—a limited-term, professional-builder missionary. In this he succeeded. At the same time he prevailed upon the Dades to give up their comfortable life in Hiram and travel to Congo to help with the building program for a few years. Lauretta and I always claimed some influence on this decision, because, we said, our successful portrayal of life on the mission field must have been appealing.

Dr. Gene Johnson recorded this change in staffing in his history of the mission:

> An important development in the sixth decade [of the mission] was the decision to send laymen to Congo whose specialty was construction. The first such builders were Mr. and Mrs. Edgar Dade who went to Congo in 1950. They were special friends of the Donald Baker family. It was to the Dades that the [two] Baker daughters were entrusted when they were left in the US by their parents to attend [high school]. Dr. Baker had admired Edgar Dade's skill in handling his contracting business, and he had a vision of what it would mean to the mission to have on the staff a man with his ability, unhampered by the need to teach, preach, or heal the sick. His suggestion was welcomed by the Foreign Division of the UCMS. Lay builders had already been sent to Congo by Methodists and Baptists. It was a time of strong support for missions in the home boards. And colonial subsidies contributed greatly to the financial possibilities for the building of schools and of hospitals.
>
> Enthusiastic reports from the field described Mr. Dade as having more than fulfilled the expectations of those who selected him for this specialized service. (Johnson, p. 49)

Great strides in the building program were made under Edgar's supervision. He repaired motors, assembled resources, improved old residences and built new buildings culminating in a large, beautiful church at Bolenge. Within the next six years three other builders were sent out to the field. What a dream come true for my father!

That change on the mission field lay in the future as I entered my sophomore year of high school. I give credit to Lauretta for easing my adjustment to American life without parents close by. She found the path alone for two years before helping me map my way. I felt secure in the great support of having an older sister—even if we did still argue about the line that invisibly divided our full-sized bed.

CHAPTER 18

GOOD THINGS COME SLOWLY

The civet cat, the python and the turtle started on a trip together. My parents retold this African tale in 1948. A different version appeared in 1979 in a folklore collection called *"On Another Day...": Tales Told Among the Nkundo of Zaire* by Mabel H. Ross and Barbara Walker (see Tale 14). Mabel Ross was a missionary at Lotumbe. In 1991 Verna Aardema chose the same story as the basis for her beautifully illustrated book for children, *Traveling to Tondo*. For my parents the story embodied the snail's pace of progress during their third term:

> Things move so slowly that it reminds us of the story of three forest animals taking a trip. They were the *yaw*, the *nguma* and the *ulu*. Hardly had they gotten started when the *yaw* (forest cat) remembered that he had forgotten some final instructions to his children. He excused himself, and while the others waited, went home and promptly forgot about the trip itself for two months. Finally, he rejoined his companions and they started again. Then the *nguma* (python) killed an antelope and ate it. Said he, "I have a weight in my stomach and must rest a bit before I go on." So they waited and waited until he had digested the antelope.
> After they had gone a bit farther, they found a big tree fallen across the path. *Ulu* (turtle) tried his best but was unable to scramble up and over it. "My body is too small," he said. "We'll just have to wait a while until the tree rots." So they were forced to wait again. (General Letter 2-15-48)

Some of the supplies ordered in January 1946 were still "on the way" to Congo two years later when Mother and Dad wrote to friends at home before I left:

> We still do not have our electric light plant or our operating light, though we do hope to have them by the end of this year. We do not have our operating table and a number of other supplies long since expected, but many of them are on the way.
>
> We do have many of the fine new instruments, considerable DDT, insect repellent, and two new drugs for malaria. We do have some resale steel army cots, four head of cattle, four new cottages for our native leaders, and another under construction. We do have a new Ford delivery truck, and are completing a garage to house it. Two cisterns have been built and a third started. Many repairs and improvements have been made on our permanent buildings. We have fifty thousand bricks ready for use and are making over a thousand a day. There is a little money in the bank to get construction started for badly needed hospital buildings. We have opened one new rural dispensary which alone gave 8125 treatments during 1947. And don't forget that we are head over heels in the daily routine ...
>
> We miss Gertrude Shoemaker exceedingly [moved to the Institute by Conference decision], and hope and pray for her return to Mondombe before the end of this year. It has put an almost unbearable load upon Hattie Mitchell. Personnel needs are our greatest handicap, and many of us who are here are getting along in our missionary careers. At one of our gatherings last year we were grouped around the piano singing folk songs. Said one of the missionaries, "Let's sing 'Sympathy.' It's old but good."
>
> One of the "younger," first term missionaries replied enthusiastically, "I just love it!"
>
> Said the first, "You wouldn't believe how old it is. I bought it when I was in high school."
>
> And the other, "Well, no. I wouldn't have thought it was that ol-uh-well-uh-uh," and she embarrassedly subsided as we all laughed.
>
> It illustrated only too well, the fact that our missionary group is aging. Even the recent recruits have not been in the lower age brackets. The youngest missionary on the field is twenty-five, and she must be plenty lonely. (General Letter 2-15-48)

The "four head of cattle" mentioned in the letter were an experiment in meeting the need for meat. To initiate the cattle business my father found a sleeping-sickness-resistant breed in the small, humped Dahomey cattle of western Africa. He experimented until he found a kind of grass strong enough to resist forest regrowth but still tender enough for the mouths of animals. This was planted on newly cleared pasturage. Lastly, a keeper was trained for a job unknown to our area. Animal husbandry was totally foreign to the Nkundo of central Africa.

The cattle lived beyond the swamp behind the hospital. They needed guarding both for their own protection from leopards and for the protection of the hospital gardens in the event that they strayed. Unfortunately, they never thrived.

Dad traveled again in the back country for a different government study:

> Doctor had a most interesting trip into two villages in June—part of a study begun in 1938, of the fertility of two tribes in adjacent villages. What a striking contrast! In one, there are 240 children for each 100 women. In the other, only 80. In physique, they differ very little. The fertile group has had very rigid family restraints and practically no venereal disease. The other village is rotten with trial marriage, promiscuity, and venereal disease. The facts might well be studied by those drawing conclusions from recent sex studies at home. Unfortunately, as is true over much of Congo under "civilization," even the virile group is slipping, and the other one getting worse. Will there be time for the church to bring them the religious and ethical standards which they need? (General Letter 8-29-48)

Three undated pages of letters sent back to the station have been preserved from that year's census trip. In them, Dad mentions Lokwa, the young man helping him on this trip. Lokwa was working for Mother at our house in preparation to his moving into nurse's training at the hospital. This personable student became a favorite of our family with his friendly, outgoing personality and his musical talents. He could play any of the various musical instruments and drums in the collection we had out on the porch. These included not only the *lokole* or "talking drum," but also assorted tom-toms and a *lokombe*, a large, thin-sided, triangular-shaped drum like a miniature A-frame with lips across the peak. It was played suspended from a shoulder beaten on both sides with indigenous rubber mallets.

We agreed that musical rhythm was in Lokwa's genes when Mother came home from baby clinic years later. She described weighing his son in the paper-lined baby scales. Less than a year old, the baby sat happily looking about and patting a pleasant rhythm on the paper under him. The genes had been passed on!

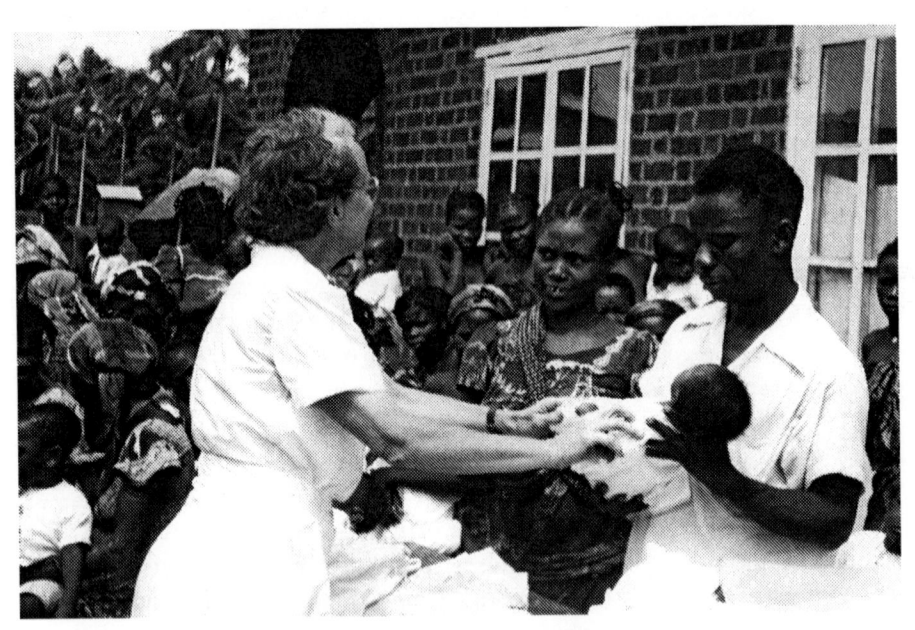

Bohambu Pierre and Aunt Stobie at Mondombe's baby clinic

Dad includes an incident of the Belgian administrator's legal imposition of punishment in a 1948 letter to his family. As a doctor, he was cognizant of and occasionally involved in healing patients who had received heavy-handed punishment. These he protested to the provincial authorities. Only a few of the administrators in our area through the years were known to apply such force. The government outlawed the practice in 1955, according to Edgerton in his history of Congo (p. 164). Dad recorded his observation:

> When Heirman [the local state administrator] was here, apparently some of the men didn't show up promptly for his *recensement* [census], and he put them in prison and gave them the *chicotte* [whip]. He has told me that he never gives the maximum of eight, and never more than six (at any one day). Whatever they did to deserve it, I

don't know, but I saw two men here with their buttocks raw. It seems a bit too much, to me. (DHB Wed. Undated 1948)

"*Betamba bia ngonda ntayalemaka fio.*" This proverb says, "The trees of the forest differ in height" and means "A long time has elapsed." The August arrival of a 1948 calendar elicited the quote of this proverb. Some pieces of mail still arrived very belatedly.

After the end of the year my parents reviewed the progress of 1948. They noted the visit of the government school inspector. The station expected educational subsidies from then on. In addition to the increased government help for education and medical work, they were assured that 50% could be given for the construction of new schools and hospitals. Already the walls of a new maternity ward reached almost to the top.

Dad felt more satisfied in the practice of medicine with fairly adequate amounts of the sulfas and penicillin for basic needs. The new operating table enhanced performing surgeries. Some day, an x-ray machine would make his work even more exact and life saving.

Meantime, I settled into the autumn routine in Hiram, as my parents started planning their own approaching trip to the States. They would stay home for two years. In that time the forest might reclaim their yards. To prevent that they planted a cover crop of the kudzu variety, which we children called "galloping gonia"—an approximation of its real name. This kept down the growth. They packed away their dishes, linens and smaller possessions in order to empty cupboards and rooms for occupancy by another missionary couple. The preparations took months for such an extensive leave.

By the beginning of April 1949 whatever needed doing was finished. Departure time arrived. As Mother and Dad waited to board the ship at the mouth of the Congo, they completed their next general letter summarizing the flurry of departure:

> The suitcases were packed. The trunks had gone on the last boat. The house was cleared and closed and locked.
>
> But no, a native nurse appeared and announced, "Doctor, there is a strangulated hernia at the hospital. Just arrived." So an emergency operation delayed our departure.
>
> It sobered us all, emphasizing as it did, what the natives had been saying. "When the next emergency comes in there will be no doctor on hand to help." As usual, our limited personnel did not permit replacement by another doctor. It is hard to work, week in and week

out, without adequate staff; it is heartbreaking to quit a full time job and just walk out on it....

Just a few days before we left, we removed six inches of stick from the thigh and abdominal wall of a ten-year-old boy. Poor little Bolongo was out in the forest and fell into an animal trap. It was a well-concealed hole about seven feet deep, whose bottom was studded with erect sticks about eight inches apart and about eighteen inches high. They were of a brashy wood, with the ends sharpened. An animal, falling in, is impaled upon them. Bolongo got one in each thigh, but this one broke off inside the skin and muscles and could not be removed in the village. He could very likely have died without our help ...

Now, we are on our way home to join the girls, Lauretta and Margaret at Hiram. Our nephew, Lyle Smith, left his parents at Lotumbe to join his brother Bryce and sister, Shirley, also at Hiram.

Mr. Ned Roberts took us to Stanleyville in the truck. And there we embarked immediately on the big Congo River boat, the latest and fastest. It is twin-screw, diesel-powered, with three decks and a bridge. The first part of the trip was new to us and we watched with interest the large villages of fisher folk and their flocks of canoes. At times the course of the boat lay close to shore, and the waves tossed the wooden shells like matches, one after the other, threatening to crush them, throwing them up on the beaches, and detaching many of them from their insecure moorings. In some villages, each canoe with a paddler in back was out in the river to ride the waves more safely away from the shore. Even then, one or two of them capsized but floated, and doubtless were rescued. These folk all know how to swim. We were told that this boat had caused the destruction of many such canoes. Each advance of civilization brings its own train of problems.

The river is enormous, spreading out for miles, with its width exaggerated by many huge islands. What a thrill Stanley must have had as he made his way downstream—the first white man to do so! It took him almost three years, including the trips around the rapids above Stanleyville, and the ones below Leopoldville. Our passage was infinitely quicker and less dangerous....

Leopoldville, the capital has been constantly building for years. It would be hard to predict a future too great for this city. The enormous wealth of this colony, actively developed by the energetic Belgians, makes us think of our own country and its diverse climate, geography and resources. Here the coal and the iron are not close together, but the hydro-electric possibilities are staggering, and the mineral and vegetable products varied and huge. Already, one twelve-story building adorns the city, and industrial plants are increasing in size and number.

At Leopoldville, our mission and others built and operate a hostel for missionaries. We were pleased to see Lutete, its Congolese manager, appear on the dock to take us to its quiet homeyness....

We find French spoken and understood by many more natives down river. Up our way, they sometimes get it a bit wrong. One commercial man told us of some applications for work which he had received. One native, applying for a place as manager of a small native store wrote, "I will gladly work for you until you go bankrupt." Another finished with a postscript, "You will locate me near the village of Yalisenga where I am constantly on strike."

After writing to our New York exporter about the loss of our stove (which the shipping company let fall in the eighteen foot depths of the Congo River at Coquilhatville), and the breakage of other articles, we received his reply. He wrote, "We are pleased to acknowledge your letter of July 6th reporting losses on shipments." We are looking for another exporter. (General Letter 4-18-49)

During the two years my parents furloughed in Hiram they took turns: one stayed home to feed the three Smiths and us, while the other traveled to churches, youth camps and meetings to describe the work of the Congo mission. They were equally requested as speakers for their fascinating narrations, but they differed greatly in the way they presented their story. Dad used his movies, now in color, for informal gatherings and spoke with great detail, facts and figures. Mother's descriptions of the work came alive with anecdotes about the people. We teased her about the parishioners she had stirred to tears with the pathos of her stories. She always seemed a bit surprised that she had moved her audience so emotionally.

CHAPTER 19

GRAPPLING WITH GROWTH IN THE FIFTIES

"... people welcomed Daddy with a whoop of joy," wrote Mother after a return from furlough. He was visiting the dispensaries and she went with him to inspect schools along the same route. Increasing requests for the little clinics and the country schools were outstripping the available staff and funds.

The whole colony bustled with activity and a burgeoning economy. Dad described the changes they observed in Leopoldville as they passed through in 1951:

> The change in Leopoldville, the capital, during two and a half years is unbelievable. During that time, the native population has jumped from 93,000 to 200,000. They continue to come in at the rate of 1000 a week. The city has expanded beyond its boundaries, creating problems in sanitation, water supply, policing and housing, as well as city planning. And still there are not enough workers for the rapidly expanding industries! During the days there is always the sound of riveting, sawing and pounding, and the hum of motors. (General Letter 12-15-51)

At Mondombe, although missionary staffing remained static, the growing effort reached farther and included more: more people, more areas, more advanced programs, more funds, more paperwork, more heartaches, more successes. The expansion was managed only with the help of Congolese mission professionals who gradually were achieving greater levels of education and experience.

The numbers of Christian students, patients and workmen increased; improved transportation brought more visitors to be ministered to and entertained. The greater ease in travel opened more distant villages to evangelization, schooling and dispensaries. All required supervision. A lot of this work had to be done by the Americans.

The advent of modern amenities, such as electricity and motor vehicles, lightened some of their work. These also necessitated constant maintenance and long hours of mechanical work by Dad and Uncle Ned—the only ones on the station who understood the functioning of the equipment well enough to keep them operating.

With electricity Dad initiated an outdoor "walk in" movie theater instead of a drive in. Mondombe took advantage of the governmental program of educational movies. Once a month films arrived by boat from the State. Dad showed them—when the generator worked—on an outside, whitened wall. Hundreds came from surrounding villages, as well as from the station, to sit on the grass and avidly watch the latest show.

Mother taught Calvert classes to five missionary children during her fourth term. My brother Maurice, the three Roberts children and Doug Cardwell from Bolenge studied, canoed and swam together. Once they left for the States to finish high school, Mother spent the rest of her term fully occupied with station activities.

Bosumbe, our beloved cook, retired. Mother attempted to train a new cook to take over the kitchen duties. The task challenged both of them and eventually ended in failure just as she needed him the most with an influx of visitors. She had taken on the work of Literature Coordinator as well, which was supposedly a fulltime job. A number of letters to us children describe Mother's increasing activities:

> The lad who is learning to cook is a pleasant, willing boy. But oh! He has so much to learn. I asked him to stir the corn. A blank stare. So I used a different verb telling him to take a spoon and turn over the corn in the pan on the stove. That "got through" to him. A pleased look replaced the dead pan as he sprang into action. He took off the lid and peeked in at the food he had taken out of a can and put into the saucepan asking in astonishment, "Is that corn?" We both laughed gaily but probably for very different reasons. (It was cream style.) (LB Letter to Family 10-7-57)

> Mother is busy with a thousand things in connection with her job as Lang. Coordinator (supposedly full-time—Ha! Ha!)—acting as station secretary and now learning under Hattie the station treasurer's work, plus teaching classes without any advance material—Christian home and pedagogy for *catechistes eleves* [the religious education students], plus running the home and anticipating Christmas, MAC Dec. 28, and a trip to Nigeria leaving here Jan. 5. She doesn't know what the All Africa Conference there is about, yet! What a business! (DHB Letter to Family 11-27-57)

Mother had just returned from the unique experience of attending the All Africa Conference in Ibadan, Nigeria, when she wrote the following letter to my sisters and me:

> How all of you would have enjoyed a peek-in here! Delegates came from all over Africa. In addition there were special resource persons from Pakistan, India, Fiji, Haiti, London, Geneva, and various parts of the U.S.
>
> The meetings were conducted in English mostly. Down front at one side sat the delegates who knew French better than English. They wore earphones and listened to the French translator. One missionary translated into Portuguese for one of the delegates from Angola. Occasionally a delegate gave his talk or remarks in French with a translator at his side.
>
> The Southern Presbyterians sent a woman delegate who knew very little English and even less French. One day she just about rolled them on the floor. We were introducing ourselves at breakfast. She stood and informed us:
>
> "I am Miz Kayinda. I come from the Belgian Congo. I am a father and a mother." (She meant a wife and mother.)
>
> The conference considered various phases of the church in relation to home and family life, politics, African culture and worship. The papers read were nearly all by Africans and were very good. Group discussion and questions and answers were most interesting. Best of all was the fellowship. There were some rare souls here. They all spoke two or more languages (except for a very few of the resource persons). Some of them, like Dr. Searle Bates, are real geniuses and saints. Alan Paton [author of *Cry the Beloved Country*] gave a splendid address.

One day we were entertained by the Premier and his wife to tea. We dressed up and they and a lot of other officials and their wives dressed up in flowing robes, fancy large turbans—for the women, and we all sat around small tables. The wife of the Premier is in the chief's family, daughter or something, so she wore her royal regalia for the occasion—a raffia rushing of purple and gold that hung over her right shoulder. Her sandals also had gold embroidery on them. In the course of the party I learned from the pretty little Nigerian beside me that the Premier is a very good Methodist.

The first part of conference I roomed with a Swiss young woman who is a missionary in Togoland. She does work with women and girls and lives and eats right in the villages. At the end of twenty months she was completely used up and was going home for a few months rest. I admire her for doing it but couldn't do it myself. The last half of conference I roomed with a cute little girl from Madagascar. She looked very Oriental, of course. Both girls spoke beautiful French. They got put with me because I know a little.

You should have seen me in one group meeting translating into French for a man on one side and into very simple ideas in English for Mrs. Kayinda on the other side. I couldn't get any notes written down for myself so had to borrow from the group scribe. He, bless him, kindly copied them all off for me (the ones he had written) so I really came out ahead. (LB Letter to Family 1-20-58)

Back from the conference "one must pay for it," she wrote, having been asked to submit at least five written reports in at least two languages to different groups wanting to hear about the proceedings. The trip had had its difficulties, as well. She wrote:

As you may have guessed by now I got back from Nigeria. But dear me! I left Congo without a *visa de retour*. We just didn't realize that the Belgians take our leaving and returning so seriously. The old man in immigration acted as if he weren't going to let me go. I thought of the money invested in that ticket and the First-Of-Its-Kind-Conference in all Africa; so I meekly asked him what he advised me to do. He explained that I'd have to get one in Brazzaville [in the French Congo] upon my return ... On my way back in Lagos I learned that there was a Belgian Consul there; so I went to see him. He could hardly believe that anyone who had been in Congo that long would fail to get one. While he didn't laugh, his eyes looked highly amused. He advised me not to go to the consulate in Brazzaville because it would take two or three months to get the visa. To make a long story a bit shorter—the [church official] was in Brazzaville to meet me and had everything fixed up. So I came in for three months on a tourist's visa. Reason given for the trip—"to join my husband" of course. Now we shall have to get a "residence" card and then I can stay on. I told Daddy I was giving him a chance to choose me all over again. (LB Letter to Family 2-6-58)

While Mother worked her way through both the tedious and the uncommon activities on her list, Dad continued his schedule at the hospital, in the operating room, on construction sites, in the back country dispensaries, at the leprosarium and in the garden. At the beginning of his new term he faced a large backlog of surgeries, which he gradually cleared. The construction work increased with more funds coming in from both the States and the Belgian government but no builder assigned to Mondombe to help.

Government medical funding increases after World War II helped develop new schools, hospital buildings and a leprosarium. Dad's pride in the leper colony showed when he wrote:

It has been quite a day—rainy, cloudy and cold. After a short time at the hospital early this morning, I climbed onto the kitchen roof to tighten some roofing about the new chimney. The rain drove me down. After a good breakfast and some work at the desk I went to the hospital and we got a pair of twin girls—1780 gms. and 1950 grams, evidently premature. Hope Stobie can keep them warm and fed. Then she and I took off for Lomina [the leprosarium]—still raining, where she gave out rations and I took stock of what is going on. It's getting to be a neat little village; maybe we can make it a model for the area. Around eighty adobe brick cottages (one room and porch), all thatch, a burnt brick dispensary building (four rooms), the chapel and a teacher's cottage, (these two with aluminum roofs). There are fruit trees all over the place, about seven acres of palms, three acres of coffee and we are about to set out more fruit trees and more palms. The folks generally look much healthier and the signs of leprosy almost universally in repression. (DHB Letter to Family 9-29-57)

By 1960, advancements in the treatment of leprosy with new medications produced such spectacular advances that Dad closed the leprosarium. Patients returned to their home villages where treatment was now available.

During the 1950s, access to medical care expanded with two commercial company doctors and two government doctors in the Mondombe area. Additional back country dispensaries gave first aid to the ill and injured. This did not diminish the number of patients on the station where those who fell ill could obtain immediate help. One emergency case arose close to the hospital staff:

> While operating one morning recently, word came that the wife of the first assistant, Lofumbwa, had fainted. Miss Stober found her almost pulseless, and revived her. It was not a clear cut case but we decided, once her blood pressure had built up, to explore for a possible intra abdominal hemorrhage. We found it, and removed the little spot on one tube which had ruptured. Lofumbwa went quietly on with his work of assisting. How would you like to trade places with him in a job like that on your own wife? We know that they have an unusual affection for each other. Things went well, and she has recovered. (General Letter 5-7-59)

A good many of the surgical cases were obstetrical emergencies. Daddy theorized that the heavy loads of firewood and manioc, sometimes eighty to one hundred pounds, carried by these small women might have something to do with it. Caesarians worked when the woman came to the hospital in good time. One woman waited through three days of labor after delivering her first by Caesarian before leaving for the hospital. She arrived too late to be helped.

Other areas of the work induced stress in the 1950s. The pension and workmen's insurance programs newly set up by the government created headaches for the missionaries. The programs increased the work of both my parents who, nevertheless, recognized the security they provided to their workmen. Dad wrote:

> I have just been summarizing the amounts paid each workman for the last two years, to send to the Legal Rep. at Coquilhatville for the government workmen's insurance.
>
> You know there is also a government pension now, obligatory for all workmen. We pay one half and they pay one half. The records!!! The "work" inspector expected to come here in June for a visit, so we

still have that to look forward to. This place is getting horribly complicated. (DHB Letter to Grace 6-5-58)

Mother got word that one of the post office checks which she had missent to the recipient instead of through the post office, had never gotten back to the P.O. and as a result, the payment, which it was to cover, was not covered, and now we owe interest on that payment between twenty and thirty dollars. I am writing of the government pension plan. It is surely a headache for us, although a fine thing for the natives. We surely hate to have to do all of the drudgery it entails. Now we are about to start a new arrangement, which is to equalize the family allocations for wife and children. (DHB Letter to Family 11-9-58)

Another worthy governmental program recognized the years of effort of outstanding Congolese:

Yesterday we had a Caesarean at church time and then at 11:00 went to Mondombe [State Post] where Nkang' Itoko and a Government Agricultural *moniteur* were given their *Cartes de Merité Civique*, such as Ntange got some years back. I had been wondering about Nkang' Itoko and am pleased that he got his [recognition]. It *is* something of an honor and he has merited it. (DHB Letter to Family 1-23-58)

Nkang' Itoko served as Dad's head nurse for all the time I can remember. His children grew up on the station and all were educated (even the girls). They held positions of responsibility. Ntange, the pastor, hosted a station banquet on his lawn in honor of the occasion. Invited to the fete were all the elders of the station.

Other advances and changes in the fifties appeared in letters from both my parents. The letters showed Dad accepting reversals to plans for future expansions and to the ongoing supervision of his dispensaries:

We have had a few disappointments, but they may work out for the best. The ambulance, which was promised us, is to be under the state man at Mondombe and, after all, that may work out for the best, since we'll have no worry about chauffeur, gas, or repairs.

They [the Belgians] have pushed me out of the dispensaries, and that was a bit difficult after all of these years. However, they put them in charge of the *agents sanitaires* and there was nothing more for me to do. If they prefer it that way, it does relieve me of a lot of work. I may be wrong, but I guess it is just a matter of a few years until most of the medical work for the natives is socialized completely, and I doubt if we'll find any very satisfactory place in that picture. They can't get enough doctors for their medical service, so it does seem like a bit early to squeeze us. (DHB to Maurice 6-28-58)

Dad took his turn as president of the Mission Conference in the summer of 1958. This responsibility passed from one experienced missionary to the next. The leader spent many days writing letters and organizing the program ahead of time. Communication was slow. Mother described one unusual aspect of handling such a meeting:

> The thing that has him bothered is terminology for conducting a meeting which is supposed to be in Lonkundo supplemented by French terminology, translated into English for a visiting secretary and some new missionaries and participated in by some missionaries who speak Lingala instead of Lonkundo. Is this a complicated, mixed sentence? Well, think what the discussion is going to be. (LB Letter to Family 7-11-58)

By the first week in August, fifty-five missionaries and as many children, plus thirty African delegates met for the conference at Bolenge/ICC [the advanced institute]. So many delegates attended that some stayed at Coquilhatville and drove the seven miles back and forth.

This was to be the first Congress. It replaced Conference that previously had been held every two years. At the Congress, along with the missionaries, the Congolese held full voting rights for the first time. Always before Africans had merely observed and met by themselves. This began the transition from a mission to an indigenous church.

Western-style decision-making differed from Congolese village methods. In the villages decisions followed much discussion and grew from the consensus that developed. No formal votes were needed as the group could see where the agreement lay. To decide matters by majority vote with losers and winners was new to the Congolese. Delegates worked together to foster a congenial atmosphere at the Congress.

It was up to Dad as president to keep things moving. Ekofo Joseph, the co-president, pastor of the Boende church near Wema, ably assisted him. Dad wrote:

> We are in the mad whirl of two weeks of meetings—one of the missionaries and one of the combined groups. We have been having inspirational spots and reports of our [Mission] Ten Year Plan committees and of the standing committees: Evangelistic and Education, Medical and Construction, and Women's and Girls' work. Mother reported today for Literature Committee and [Printing] Press. She had a nicely organized and presented report. Previously, it has been a rather minor committee and its work has dragged ...
>
> We have been pleased with the understanding and cooperation of the native delegates, although, so far, I have not had any money issues ... (DHB Letter to Family 8-6-58 through 8-11-58)

After the delegates returned to their home stations from the Congress, there was a mixed reaction from Mother about its accomplishments. She felt almost smothered or overcome by the speed with which life was changing. Her feeling arose partly from the rapid integration of the Congress delegates and partly from the overwhelming task the committees met in trying to flesh out their ten-year plans. The mission had grown into virtually a large business with extensive fields and a huge budget. Managing this in several languages with many levels of experience of both Congolese and missionaries presented more decisions than could be settled in one two-week session.

The coming years boded unlimited challenges. No one had the slightest inkling how boundless those challenges would be.

CHAPTER 20

THE LULL BEFORE THE STORM

A whirlwind of independence movements swept across the colonies in Africa in the nineteen fifties. In 1956 Ghana, situated in the western hump of the continent, was the first colony to gain some self-determination, setting it on track for complete self-government in 1960. Kwame Nkrumah, Ghana's charismatic leader, wrote in his autobiography that he knew the success of the new government depended on his ability to convince the British civil servants to stay on after independence to assist in making the transition. Ghana had five centuries of commerce with the Western world and several generations of university graduates by then. I met a Ghanaian student in the States in 1957 who told me proudly his grandfather was an Oxford University graduate. Ghana, with its sometimes rocky but successful independence, led the continent into a new era.

Congo began to stir politically in the fifties. For an excellent history of this period read Alan P. Merriam's *Congo: Background of Conflict*.

The paternalistic Belgian colonial administration by now supported mass education in three systems—Catholic, Protestant and State. It began to emphasize advanced schooling now that primary schools successfully provided a wide base of students to move up the pyramid of education. Two universities officially opened in the colony in 1956. At first few students qualified for admission, but enrollment increased steadily.

The government instituted its Ten-Year Plan in 1952 for the colony. The plan would increase economic development and raise the standard of living. This expensive program succeeded in many projects, advancing social progress and providing a more secure future for its workforce. Its emphasis on lifting the mass of population starkly contrasted with the French and British colonial approaches of concentrating on an educated and ruling elite. This privileged group, educated in Europe, furnished the leaders who were demanding and organizing the movements toward self-government over much of Africa. In the Congo in 1958 the Belgians still offered no timetable toward emancipation, but with the Ten-Year Plan the colony's economy expanded rapidly.

The pressure of preparing the Congolese for the future creeps into letter after letter in my parents' last years of service. The length of time until independence, a matter of much discussion, failed the predictions colossally. Everyone counted on many remaining years. Dad wrote to the family:

> We have been building up our teaching force at the advanced schools at Bolenge, and are short now on the stations. One of these days, someone is going to have to decide where we are going and what we must lop off. We keep hoping that better days are just around the corner, and in truth, we do have more missionaries than we ever had before. However, the work grows and will keep on growing, and it is at the graduate level that we must concentrate, or we can't get our Congolese leaders trained adequately to do what must be done. We were advised to accept the figure of 100 missionaries as maximum on the list for 1970, whereas we had hoped to have 120 by 1960.... (DHB Letter to Family 9-28-58)

A number of successful Mondombe students completed advanced medical training as nurses. Bohambu led the way in 1948 at a school in Yakusu near Stanleyville, which qualified him for a good government salary. He was followed by two more of Dad's qualifying nurses. Now two nurses were in training at the down-river school in the lower Congo. These nurses were well trained and a tremendous help at the hospital, as Dad wrote:

> We had two nurses come back from Kimpese, our medical school along the railroad in lower Congo between Leopoldville and Matadi.... Both of these young men have made a very nice development and are fine fellows. Our corps at the hospital is, for the most part, an unusually fine group of steady and earnest Christians and good workers. (DHB Letter to Family 9-9-58)

The fact that his nurses more generously supported the mission both by their work and by their contributions in greater amount than the teachers, who were more numerous and drew higher salaries, pleased Dad immensely. He felt there was a greater devotion to their work, on the whole, than among the teachers, particularly the younger teachers.

Dissatisfaction among the younger Mondombe educators became more pronounced as the years progressed. They went so far as to accuse the missionaries of misappropriating the government funds allocated to the school and withholding the bigger salaries they wanted. They put that in writing in a letter to government officials. Their libel cut to the quick. The missionaries knew that the teachers had a limited background in understanding budgets, timelines and large funding accounts. Knowing that did little to assuage the hurt. Such suspicion and unrest directed toward those who had given a lifetime of service foretold more ominous days ahead.

Increased traffic on the river indicated new successes of the government's Ten-Year Plan. With all the construction going on everywhere, commerce was booming. Educated Africans could earn a good salary in many capacities. These rates were generous, Dad wrote:

> Last year the [State] administrator told us, the average income for the back country villager was 1700 frs. Or $34. The total average for the territory is higher. He was telling us that he has a clerk in his office who gets 7000 frs. per month or $140. Then he added, "That's more than my father ever earned in a month." I got to wondering about it, and guess that it is as much or more as many of our fathers earned, even in the States. (DHB Letter to Family 10-11-58)

By the end of 1958 Mother had pretty well conquered the treasurer's work, which freed some of her time to work on Lonkundo lessons with a new missionary couple stationed at Mondombe for six months of language study. She continued teaching Lonkundo to new missionaries with the collaboration of a Congolese teacher until she retired.

Meanwhile, I completed my work in history at Hiram College. A special summer program at Kent State University prepared me for certification in elementary education. With three and a half years of teaching completed, I decided to return to Congo for a visit the following summer.

Plans for my trip to Congo in 1959 began to appear regularly in letters. I hoped to teach for a year in Europe in a US Army Dependent School after leaving Africa. My parents floated tentative ideas for their travel home on furlough in 1960. We might be able to meet in Europe after my school year ended.

By the time Mother and Dad completed this furlough, only one more year of service would remain until time for full retirement. Dad wanted to spend that last year on the field.

As 1958 came to a close Mother wrote about Christmas celebrations:

> On Friday night the schoolchildren gave a Christmas pageant which can be "carried" into the villages. That is, it is the type of program the school children can have their village reproduce. It was nice to have the school kids move out and give us a little peace and quiet for a few days before Christmas. Early this morning folks were out caroling. At least that was the program. Then there was an early church service which was well attended—church packed—according to Daddy's report. I stayed home to finish a Christmas gift and get dinner organized. Then after a baptismal service at our beach (again I did not go) there was a communion service. I played the organ and Aunt Gertrude led singing because the regular leader is having a fight with his wife. The church was beautiful. All the posts and, at the front, the crossbeams as well, were fringed with palm fronds brightened at intervals by bunches of brightly colored leaves and flowers. It made the church look special and festive. Again it is an idea the school children can use at home.

Church at Mondombe

>When Ntange gave his communion talk he "beamed" its message at the group of newly baptized. It sounded so very much like a Mondombe version of Paul speaking to some of the young New Testament churches. Ntange is so devoted to his people and such a sincere Christian and so practical and down-to-earth in his approach to Christianity. His life and example are a wonderful blessing to this area.... (LB Letter to Family 12-25-58)

After these festivities with the Congolese, the missionaries celebrated with each other, upholding their American traditions. The tree was a palm, and the turkey, stuffed duck, but the fruitcake and suet pudding were the real thing. The gift giving differed only in the many handmade presents. Christmas music and a reading of Dickens' *A Christmas Carol* completed a full day.

Two days after Christmas Mother's thoughts turned to days immediately ahead:

>Daddy and I <u>are</u> working hard, but we are in good health and we enjoy the great variety of our duties. We've both eased up just a bit (deliberately so, because we feel we're entitled to it) on the heaviest physical labor. We both ride several miles a day on our bicycles (in short stretches). Each evening Daddy works an hour or more in the garden. I manage several hours a week with flowers, when extra afternoon duties with the dorm boys don't crowd them out. Both of us have a lot of deskwork. However, we "know the ropes" in most of the fields of work and don't waste much time worrying or fussing around—as I once did.
>
>Margaret, will you be going to the Passion Play in 1960? We'd like to see it but don't know about the time. The Disciples of Christ World Convention will be in Edinburgh in August and we shall be planning on it. Maybe we could see the Passion Play just before, if we can break away from Mondombe in time. It would be less expensive to see it as we come through Europe from Congo on our way northward to Scotland. (LB Letter to Margaret 12-27-58)

And more parental worrying:

>Our "short" dry season seems finally to be ended. It actually turned into quite the longest short one we can remember. The big rose apple tree down in the chicken yard died either because of that or because

of something else which we can't explain. I'm so sorry, for that was one thing that was not going to look smaller to Margaret than as she remembered it. So much does look smaller and less impressive when one revisits childhood scenes.

Margaret, we keep wondering whether you have your teaching job in Europe for next winter. If you don't get it, can you still afford the trip? I'm hoping so, naturally, but we keep wondering whether you have heard. (LB Letter to Family 4-6-59)

My plans to teach for the Army Dependent Schools in Europe hit a snag at the last moment. In late May, when the Army finally notified me that I was indeed selected, I also learned that I couldn't report for work in Germany as I returned from Africa. The Army required me to leave from the States.

By the time I learned this I was in the last month of the school year in Shaker Heights, a suburb of Cleveland, Ohio, where I was teaching. Flight reservations for the trip to Congo with a friend had been completed with several stops in Europe to visit friends. My traveling companion had delayed her trip in order to fly with me. She was visiting her daughter and family in Leopoldville. After my visit to Mondombe I had a return ticket only as far as Germany.

Upon further questioning, the Army representative volunteered that they sometimes hired teachers locally, just before school started, to fill unexpected needs. They were willing to send my portfolio to Europe to assure my being selected in such an eventuality. I took a chance, shipped two packed footlockers by sea from Cleveland to a friend in Norway, and set off in mid-June for Africa.

The last leg of the trip, by SABENA Airlines turbo-prop airplane, began for me in Rome in the early evening and ended in Leopoldville in the late morning the next day. Those passengers who had started from Belgium had spent another four or five hours on the plane. With admiration we watched one young Belgian mother de-plane with her four pre-school youngsters all neatly combed and dressed in fresh, bright blue outfits, alert and eager to rejoin their father, we surmised. The rest of us straggled off the plane bleary-eyed and disheveled into the blinding sunshine and wilting humidity.

I spent the rest of the day and night with the family of my traveling companion. The husband served in the American Consulate as its economic specialist. I was dismayed that he had visited each provincial capital, but had never been outside the cities. I invited him to meet my parents in the interior where he could see an example of rural life. He seemed a bit uncertain as to why that should interest him but warmed to the idea as we talked.

The following day with great anticipation I flew into Coquilhatville for the first time—the first time by air, that is. How strange everything looked from the sky! How reduced the Congo River appeared—just a dark brown ribbon. The seven-mile drive to Bolenge showed much development. The station's path along the Congo, lined with familiar missionary homes, still presented its breathtaking panoramic sweep across the channel to the first island a mile away where Stanley stopped. Beyond it, I knew, more water and more islands continued for another six miles. Seeing no *Oregon* moored along the beach felt hollow to me, but I had heard of its sale.

I rode up river with missionaries attending the representative conference at Monieka where I would reunite with my folks. The journey took a day by sturdy car on a narrow dirt road frequently eroded by torrential rains. We were lucky the weather stayed dry.

My arrival in July coincided with the Central Committee meeting, the old M.A.C. It also coincided with the arrival of three other visitors from the States, all of whom wished to see Mondombe. As Dad was the Mondombe delegate to the conference, the rest of us visited with each other while the decisions apportioning the resources of the mission were made. Mother was present for the fellowship, which gave us time to exchange our news.

I'd forgotten how truly funny and stimulating conversations around the meal table could be with this highly educated and capable group. The wholesome joking proved they could take a break from their serious work and their sometimes fiercely competitive stances.

After two weeks my limited facility with Lonkundo returned. Gradually the lovely musical syllables formed into recognizable words, and I began to hear sentences. My childish vocabulary proved to be disappointingly inadequate for adult conversations. My French was a little better. The Africans slipped easily between the languages.

Dad drove the panel delivery truck to Mondombe packed with African delegates, American visitors and my family. In spite of the improved and widened road the trip contained many breathless moments as Dad crossed over poor bridges with rotted beams or slid on rounded, slippery clay topping. The ferry at the Loile River carried us smoothly to the other side.

Driving in the interior always furnished an adventure. One of the American guests, an electrical engineer, showed constant amazement at the skill Dad displayed in lining up the wheels of the truck with the logs of the bridges. The placing of the logs didn't always match the distance between the wheels. The visitor generously expressed his admiration of Dad's ability to cross successfully without losing any tires wedged in the gaps.

We arrived long after darkness had fallen. For miles ahead of us the talking drums beat out messages of our passing through the villages. The mission folk kept abreast of our progress. As we crossed the white clay dike across the swamp and drove up the road into Mondombe, I could hardly contain my excitement. I was home! A large crowd stood waiting to greet us near the church. What a rousing welcome for my return! A daughter of the mission had returned and they couldn't have been more pleased. The greeting astounded me with its enthusiasm.

The beauty of the station remained unchanged flanked by the grandeur of the river and the rich green of the forest walls. The palms still arched above the main path with their encircling fern mantles. The bougainvillea, cannas and other cultivated tropical flora flashed their brilliant colors. I felt wonderful joining in the work and worship of my childhood with the women in their colorful dress and satin head scarves and the men neatly attired in shirts and pants. But it was difficult to reject the entreaties of the Congolese to come back as a missionary. Their needs were great and wasn't I a teacher?

The too-short time at Mondombe passed in a rush. At the baby clinic I found the mothers and babies healthier and better clothed than before. Always good linguists, the educated Congolese spoke better French than I as we found discussion topics in common. Typing came in handy in helping my parents. And the delicious tropical dishes and fruits—what gustatory joy! If some objects appeared smaller than I had remembered them, the trees exceeded all memories. Eighty feet tall, the lovely *bokungu* tree beside the church spread its tiny fernlike leaves in layered, airy benediction. One more fishing out a lake, one more visit with Belgian friends, one more church service and then, reluctantly, the trip back to the airport at Boende.

Heading only as far as Europe for the school year made it easier to say goodbye. In less than eleven months my folks would join me there for the Passion Play in Oberammergau, Germany, the town famous for its re-creation every ten years of Christ's death. After the play we'd be together again for their year's furlough in the States. That was the plan.

Arriving in Germany I headed immediately to Heidelberg and the Army Dependent Schools Headquarters. What a blighted hope to find everyone but a few secretaries on vacation for the last two weeks before school started! Where could they get in touch with me, if I were needed, they asked? By great good fortune my Norwegian friend invited me to spend the time in Oslo. After a week there, and still hearing nothing from Germany, I flew to England.

It was midweek before Labor Day by now. In London I found a "local hire" job teaching for the United States Air Force Dependent Schools in England. On

Friday before Labor Day I received my papers, took the train a hundred miles north to Leicester and from there was driven to Bruntingthorpe Air Force Base. The small, recently re-opened base had been closed since Would War II during which the RAF loaned it to the USA. There I met the rest of the staff recently arrived from the States. "In the nick of time" took on new meaning for me!

The year proved to be a valuable teaching experience in improvising. The staff coped with a rapidly expanding enrollment and shortages of everything. DeGaulle had rejected having nuclear military units in France. When they moved to Germany, other groups were moved to bases in England to clear space for them. Our classes met in WWII vintage Quonset huts, which little resembled the beautiful, well-supplied Army schools in Germany. (We heard that teachers in Germany even had their own ski lodge.) The children were savvy—capable, independent and flexible.

Having to live off base gave the teachers the better of two worlds. A generous housing allowance and commissary privileges overcame any deficiencies in English living, such as a lack of central heating or refrigeration. Four of us teachers lived together in a house with hunting pictures on the walls and cretonne-covered chairs grouped around the fireplace. We rented heaters for every room, a small refrigerator and a T.V. The off-base house planted us in the midst of storybook Robin Hood country.

Life among the English introduced us to the resourceful British, who had just ended the last of their wartime rationing. Our neighbors proved to be delightfully warm and friendly—as we experienced all the British to be. Their cold and standoffish image proved to be inaccurate. Instead we found them shy and reserved.

They were kind to us, enjoyed our differing ways, teased us gently, and looked out for us. Our household was a phenomenon to them, because we were willing on Thursday to plan a weekend trip to a destination two hundred miles distant. The British spent a year planning such a holiday. With only 1,000 miles separating the farthest southwestern point at Land's End to the most distant northeastern tip of Scotland at John O'Groats, and with us in the Midlands, no part of the island exceeded our American scope during a weekend or a longer break from school.

The four of us left for Cornwall during spring break. The grass had started to grow and the flowers were beautiful. We returned to a back lawn groomed to resemble a golfing green. One kindly neighbor had spent untold hours reducing the fine, thick grass to a height we could handle. In cool, moist England, we were told gently, lawns needed twice-weekly mowing.

Another time one neighbor asked if she could cut something in our garden. "Of course," we said. "Help yourself."

"You don't have any idea what I am going to cut, do you?" she chuckled and gave the common name for a flower. Gardeners in England referred to plants precisely by their Latin names.

While thus occupied, letters from my parents brought disquieting news from Congo. The future there seemed more and more uncertain.

CHAPTER 21

THE END AND THE BEGINNING

When would the Belgian Congo gain its independence? The question resounded through the letters of the last years my parents spent in the field. Though the colony was modernizing, humming with activity, pushing its accomplishments, it was still hampered by a lack of trained and skilled workmen and inadequate supplies. In most colonies the government held back their wards. In the Belgian Congo, Dad felt, they were pushed beyond their readiness, so great was the need for well-trained workers. Seventy-five years, he said, proved not to be a long enough time to prepare a large percentage of an aboriginal population for a modern industrial economy.

The political awakening of the Congolese appeared first in the urban areas. As the years passed, expressions of these stirrings disturbed the peaceful tenor of the days in the interior as well. By 1958 Dad wrote, "In many ways there is a different spirit of independence present among the younger folks. It isn't always best for them, and it certainly makes it more difficult for us." Insolence resulted in firings, leaving some Africans out of jobs and some Westerners without help. The libelous action of the teachers at Mondombe, already mentioned, did not result in any dismissals, but it certainly tainted the atmosphere.

In 1958 some visitors from Texas to the mission had been told at mission headquarters in the States that ten years was all the time the mission work could count on before missionaries would have to leave the Congo. As they traveled to the various stations and government posts finding out about programs, goals and difficulties, they tried to verify the timeline. At Mondombe in a meeting with both missionaries and Congolese the visitors asked about the ten-year timeline.

Ntange countered with, "Who are these people who tell you we want the missionaries to leave? I've heard nothing about it. From the beginning there has been work the missionaries could do and work we could do. We haven't seen that the work or the need to work together is finished." The visitors found neither missionaries nor state men thinking in terms of ten or fewer years.

About the time of the visitors to Mondombe, Dad privately made a prescient prediction in a letter to me:

> If the Belgians should happen to be forced out of here by a few demagogues of Congo origin, plus the Communist propaganda, plus well-meaning but ill-informed people in the States and elsewhere, within the next twenty-five years, the devil will be to pay for it. These people are a lot further away from handling their own affairs on a national scale than most people can even imagine. As it is, the country is making a nice development. (DHB Letter to Margaret 6-21-58)

But Congolese political leaders found words to express the yearning in their followers for self determination. The fever of independence on the continent of Africa struck with rioting and protests against colonial governments. The first riot in the Belgian Congo rocked Leopoldville in January 1959. From up river it was hard to evaluate the causes. My parents reported from the interior:

> Four months after the rioting in Leopoldville the masses in our Mondombe back country villages, including our teacher/preachers, have still not heard about the incident or of its details. Why? Because of the distance and lack of common interests and general communication.
>
> The effects of the tragedy will be much more widespread than we had even supposed. Investors, Belgian and others, will hesitate about placing capital in an uncertain situation. It means a real exodus of Belgian women and children from Congo, and an increased lack of confidence in the future of the colony. We are told that the Belgians lack 300 Belgian teachers in their schools here. One of the Belgian agricultural workers tells us that in one of his classes, as he prepared for his work here before coming, there were forty students. Today there are none, and the class has been abandoned. We have been told that the Belgian medical service cannot find an adequate number of Belgian doctors for Congo. So they set out to recruit doctors in other countries, seeking one hundred. They succeeded in getting only thirty. The conclusion seems to be: missionary doctors will be

needed in Congo for a long time to come. Incidentally, subsidies for our medical work are to be increased. (General Letter 5-7-59)

Even with the rioting, imminent independence still seemed unbelievable to Dad as he responded to a letter from Lauretta:

> Lauretta asked about the Belgians "pulling out." It is unthinkable to us that they could get out of here in some years yet. There simply are no highly skilled Congolese of any category. Possibly one or more of this and that. It seems that the Belgians even have one Congolese in training for assistant (District) *commissaire*. (DHB Letter to Family 11-22-59)

One can see a split between Dad's evaluation and that of some of the Congolese who heard many rumors. One clerk at the nearby state post informed Dad that the Belgians had promised independence by March 1960. He had a vague notion that the Belgians would turn everything over to the Congolese, but no idea how they would carry on the work in government, medicine or agriculture. The clerk had heard it on the radio and in magazines.

Although the Belgian Congo had achieved an overall literacy rate among the highest in sub-Saharan Africa, the lack of highly educated Congolese became a constant obstruction to moving forward at the speed necessary to keep up with the demands of the period. The Protestant mission successes mirrored the Catholic and government advancements. Their difficulties were also reflected in all the school systems.

With the difficulties the mission experienced finding enough trained teachers at the lower grade levels, the missionaries worried that they could even educate enough students successfully to qualify for the school subsidies. College preparation expanded their concerns.

At the end of 1959 my parents took the time to review the mission achievements during their nearly thirty years of work. Looked at over a long period they could rejoice in the numbers who had come forward to be educated, to join the church, to be treated at the hospital. Now the women yearned to move and change with the men.

Improvements in material goods such as clothes, nutrition and housing, in income and savings, and in the spread of information showed the influence of the missions. The speed of change, however, seemed to have reached a frenzied pace.

Rumors abounded with little way of testing their truth. The whites would all be gone next year. A Congolese from down river was to take over from the Belgian administrator. The local Africans were to choose which whites they wished to remain.

Certainly everybody wanted *Independence*. The French word was used, since there was no word and no conception of the meaning in the Congolese language. Some of the simple folk, it was said, took a suitcase to a meeting called to discuss a coming election, so that they could carry home their *Independence*. When the American pastor was asked about the election, he explained that it meant their representatives to the council could decide how their taxes would be spent. Jaws dropped as they gasped, "You mean we're still going to have taxes after we get our *Independence*?" Few recognized the responsibilities inherent in gaining self-rule.

Elections scheduled by the Belgians started with local councils. Over time, presumably four years, more elections would lead to the selection of councils at the provincial and colonial levels of government.

At Mondombe on Election Day in December the chief, the government official and two policemen arrived with eleven locked ballot boxes—one for each candidate with a name, a photo, and a long slit in each to insert one's ballot. The voting proceeded smoothly. Mondombe was literate. Elsewhere, problems ensued, wrote my parents:

> We were told that elsewhere the officials had found ballots hung on nails, stuck into cracks, and even wadded and thrown on the floor. The problem for the nominees was to get the votes of the illiterates who not only couldn't read the name on the box, but very frequently couldn't "see" the photo of the face which belonged with the name. Our local chief, one of the nominees, solved the problem. He had stabbed a spearhead into his box. Another nominee used an eagle feather. Maybe they would have won without their attention-getters. Maybe these were but evidences of inborn shrewdness which wins success. In any case both men are on the territorial council. (General Letter 2-23-60)

Meanwhile, there had been an outbreak of violence in Stanleyville. Rumors claimed that three times as many people had been killed as reported in the news. When Mondombe's American pastor returned from a trip to the up-river state post at Ikela, he reported that someone from the big city was to visit in January "to stir up our province, the Equatorial," Mother wrote. He was so disturbed by what he had heard that he resolved not to travel any more so as not to leave his family alone. Anxiety clutched the interior about what the urban areas were doing or might do.

Stanleyville served as Lumumba's base. His political activists traveled throughout the DCCM area demanding support. Those who could afford it paid the $1.20 for a party membership card—as insurance, I heard, against being roughed up later. Few other parties penetrated that far into the area. In a letter to Lauretta Mother expressed her unease:

> If only we could have had one more generation before this trouble started! ... But it may, through no fault of ours, just take more time than history allows us. We still hope such is not the case, but it isn't beyond the realm of possibility at all that the whole thing could "blow up" within the next few months. We pray and dare to hope that it won't. (LB Letter to Lauretta 12-? 59)

Was racial bias stirring the pot in the cities? Did racism exist in the Congo? Of course it did—just as segregation, prejudice and epithets endured in the States at that time. Leopoldville had its white and black residential areas. It is worth noting, however, that the first African who crossed the barrier moved into a white neighborhood in Leopoldville in 1958. That preceded by one year the first African-American family buying into Shaker Heights, Ohio, the wealthy, previously all-white bedroom community in which I taught. There, as here, racial discrimination caused unrest and revolt.

By mid-January of 1960 Dad wrote that there were several different turns the colony might take and none of them were "very pleasant in anticipation." He found himself not seeing "eye to eye" with some of the direction from the home mission board, which remained optimistic. The Belgians working in the Congo, also, complained about decisions being made in Belgium by their superiors who had never worked in the colony.

On February 10, 1960, the Round Table Conference in Brussels moved from commission meetings to plenary sessions to hammer out an agreement for the independence of Congo. The time had come to face the inevitable. Convened were fifty-five Belgians and ninety-six Congolese.

All preparations telescoped to accommodate the impending onset of self-rule. The Congolese wished to retain their Belgian judges and teachers in Congo but not the administrators. The Belgian Foreign Service was asked to prepare the Congolese within two months to take over their own representation in foreign capitals. Amazingly, the date set was June 30, 1960. Independence in less than five months.

How did it happen that Belgium so hastily bailed out on its colony, set the date for independence a scant four months away, and thereby ensured the tragedy that followed? Perhaps my mother's theory—based only on her knowledge of Bantu culture and not on any political information—furnished the answer. She figured that in true Congolese bartering style the delegates asked for an impossibly short time and expected to negotiate a more reasonable duration with the Belgians, who were looking at least four years down the road. (Before the Round Table discussions my parents heard that the government in Belgium had taken over from the colonial administrators who would have recognized the ploy.) If this theory is true, the Congolese must have been as flabbergasted as the rest of the world to have their first request accepted.

Alan Merriam's book supports this supposition. It quotes in a news report of *Inforcongo* that most of the Congolese present for the announcement of the June 30th date showed astonishment, elation and apprehension. Mother's hypotheses might explain how it happened, but it still doesn't account for why the Belgians would cave in without a more thoughtful timetable. Merriam, who made his observations from his year in southern Congo, describes the pressures from the UN, the US and the budget that undoubtedly squeezed Belgium into agreeing to this date.

In *Who Killed the Congo* Philippa Schuyler details the burgeoning cost of the Ten-Year Plan. Belgium covered a $50,000,000 budget deficit in 1959. The budget shortfall for 1960 would be as large or larger. She concluded that the Belgian government "freed the Congo so suddenly for three main reasons: they hoped to avert bloodshed; they were under great international pressure and national leftist pressure to do so; and they foresaw having to spend huge sums of money if they held on any longer."

The exodus of Belgians from the colony started almost immediately after the Round Table decision when administrators started sending in their resignations. Many of the women and children had already left Stanleyville. The official position stated that there would be a Belgian presence for at least two to four years. However, if the personnel were unwilling to stay on, my parents didn't see how that would be possible.

The uncertainty of the future in Congo continued to feed on rumors throughout the spring, as my parents prepared to leave Congo. They had decided to leave for good. Determined to get their things away while the transportation routes still maintained normal operation, my parents were delayed by work and guests. Nevertheless, they completed packing and shipping their belongings in May.

In May, also, they wrote and sent home their last general letter to be duplicated and mailed. The letter drew too pessimistic an evaluation of the situation for the home office, which appended a disclaiming postscript. That infuriated my father. The note served as one more symptom of the period that the mission department, which held a rosier view of the future than my parents, felt it necessary to annotate a personal letter:

> A widely quoted review of the Congo situation of December 1959 said, "Estimates vary from a gloomy pessimism to a stubborn optimism." By now, even our local "stubborn optimist" has left for Belgium....
>
> The present government doesn't do anything without consulting a group of Congolese, at every level. The Belgians seem already to have abdicated. We know of no arrangements for administration after July 1st. The Belgians say that their government has sold them out.
>
> We Bakers have plane reservations to leave Congo on July 15th for Rome, Geneva, Zurich and Oberammergau for the Passion Play on the 20th. [The rest of the letter covered more normal activities of the station.] (General Letter 5-8-60)

Cautiously, my parents planned to travel down river to Coquilhatville before the day of independence to spend two weeks there before departure from Leopoldville. Surprisingly, they did leave Leopoldville on July 15th, but nothing else about their departure went according to plan.

* * *

Independence Day in Leopoldville dawned calm and expectant. King Baudouin of Belgium had flown in the day before. At the ceremonial turning over of power, the King and President Kasavubu, of the Bakongo tribe, made polite speeches. The King unfortunately referred to the days of King Leopold II with praise. This infuriated Prime Minister Lumumba. In his response, according to the Historian Robert B. Edgerton, Lumumba accused the King of presiding over "a regime of injustice, suppression, and exploitation. We have known that the law was never the same for a white man as it was for a black...." What seemed a rude and unstatesmanlike speech to Westerners apparently encouraged an acrimonious reaction in many of the Congolese.

Day after day the stability in the cities deteriorated as tribe set against tribe; workers tried to compel payment on wild promises made for vastly increased wages; and the army overthrew its Belgian officers. The soldiers then rampaged. Belgian paratroopers sent to Congo to bring order and facilitate the evacuation of the frightened Belgian nationals were replaced by UN forces, as whites fled by the thousands.

Back in Germany, I, and the teacher with whom I was traveling, stopped at the American consulate in Frankfurt on July 15th to find out whether my parents had been able to leave Congo. It seemed dubious that they could depart, when we heard the news of the fighting in Leopoldville. The consul promised to try to find out through diplomatic channels; we should call her in a couple days.

Instead of staying in Frankfurt as agreed upon to meet my folks, we drove on to Oberammergau full of worry, hoping we could find news there. No one in the large reception room had information for us, nor did they show any surprise at our predicament. We were assigned to rooms in a private home where we went and unloaded our baggage. After a brief nap we returned to Passion Play headquarters to buy some stamps. As I turned to leave, my parents walked in the door. What joy! What relief! How tired they looked.

My dazed and exhausted mother recounted in cathartic detail the events surrounding their evacuation. She talked about the disintegration of order in Leopoldville and the colony after Independence Day; the US military delivering UN peace-keeping personnel while a battle took place in the airport; the gathering of whites at Coquilhatville for immediate removal; the uncertainty when women and children packed the only plane and the men stayed behind; the thrill she felt seeing head of the UN peace keepers, Ralph Bunche, stride through the bullet-riddled airport in Leo surrounded by the blue-helmeted soldiers; the crowded conditions on the US transport evacuation plane with a child on every woman's lap; the lull that night as they sat on the tarmac for several hours to allow the exhausted Air Force crew time to sleep before the long haul back to North Africa; the loud rapping on the door as frantic Belgian military officers begged passage out. Lumumba had guaranteed their safety only until six the following day. The American crew assured them that they would be flown out before then.

During the seemingly interminable flight to the American military base in Libya, Mother heard whispered stories of brutality against Belgians attacked up river—some had made their way to this flight; some had not made it out. That added to Mother's worries about the men left behind in Coquilhatville. She felt anguish for the Congolese caught helplessly in these unsafe conditions.

Mother collapsed into bed at last in the barracks on base. From a deep sleep she was happy to be awakened with the news that Dad had arrived shortly after she had. She learned that an unscheduled plane arrived in Coquilhatville after she left. It evacuated the rest of the travelers to a second Globemaster in Leopoldville. Without knowing it my parents had been adjacent on the flight line in Leopoldville in their separate planes. They were two of the 2,478 evacuees rescued by US forces.

Reunited and sharing a passport once more, Mother and Dad continued on to Brussels and then Frankfurt. Confused at not finding me, they took the train to Oberammergau.

The Passion Play was unforgettable. We treasured two weeks together afterwards driving across Germany, up England and around Scotland. I left them in Edinburgh for their International Convention and boarded the *Empress of France* for the trip back to the States. They would join me in the Cleveland area for their retirement.

EPILOGUE

After its missionaries fled in July 1960, Mondombe gradually regained a skeletal American staff. The missionaries evacuated only as far as Belgium returned in September. By the time those missionaries who had taken furlough in the States returned a year later, Lumumba was already deposed and murdered. Congo had split temporarily into two parts. Government instability continued.

The next and final evacuation of Americans from Mondombe took place in 1964. The rebel "Simbas" invaded from Stanleyville, now renamed Kisangani. Their witch doctors claimed to have endowed them with invincibility to bullets. The intruders marched across the province essentially unopposed. Resistance melted away before the oncoming army, usually without a fight, because both the rebels and their opponents believed in this invisible, protective shield. The invaders targeted educated people for execution and pillaged and destroyed buildings and belongings.

The story I heard of the occupation of Mondombe, perhaps apocryphal, told of the flight of the inhabitants into the forest. There they hid for six weeks in great distress without food, medicines or protection from the elements. Only Bohambu remained at Mondombe, in total risk to himself, to save the station. When the rebels arrived, they found this one elder, the first governmentally licensed of Dad's nurses. With tremendous bravery this small, capable man warned the soldiers that God's punishment would be great, if they were to destroy or desecrate any building within the mission area. In spite of shackles so tight on wrists and ankles that the flesh swelled and ulcerated, he maintained his conviction of divine retribution. Awed by such deep faith and cautious as to whose spiritual backing were the stronger, the rebels not only let Bohambu live, they also left the station buildings standing and undemolished. When the Simbas finally fled back to Stanleyville, the inhabitants of Mondombe returned and revered Bohambu. He came as close to sainthood as Protestants get.

The same year as the Simba rebellion–1964–the Church of Christ in Congo (Disciples of Christ), representing 125,000 members, became the legal owner of the mission property formerly known as the DCCM. The direction and administration of the whole enterprise now lay with the able, autonomous Congolese leaders. The church in the United States and the missionaries worked to help their friends in Congo as their assistance was requested.

After the occupation by the Simba rebels American staff deemed Mondombe too remote and unsafe to be stationed there. For four years, 1967 to 1971, the hospital continued to benefit from the training, supervision and assistance of Dr. Gene Johnson working from the regional hospital at Boende. The Congo church gained permission to use the former government facilities and talked two medical missionaries into staffing it. The staff later grew to four doctors.

Dr. Johnson, the missionary doctor previously at the Monieka station, returned with his family from his retirement practice in the States to join the hospital at Boende for one term. He flew to the hospital at Mondombe and six other hospitals in his Piper Supercub to keep them supplied and to perform complicated surgeries. Dr. Johnson landed his plane at Mondombe on the main path where the perimeter palm trees had been cut down in 1962 to create a landing strip for a mission plane. Under his tutelage the chief nurse at each hospital learned to do simple surgeries, such as hernias and Caesarean sections. Congo by this time was again one nation. Mobutu had consolidated his control of the government, a dictatorship that would last for thirty years.

Communications from Mondombe trickled thinly to Ohio where Dad and Mother settled into new professional lives. Many a night Mother tossed and turned unsleeping as she worried about the latest bad news from the Congo and wondered about its implications for the people she knew. Dad slept soundly. When queried by Mother, he shrugged his shoulders and said in his pragmatic way, "There is nothing we can do about it. Why lose sleep over it?" At one point they heard with pride that nurses trained at the Mondombe hospital were administering four of the hospitals in our region.

At least three times invading troops from eastern Congo and Zimbabwe overran Mondombe. One group burned all the books. The last time the place was stripped. Windows, doors, blackboards, tools and instruments—all were taken or burned by the rebel soldiers. The people who had survived earlier occupations once more stood in genuine risk of starvation, unable to care for themselves without implements for cultivating food and mending their houses. Again they pulled together.

In 2004 Dr. Johnson returned to the Equator Province to the area of the former DCCM to assess, for the church in America, the medical needs of the hospitals. Because of the uncertainty of government payment, the church in the States undertook the expense of paying the salaries for doctors in this area. The Division of Overseas Ministry wanted to know what condition the hospitals were in. Dr. Johnson traveled as far up river as Mondombe by means of motorboats—one for the delegation and another to transport fuel, which was unobtainable in the interior. This turned out to be very expensive, but no other transportation existed except dugout canoes and the occasional commercial craft.

In his report of the trip Dr. Johnson wrote of his visit to the Mondombe hospital:

> I had been told that everything had been pillaged … so I was surprised to find that they had quite a bit of medicine. They had received a gift of $3,000 from the German churches and had used it to buy a stock of medicine. When they sell the medicine they keep that money in a separate fund so they can renew their stock.
>
> The only surgical instruments belong to the nurse who does most of the surgery. He was there back when I visited the hospital by airplane until '71. He had been doing surgery in the doctor's absence and showed us several post-op cases who were getting along OK.... The laboratory had nothing but one microscope, but it is by far the nicest I have seen out here. It was a gift from some organization whose name I didn't recognize.
>
> … I was positively impressed by the attitude of the people and the work they were doing in spite of many obstacles. The hospital buildings are solid, the roofs don't leak, but nothing has been painted for 50 years. (E-mailed report dated 5-6-04)

The Congolese doctor appointed to Mondombe after the last rebel incursion traveled up river with the boat delivering fuel for Dr. Johnson's delegation. It was his first trip to Mondombe. He went back down river with Dr. Johnson to retrieve his wife from Leopoldville, now named Kinshasa. I don't know when or how he will be able to return to his new post. Until then the nurses will carry on.

Travel to Mondombe now must be by private boat or canoe. The untended roads are impassable by car and the streams lack ferries. There is no mail service, no State boat and no air service beyond Boende. Government salaries are infrequently or never paid. Diseases such as yaws and leprosy are undoubtedly making a comeback without regular treatment in the villages. At the same time tuberculosis and AIDS are flourishing, transmitted by the soldiers and fueled by the poor living conditions. I am willing to believe that the schools are still holding classes, probably with few books. Religious convictions remain strong, and the church continues to grow supported entirely by the worshippers' contributions. Tremendous strides were accomplished during the missionary period. The Congolese, from what used to be the DCCM area, continue to build on that foundation. When the nation achieves a peaceful existence with a stable government, the Equator Province will be in position to advance again rapidly.

*   *   *

My parents retired from the mission field to Cleveland, Ohio, where Dad practiced medicine until age seventy-one and Mother taught pre-school classes for 3-and 4-year-olds. In 1977 Dad heard from Lofumbwa, his chief surgical nurse, who had helped with the operation that saved his wife's life. Lofumbwa's son had just graduated from the University of Kinshasa, School of Medicine. "What a wonderful surprise for us, after all these years," Dad wrote.

Dad died just short of his eighty-ninth birthday in Albuquerque, New Mexico, where he moved to be near my family and me after Mother's death. To the very end he continued his love of gardening, concentrating on flowers in the later years. The other three Bakers and their families are scattered from Ohio to Florida. None of them has lived abroad since their Congo days, although they share a love of foreign travel.

BIBLIOGRAPHY

Aardema, Verna. *Traveling to Tondo*. New York: Scholastic, 1991.

Edgerton, Robert B. *The Troubled Heart of Africa: A History of the Congo*. NewYork: St. Martin's Press, New York, 2002.

Forbath, Peter. *The River Congo: The Discovery Exploration and Exploitation of the World's Most Dramatic River*. New York: Harper & Row, 1977.

"Congo Portfolio-Mondombe." Brochure of the Disciples of Christ Congo Mission, 1952.

"Gripsholm 1925-1954." http://www.salship.se/grip2.asp.

Johnson, Dr. Gene E. *Congo Centennial: The Second Fifty Years*. Galesburg, IL, First Christian Church, 1999.

Merriam, Alan P. *Congo: Background of Conflict*. Evanston, IL: Northwestern University, 1961.

Moon, E.R. *I Saw Congo*. Indianapolis, IN: The United Christian Missionary Society, 1952.

Ross, Mabel H. and Barbara Walker. *"On Another Day..." Tales Told Among the Nkundo of Zaire*. Hamden, CN: Archon Books, 1979.

Schuyler, Philippa. *Who Killed the Congo*. New York: The Devin-Adair Company, 1962.

Smith, Herbert. *Fifty Years in the Congo*. Indianapolis, IN: The United Christian Missionary Society, 1949.

INDEX

All Africa Conference 182
Ambulance 98, 186
American Baptist Mission 77
Ants: driver ants 107, 124, 167
    Termites 92, 101-102, 125
Arab slave traders 1, 3, 54
Arab War 3
Avocado 71

Baby clinic 57, 66, 71, 72, 196
Baker, Lauretta 18, 20, 27, 30, 34, 51, 52, 56, 58, 74
Baker, Maurice 81, 136, 156, 181, 187
Baker, Ruth 73
Bantu xiv, 2, 4, 16, 47, 66, 113, 114, 204
Baptism 77, 151
Barber, Lelia 7
Basenji dog 61
Belgian colonial policy 4
Belgian Congo xiii, 1, 2, 3, 4, 15, 21, 152, 182, 199, 200, 201
Belgium 2, 3, 4, 5, 17, 19, 20, 21, 41, 43, 74, 77, 146, 147, 149, 194, 203, 204, 205, 209
Berlin Conference 3
Blacksmith 109, 116
Blackwater fever 38, 133
Boende 146, 187, 196, 210, 211
Bohambu Pierre 177, 191, 209
Bokese Paul 24, 86
Bolenge 1, 6, 22, 23, 24, 39, 44, 49, 53, 58, 67, 77, 78, 143, 144, 148, 150, 151, 152, 161, 162, 165, 171, 181, 187, 190, 195
Bongelemba 116
Bonjimba 55, 56

Bosumbe 126, 181
Boys' dormitory 83, 121
Bride price 111
Brussels 20, 22, 49, 203, 207
Building program 24, 165, 171
Butterflies 14, 15, 56, 132

Calvert Correspondence Course 125, 127, 129, 181
Camera 125
Captain John Inkima 140, 143-145
Cassava 71
Census 32, 48, 49, 52, 53, 54, 55, 56, 68, 74, 117, 176
Childbirth 38, 66
Christmas 20, 29, 182, 193
Conference 2, 8, 9, 22, 23, 44, 45, 73, 74, 122, 123, 144, 146, 165, 182, 183, 187, 195, 203
Congo Christian Institute 150
Congo Free State 2, 3, 4, 15, 41, 54
Congo River 1, 2, 4, 5, 6, 21, 22, 44, 143, 149, 157, 167, 178, 179, 195
Congress 187, 188
Consultation 164
Coquilhatville 22, 45, 49, 78, 146, 167, 168, 169, 179, 185, 187, 195, 205, 206, 207

Dade, Barbara 170
Dade, Edgar 171
Dancing 27, 43, 55
DCCM—See Disciples of Christ Congo Mission
DeNoya, Oklahoma 11-14
Depression 4, 21, 40

215

Diabetes 27, 28
Disciples of Christ Congo Mission (DCCM) 6, 15
Dye, Dr. 138

Ekitelo 48
Election 157, 202
Electricity 99, 181
Elephantiasis 22, 24
Equator Province 22, 59, 116, 210, 212
Evacuation 206, 209
Evangelism 24

Fetishes 114
Fishing 37, 74, 117, 118, 196
Folklore 43, 115
Furlough 15, 40, 45, 57, 58, 69, 73, 74, 75, 123, 125, 148, 153, 160, 161, 163, 180, 196, 209

Girls' dormitory 25, 57, 84, 85
Gripsholm, M.S. 160

Henderson, Dr. and Mrs. 149, 154
Hensey 15, 16, 17, 23
Hiram College 8
Horner, Dr. William Howard 133, 154, 165
Horton, Dr. George 15, 22, 94
Hospital, Mondombe 78, 210, 211
House 11, 12, 14, 25, 27, 38, 42, 47, 49, 54, 58, 67, 74, 75, 99, 114, 121, 122, 124, 134, 143, 153, 158, 160, 164, 170, 171, 177, 197
Hurt, Mrs. Ambra 38, 80, 81
Hurt, Mr. Lewis 24
Hurt, Virginia 38, 80
Hygiene 57, 66, 70, 71, 72

IcyBall 51, 52
Ikela 202

Independence xiii, xiv, 4, 169, 189, 190, 199, 200, 201, 202, 203, 204, 205, 206
Institute School (ICC) 67, 81, 112, 150, 162, 166

Jaggard, Dr. 148
Johnson, Dr. Gene 144, 171, 210

Kennedy School of Missions 14, 17, 24
Kigoma 149, 168, 169
Kimpese 190
Kinshasa—see Leopoldville
Kisangani—see Stanleyville
Klim 20, 21

Ladia 39
Last Battle 36
Leopard: Spotty 135, 136
    wild leopard 45, 49, 50-54, 94, 95, 123, 135, 175
Leopold II, King 2, 205
Leopoldville 21, 77, 78, 157, 168, 169, 178, 179, 180, 190, 194, 200, 203, 205, 206, 207, 211
Leprosy 24, 32, 106, 185, 211
Lingala 2, 39, 169, 187
Lofumbwa 185, 212
Lokole 5, 48, 175
Lokwa 175, 176
Lonkundo 4, 15, 16, 39, 57, 73, 187, 195
Lotumbe 44, 76, 78, 142, 149, 150, 151, 152, 178

M.A.C. 58, 76, 168, 195
Mail boat 153
Malaria xiii, 22, 24, 25, 38, 67, 73, 115, 132, 133, 163
Manioc 1, 2, 6, 71, 99, 185
Marriage 9
Mata Bondo 66
Matadi 2, 20, 21, 77, 190
Mbandaka—see Coquilhatville

Miliama 86, 87, 165
Mission Advisory Council. See M.A.C.
Mitchell, Hattie 40, 48, 57, 153
Mondombe xiii, 6, 23, 24, 25, 29, 37, 38, 39, 40, 41, 42, 43, 44, 46, 48, 49, 53, 58, 66, 67, 69, 70, 71, 73, 74, 75, 76, 78, 79, 86, 98, 112, 114, 115, 117, 131, 143, 144, 148, 149, 150, 151, 152, 153, 161, 162, 163, 165, 180, 181, 184, 185, 186, 190, 191, 193, 194, 195, 196, 199, 200, 202, 209, 210, 211, 213
Monieka 148, 195, 210
Moon, E.R. 114, 124, 139-140
Motorcycle 68, 88, 131, 133, 152, 167
Movies 55, 179, 181

Nkang' Itoko 186
Ntange Timothy 24, 86, 151
Nurses 25, 27, 28, 29, 66, 69, 77, 99, 113, 150, 160, 161, 162, 190, 209, 210, 211

Offering 8, 147, 163
Oregon 23, 44, 45, 76, 78, 122, 142, 143, 144, 145, 146, 149, 151, 163, 168, 195
Oregon, S.S. 44, 168

Philathea Class 19, 20, 25, 38
Polly 134, 135
Proverb 115, 145, 177

Quinine 22, 133

Rebellion 209
Rebels 209, 210
Roberts, Jewell 126
Roberts, Ned 86, 87, 178
Round Table Conference 203

Scarification 110, 119
School, women's 25

Schools xiv, 39, 57, 150, 153, 162, 163, 165, 166, 171, 177, 180, 184, 189, 190, 194, 196, 197, 200, 211
Shoemaker, Gertrude 24, 34, 49, 56, 72, 75, 79, 80, 81, 84, 154, 165, 174, 192
Sleeping sickness 32, 68, 98
Smelting 7, 109
Smith, Elizabeth (Aunt Betty) 16, 38, 39, 60, 95, 153, 160
Smith, Everton 16
Stanley, Henry Morton 1
Stanleyville 167, 168, 169, 178, 190, 202, 203, 204, 209
Stober, Buena 24, 39, 40, 45, 53, 66, 74, 80, 85, 99, 103-105, 153, 156, 161, 176, 185
Student Volunteer Movement Conference 9
Subsidy 4, 165, 171, 176, 201

Topoke 110
Tschuapa River 6

United Christian Missionary Society (UCMS) 14

Voting 187, 202

Wema 44, 74, 133, 144, 164, 167, 168, 187
Witch doctor 28, 47, 67, 69, 87, 88, 99, 114, 163, 164, 209
World War II 4, 127, 132, 144, 146, 160, 165, 184

Yaws 24, 26, 32, 68, 70, 98, 211

Zamzam 148, 149

978-0-595-46631-3
0-595-46631-1